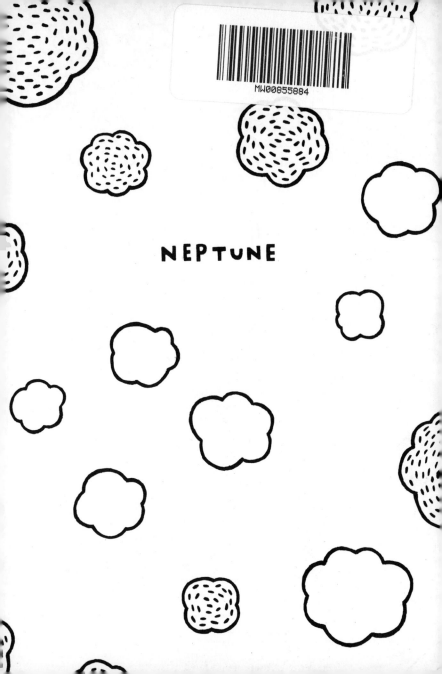

NEPTUNE

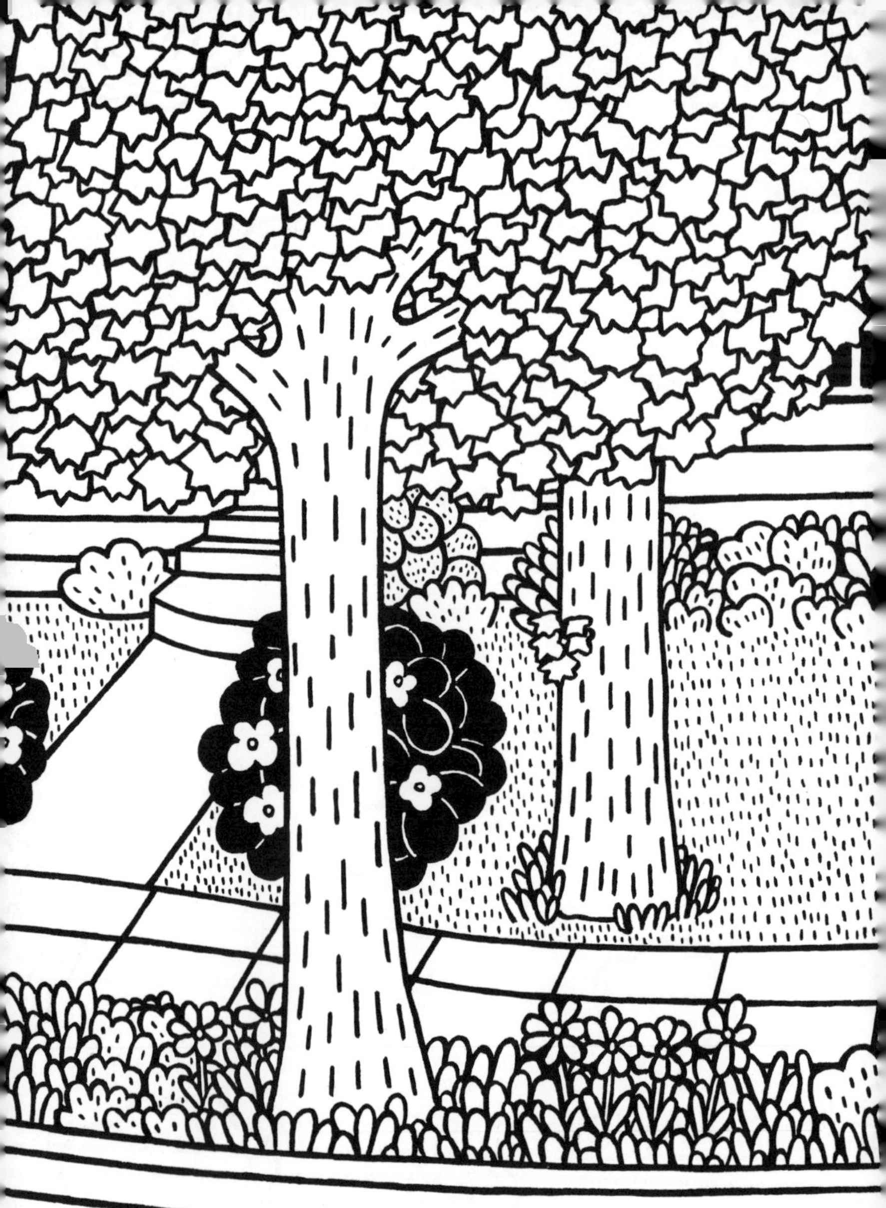

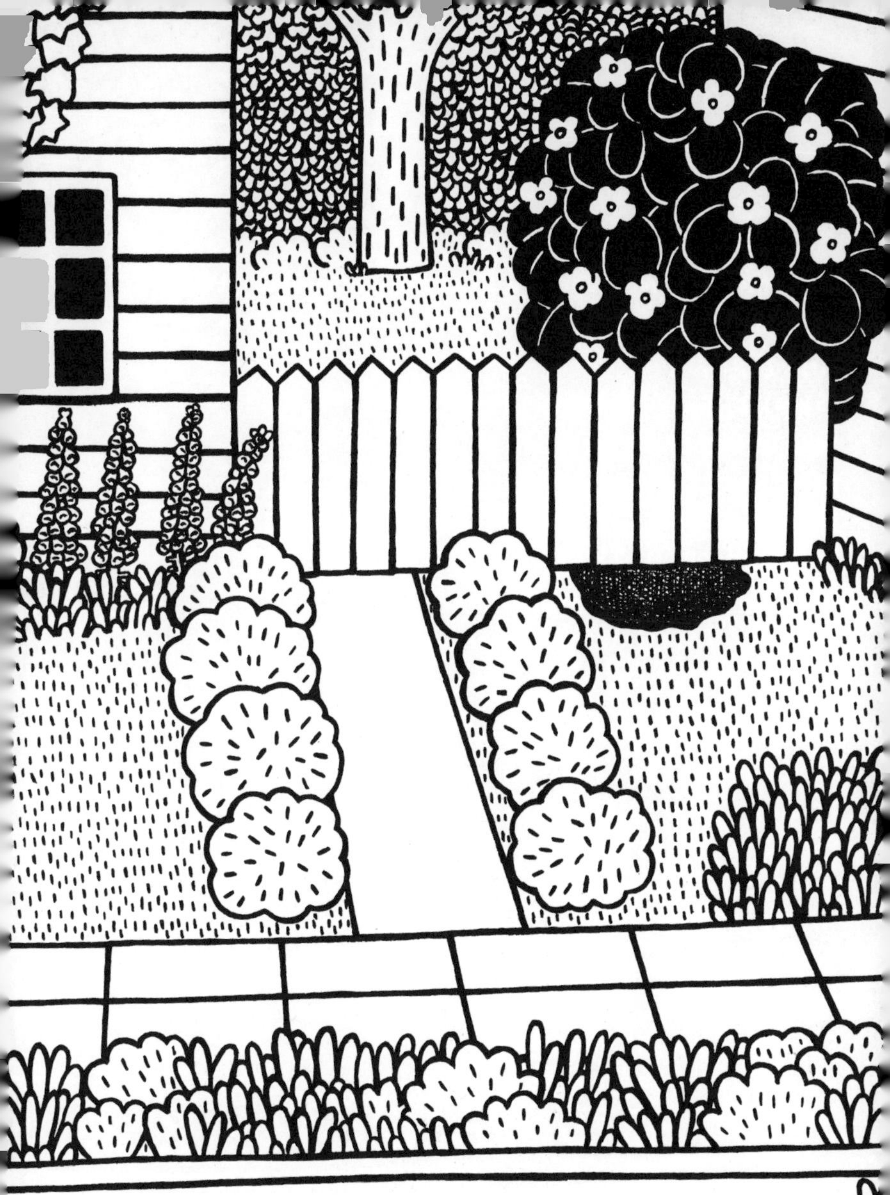

First Edition
ISBN: 978-0-97974652-9
Send Letters of appreciation to:
Aron Nels Steinke
PO Box 14883
Portland, OR 97293
www.aronnelssteinke.com
This book was printed with care by
Brown Printing of Portland, Oregon USA

Published in North America by:
Tugboat Press
PO Box 12409
Portland, OR 97212
www.tugboatpress.com
and
Sparkplug Comic Books
PO Box 10952
Portland, OR 97296-0952
www.sparkplugcomicbooks.com

FOR ARIEL

WITH ALL MY LOVE

♥

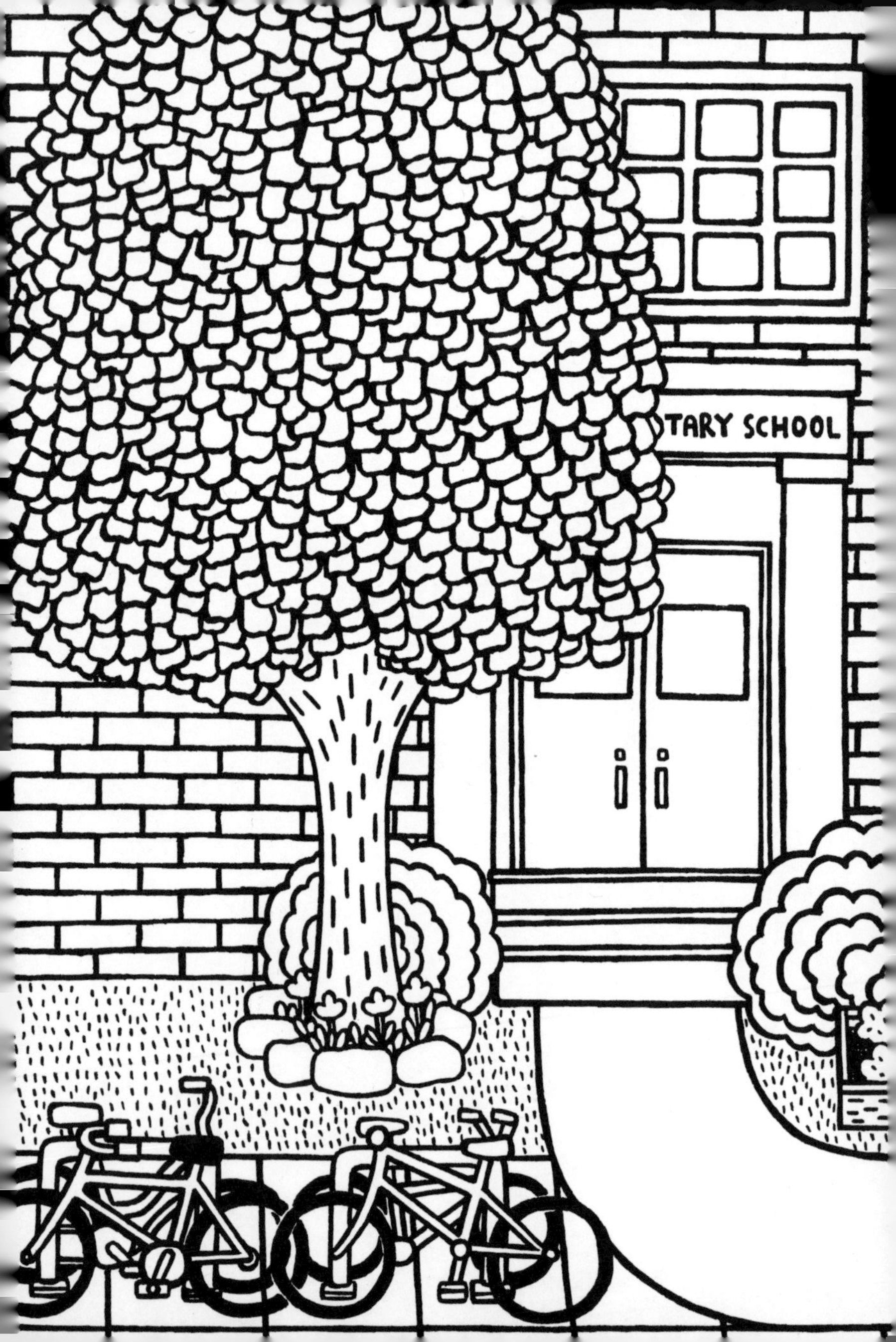
TARY SCHOOL

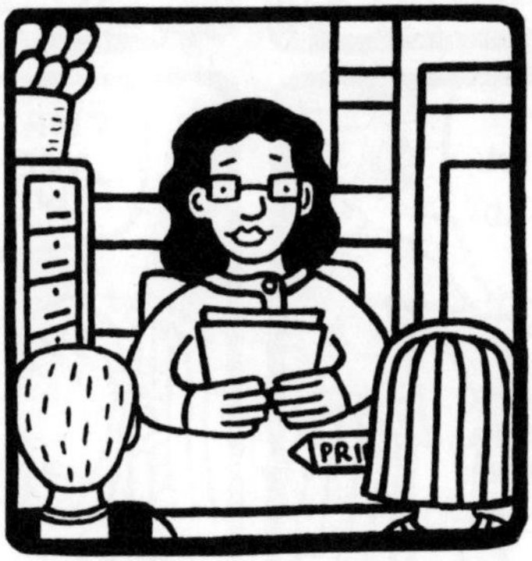
PRI

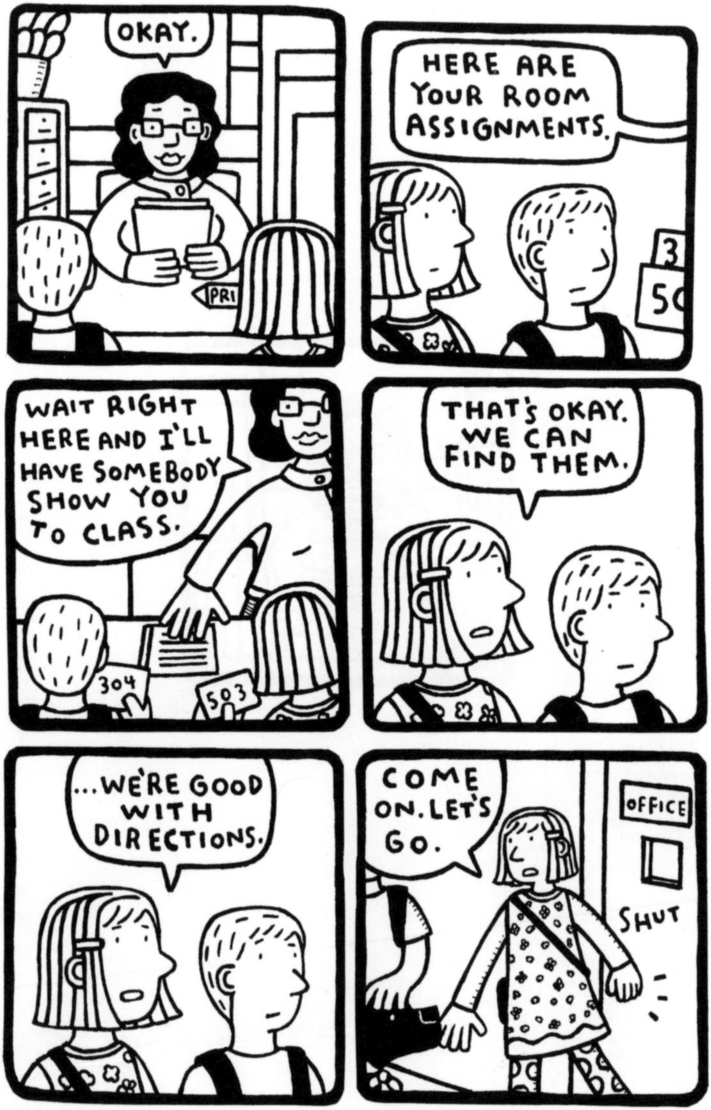
OKAY.
PRI
HERE ARE YOUR ROOM ASSIGNMENTS.
WAIT RIGHT HERE AND I'LL HAVE SOMEBODY SHOW YOU TO CLASS.
304
503
THAT'S OKAY. WE CAN FIND THEM.
...WE'RE GOOD WITH DIRECTIONS.
COME ON. LET'S GO.
OFFICE
SHUT

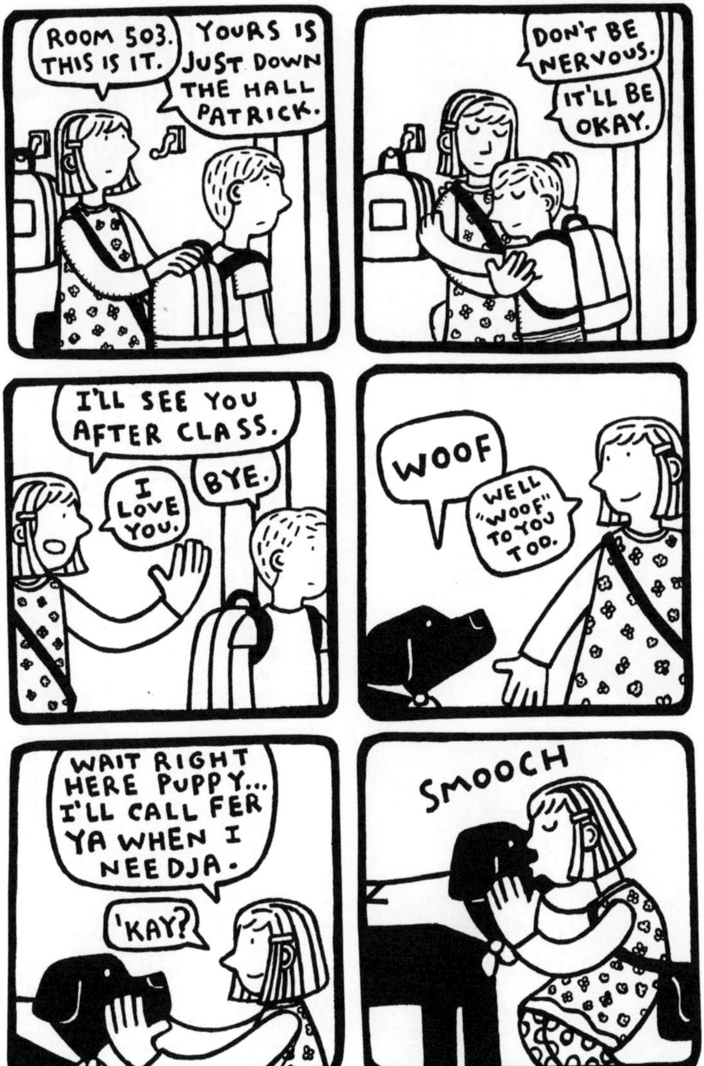
ROOM 503. THIS IS IT.
YOURS IS JUST DOWN THE HALL PATRICK.
DON'T BE NERVOUS.
IT'LL BE OKAY.
I'LL SEE YOU AFTER CLASS.
I LOVE YOU.
BYE.
WOOF
WELL "WOOF" TO YOU TOO.
WAIT RIGHT HERE PUPPY... I'LL CALL FER YA WHEN I NEEDJA.
'KAY?
SMOOCH

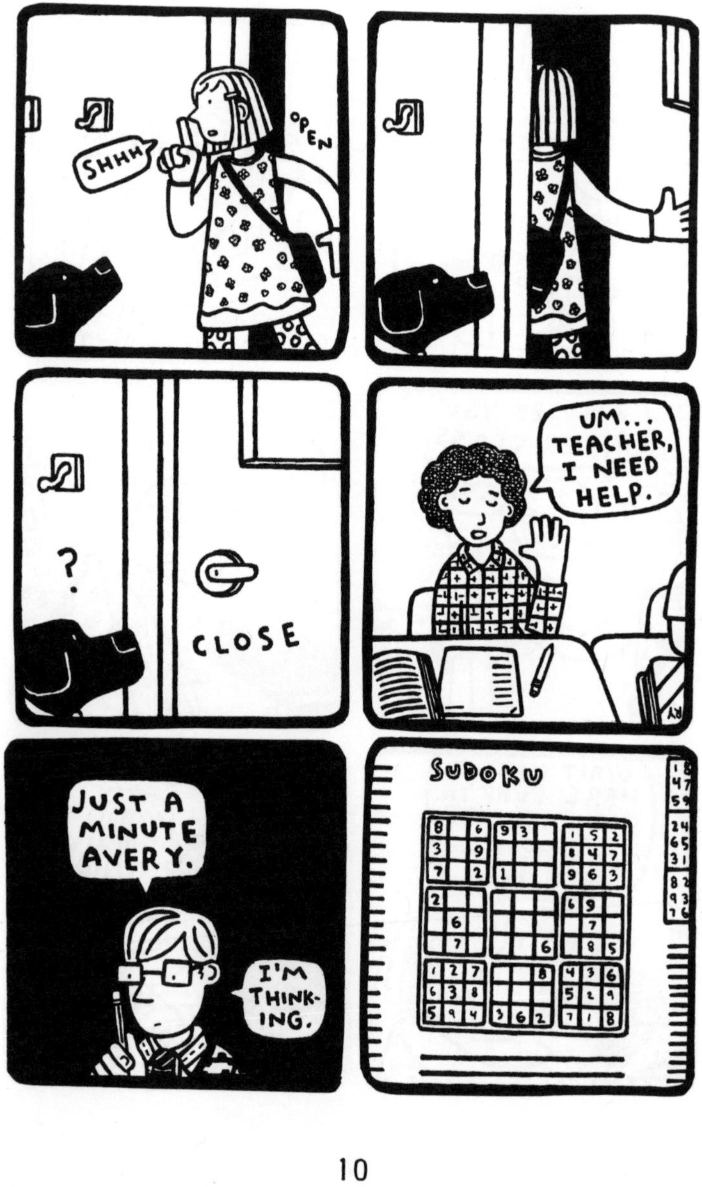
SHHH
OPEN
?
CLOSE
UM... TEACHER, I NEED HELP.
JUST A MINUTE AVERY.
I'M THINK-ING.
SUDOKU

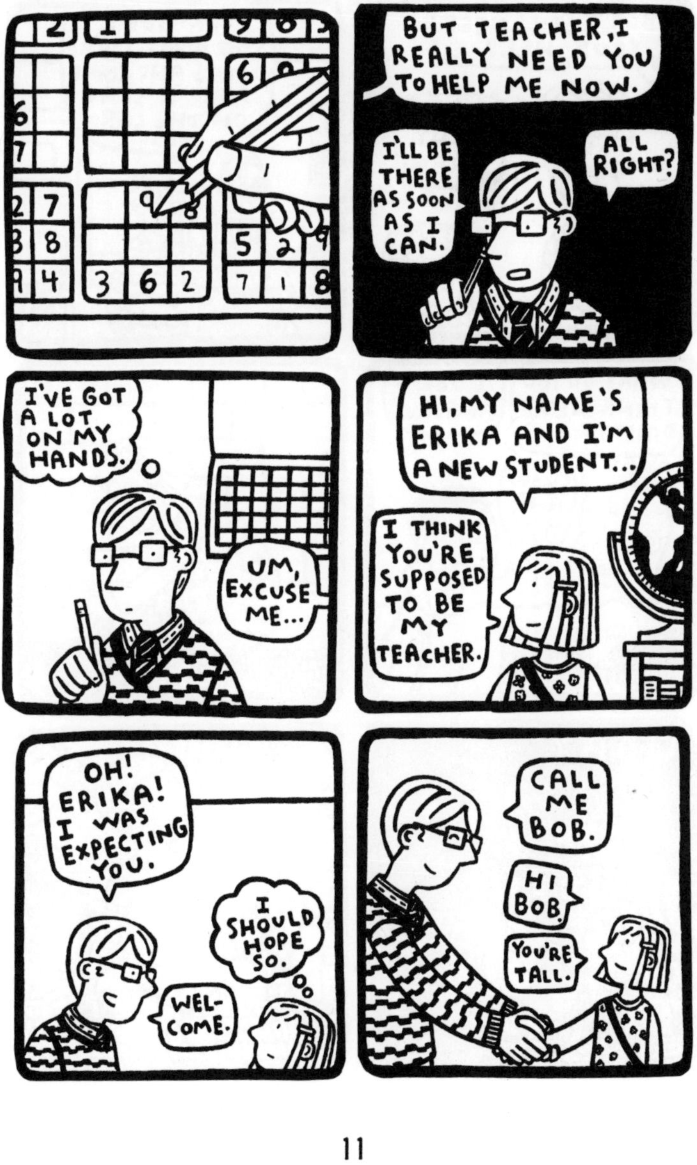

BUT TEACHER, I REALLY NEED YOU TO HELP ME NOW.
I'LL BE THERE AS SOON AS I CAN.
ALL RIGHT?
I'VE GOT A LOT ON MY HANDS.
UM, EXCUSE ME...
HI, MY NAME'S ERIKA AND I'M A NEW STUDENT...
I THINK YOU'RE SUPPOSED TO BE MY TEACHER.
OH! ERIKA! I WAS EXPECTING YOU.
I SHOULD HOPE SO.
WEL-COME.
CALL ME BOB.
HI BOB.
YOU'RE TALL.

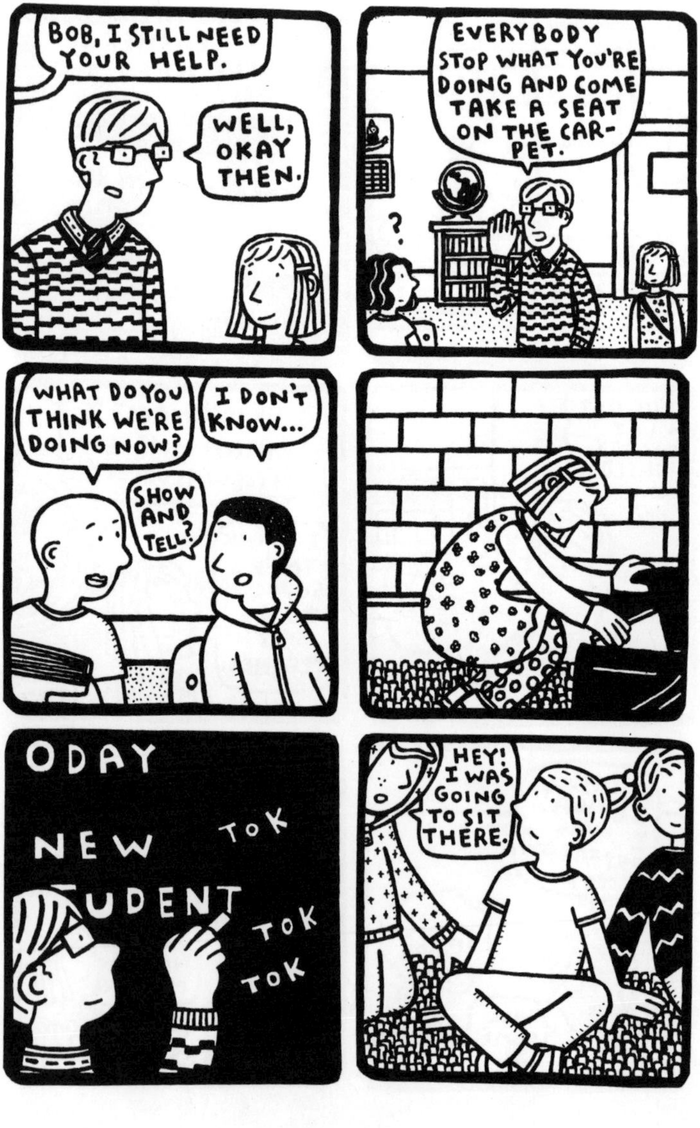
BOB, I STILL NEED YOUR HELP.
WELL, OKAY THEN.
EVERYBODY STOP WHAT YOU'RE DOING AND COME TAKE A SEAT ON THE CAR-PET.
?
WHAT DO YOU THINK WE'RE DOING NOW?
I DON'T KNOW...
SHOW AND TELL?
ODAY
NEW
UDENT
TOK
TOK
TOK
HEY! I WAS GOING TO SIT THERE.

ALRIGHT CLASS LISTEN UP.. IT'S SHOW AND TELL TIME AND I KNOW YOU'RE ALL REALLY EXCITED TO SHARE SOMETHING WITH THE REST OF THE CLASS...
BUT FIRST YOU'VE PROBABLY NOTICED THAT WE HAVE A NEW STUDENT. I THOUGHT WE'D LET HER GO FIRST.
OH MAN.
THIS IS A LOT OF PRESSURE.

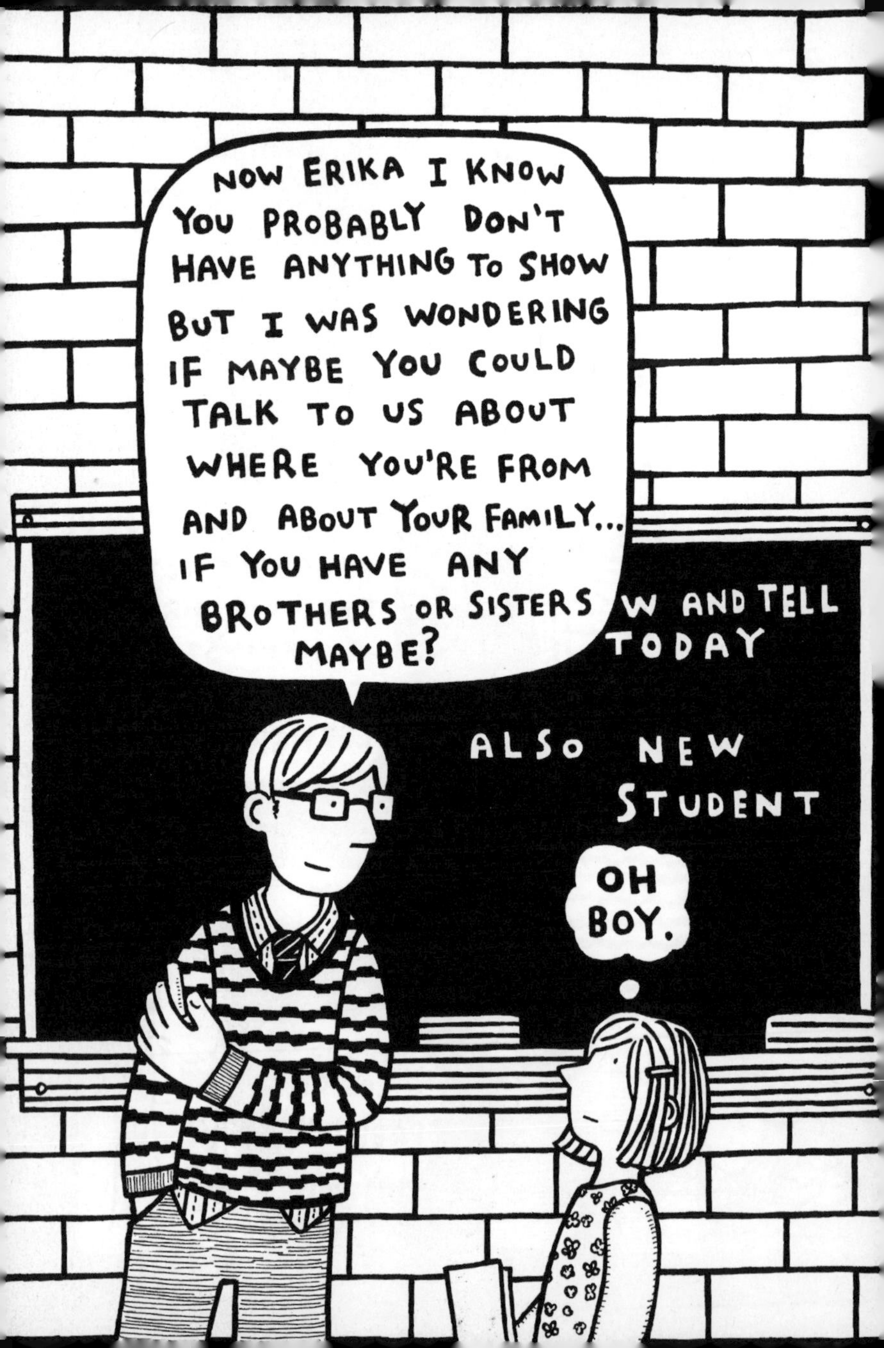
NOW ERIKA I KNOW YOU PROBABLY DON'T HAVE ANYTHING TO SHOW BUT I WAS WONDERING IF MAYBE YOU COULD TALK TO US ABOUT WHERE YOU'RE FROM AND ABOUT YOUR FAMILY... IF YOU HAVE ANY BROTHERS OR SISTERS MAYBE?
W AND TELL TODAY
ALSO NEW STUDENT
OH BOY.

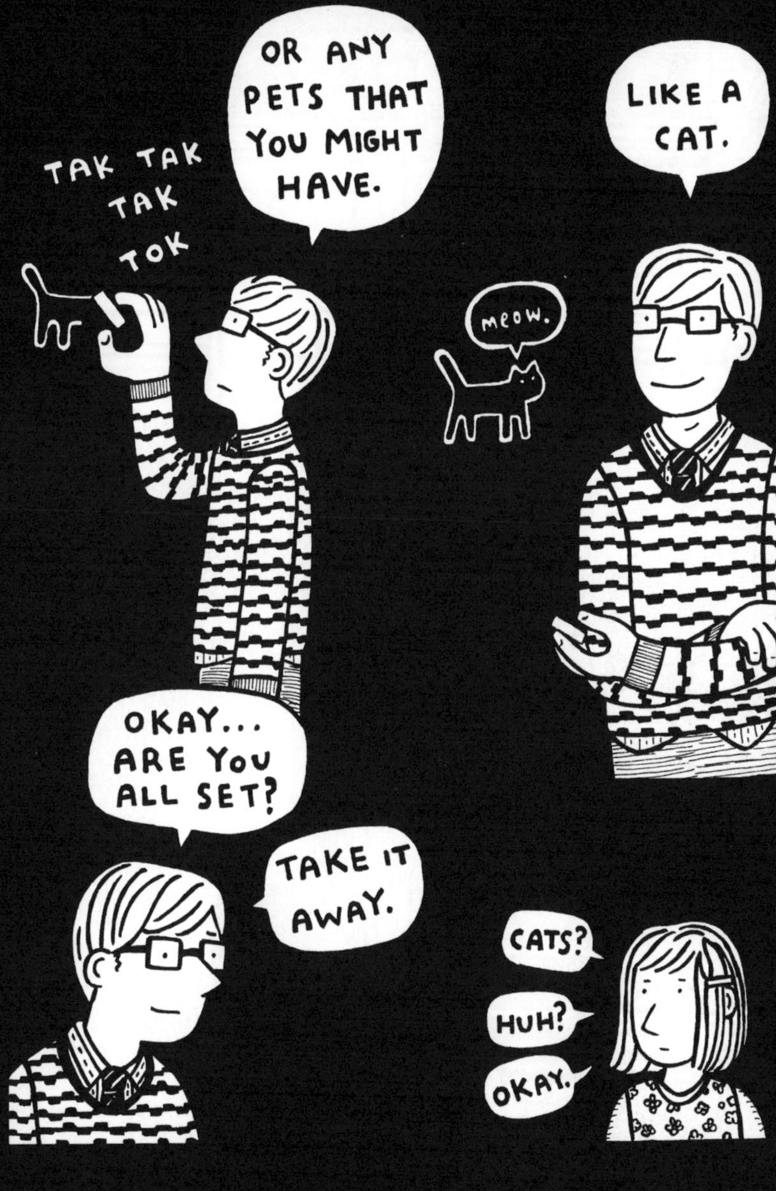
OR ANY PETS THAT YOU MIGHT HAVE.
TAK TAK TAK TOK
LIKE A CAT.
meow.
OKAY... ARE YOU ALL SET?
TAKE IT AWAY.
CATS?
HUH?
OKAY.

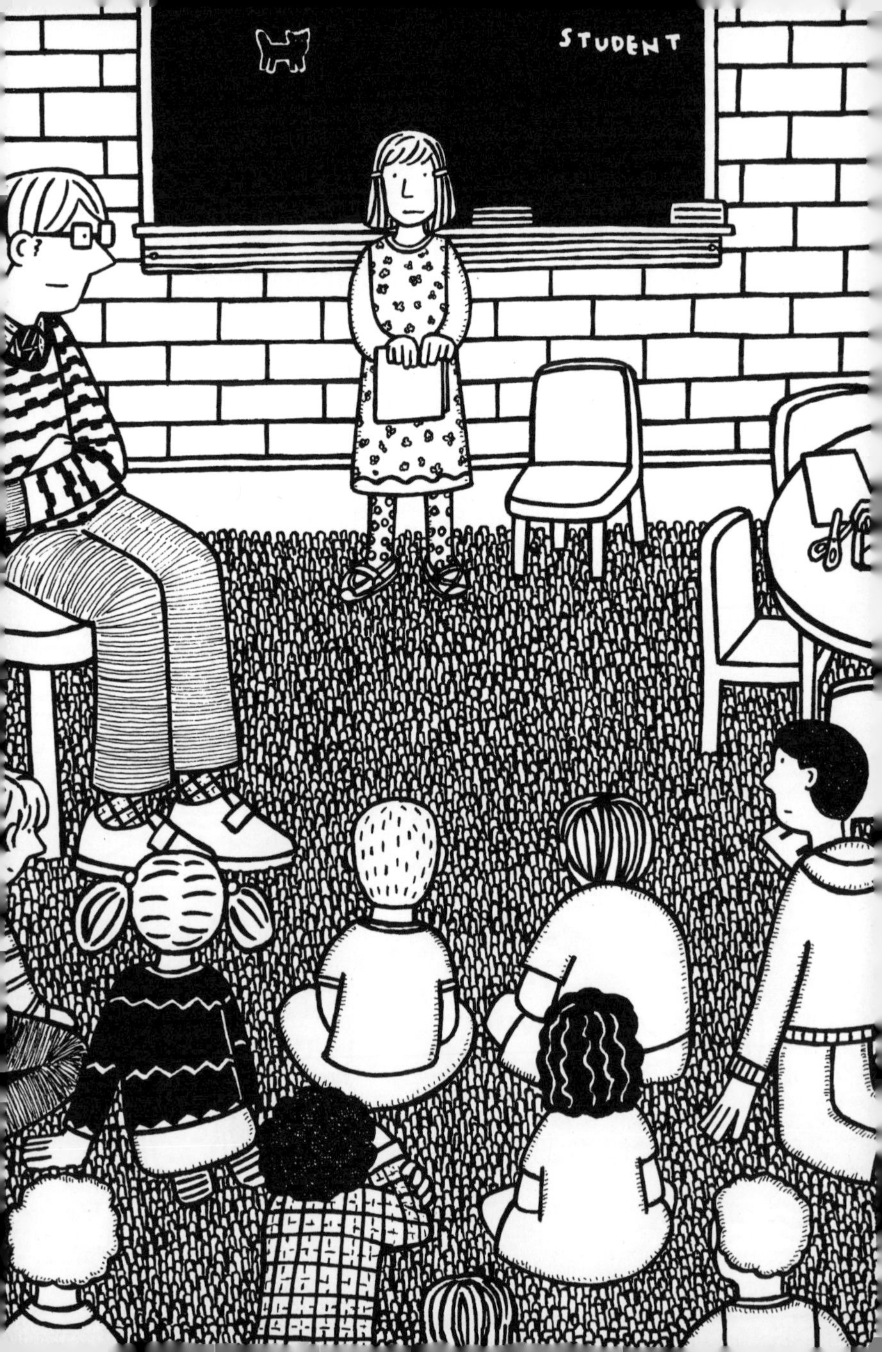
STUDENT

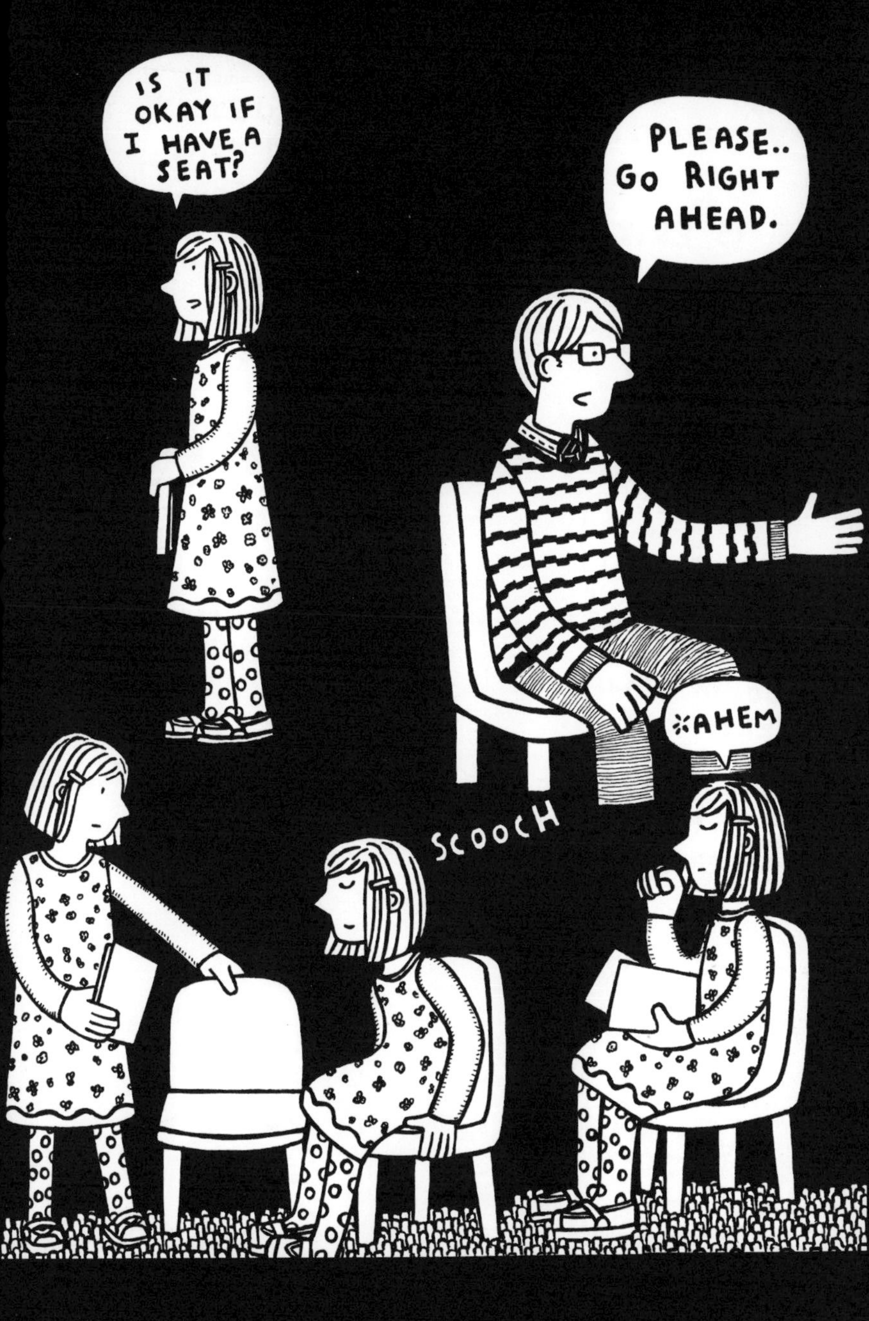
IS IT OKAY IF I HAVE A SEAT?
PLEASE.. GO RIGHT AHEAD.
*AHEM
SCOOCH

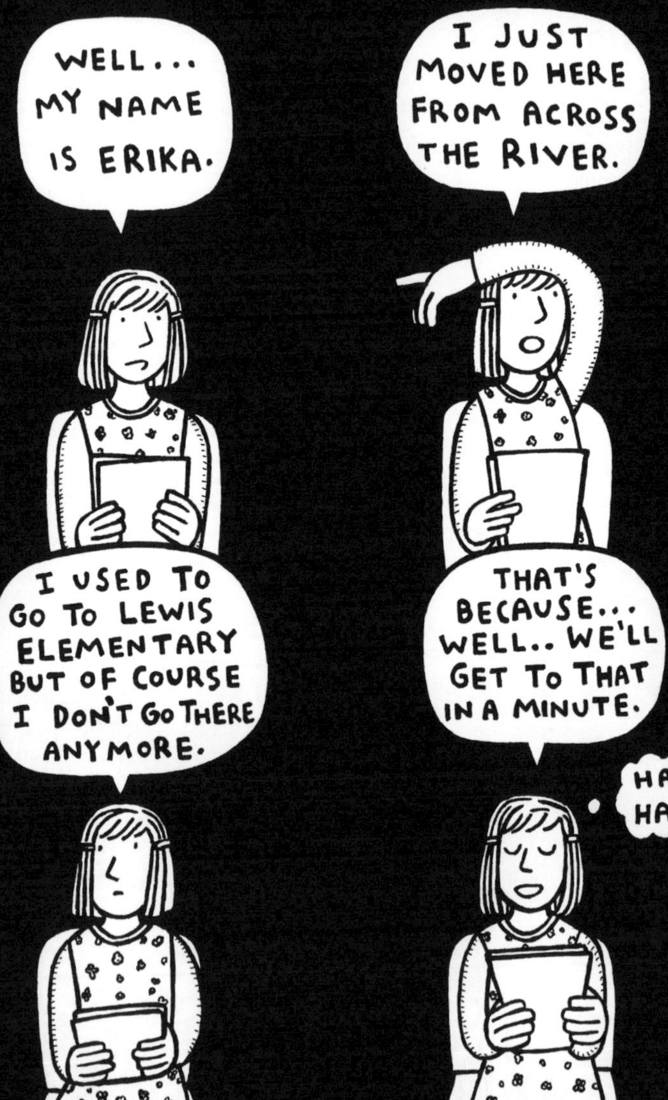
WELL... MY NAME IS ERIKA.
I JUST MOVED HERE FROM ACROSS THE RIVER.
I USED TO GO TO LEWIS ELEMENTARY BUT OF COURSE I DON'T GO THERE ANYMORE.
THAT'S BECAUSE... WELL.. WE'LL GET TO THAT IN A MINUTE.
HA HA

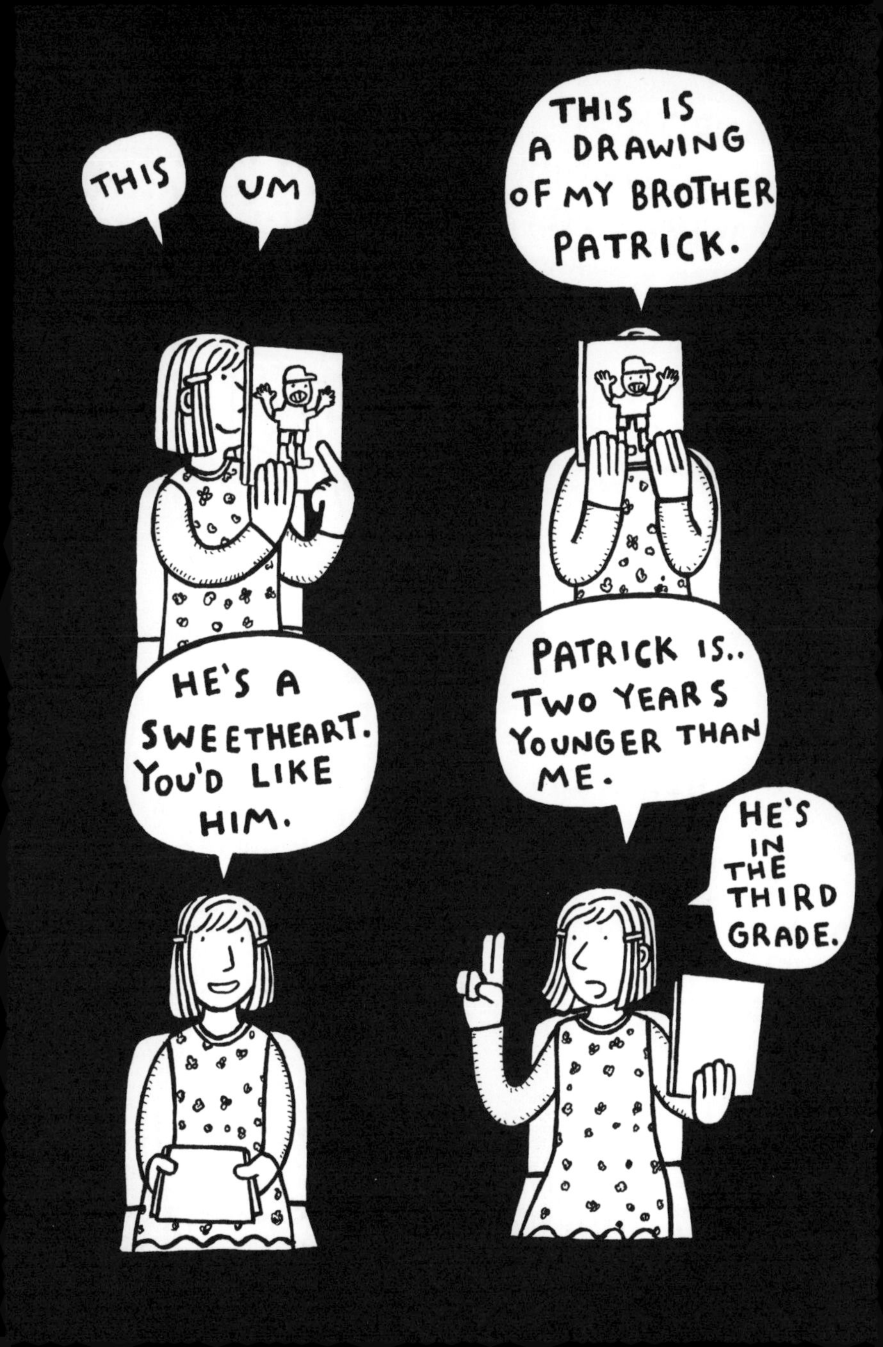
THIS
UM
THIS IS A DRAWING OF MY BROTHER PATRICK.
HE'S A SWEETHEART. YOU'D LIKE HIM.
PATRICK IS.. TWO YEARS YOUNGER THAN ME.
HE'S IN THE THIRD GRADE.

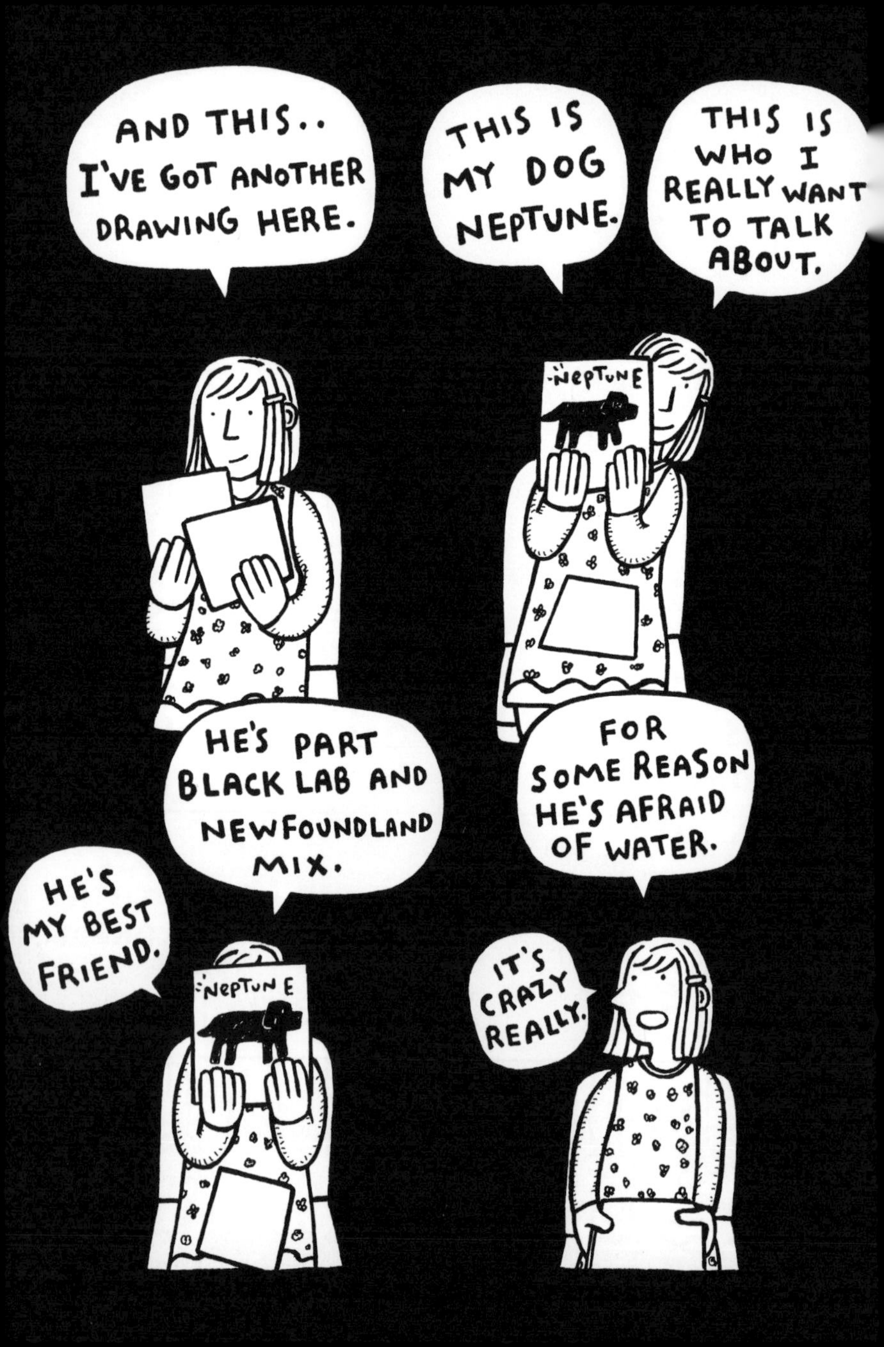
AND THIS.. I'VE GOT ANOTHER DRAWING HERE.
THIS IS MY DOG NEPTUNE.
THIS IS WHO I REALLY WANT TO TALK ABOUT.
NEPTUNE
HE'S PART BLACK LAB AND NEWFOUNDLAND MIX.
FOR SOME REASON HE'S AFRAID OF WATER.
HE'S MY BEST FRIEND.
NEPTUNE
IT'S CRAZY REALLY.

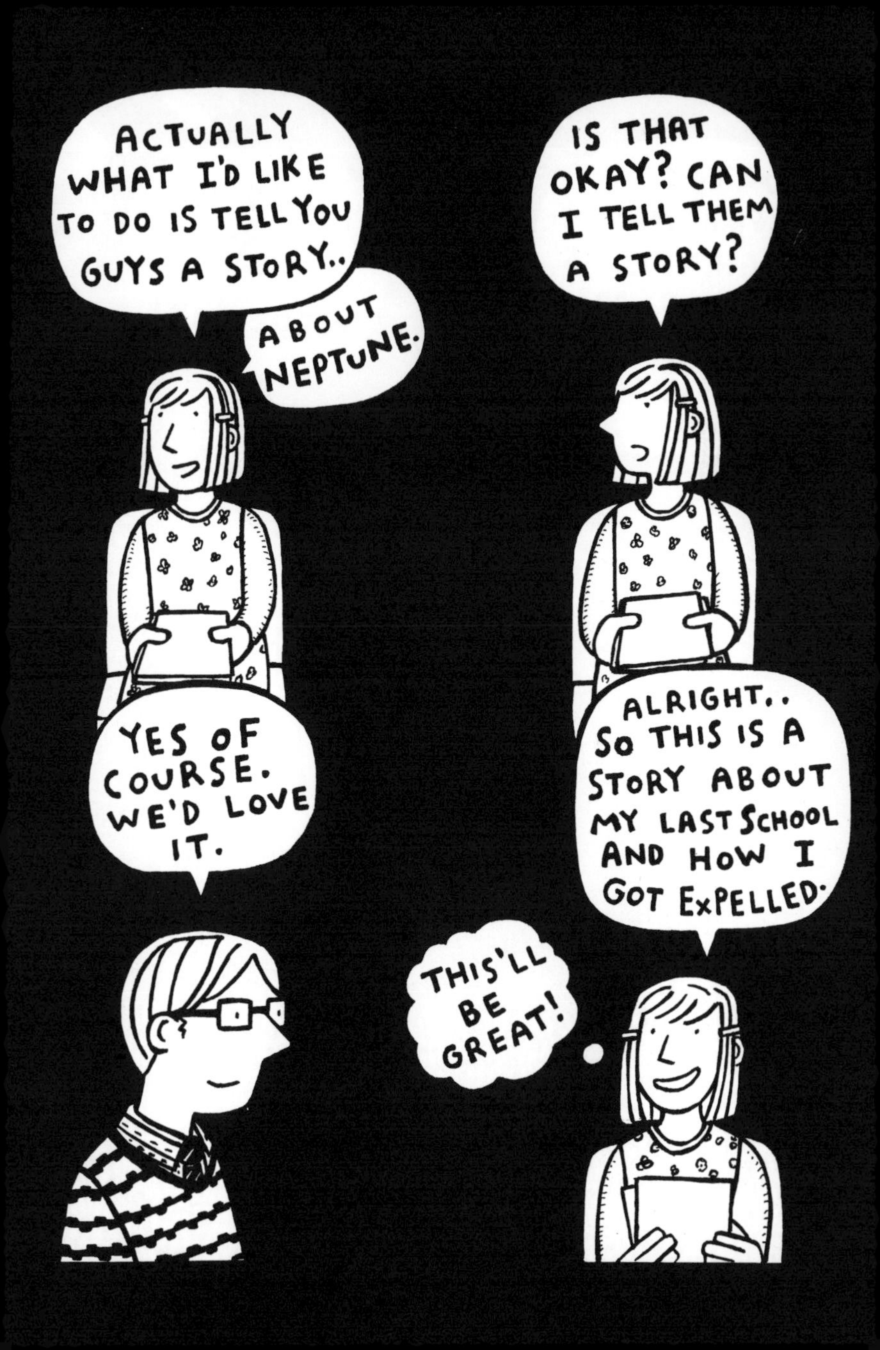
ACTUALLY WHAT I'D LIKE TO DO IS TELL YOU GUYS A STORY..
ABOUT NEPTUNE.
IS THAT OKAY? CAN I TELL THEM A STORY?
YES OF COURSE. WE'D LOVE IT.
ALRIGHT.. SO THIS IS A STORY ABOUT MY LAST SCHOOL AND HOW I GOT EXPELLED.
THIS'LL BE GREAT!

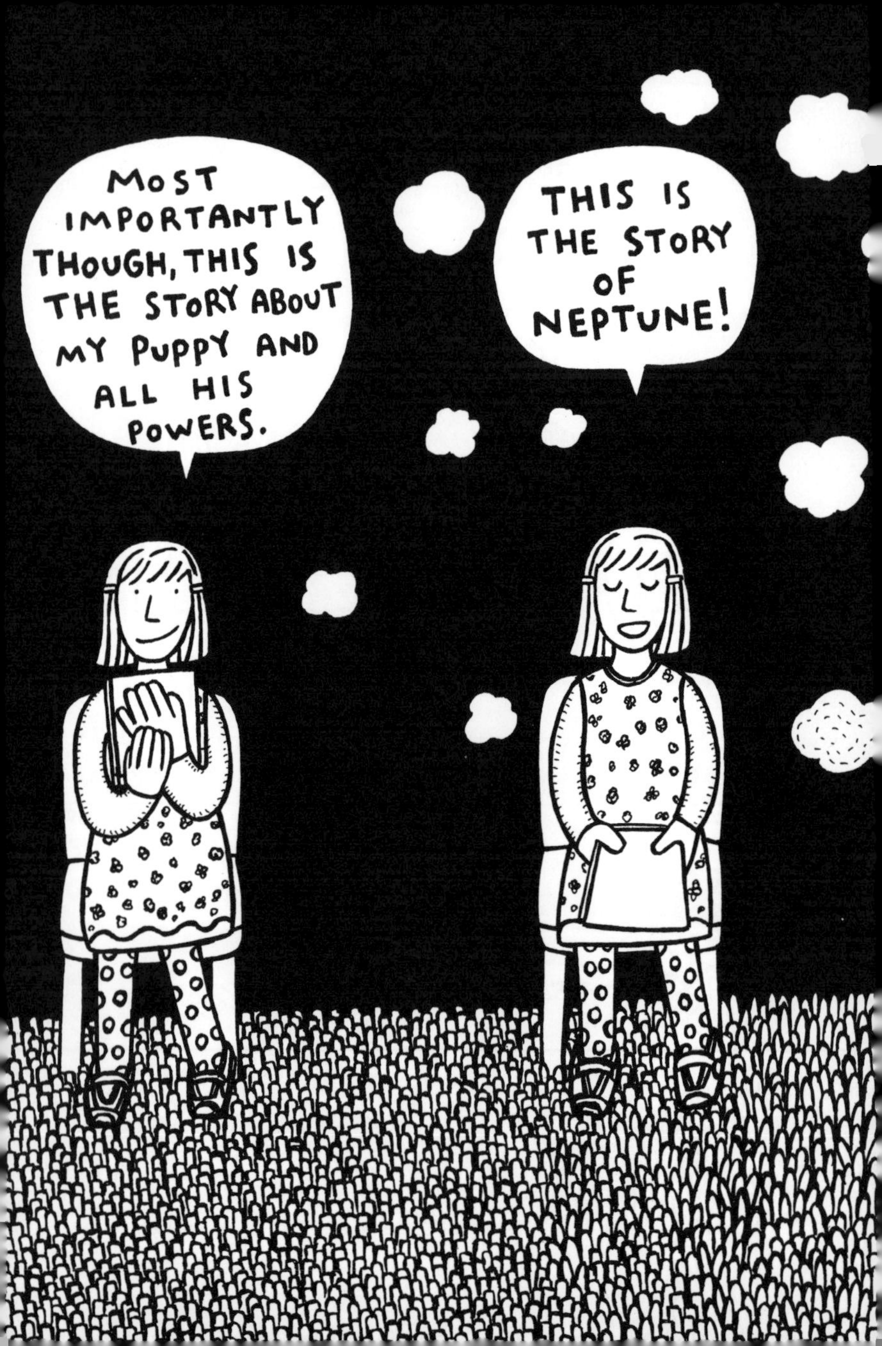
MOST IMPORTANTLY THOUGH, THIS IS THE STORY ABOUT MY PUPPY AND ALL HIS POWERS.
THIS IS THE STORY OF NEPTUNE!

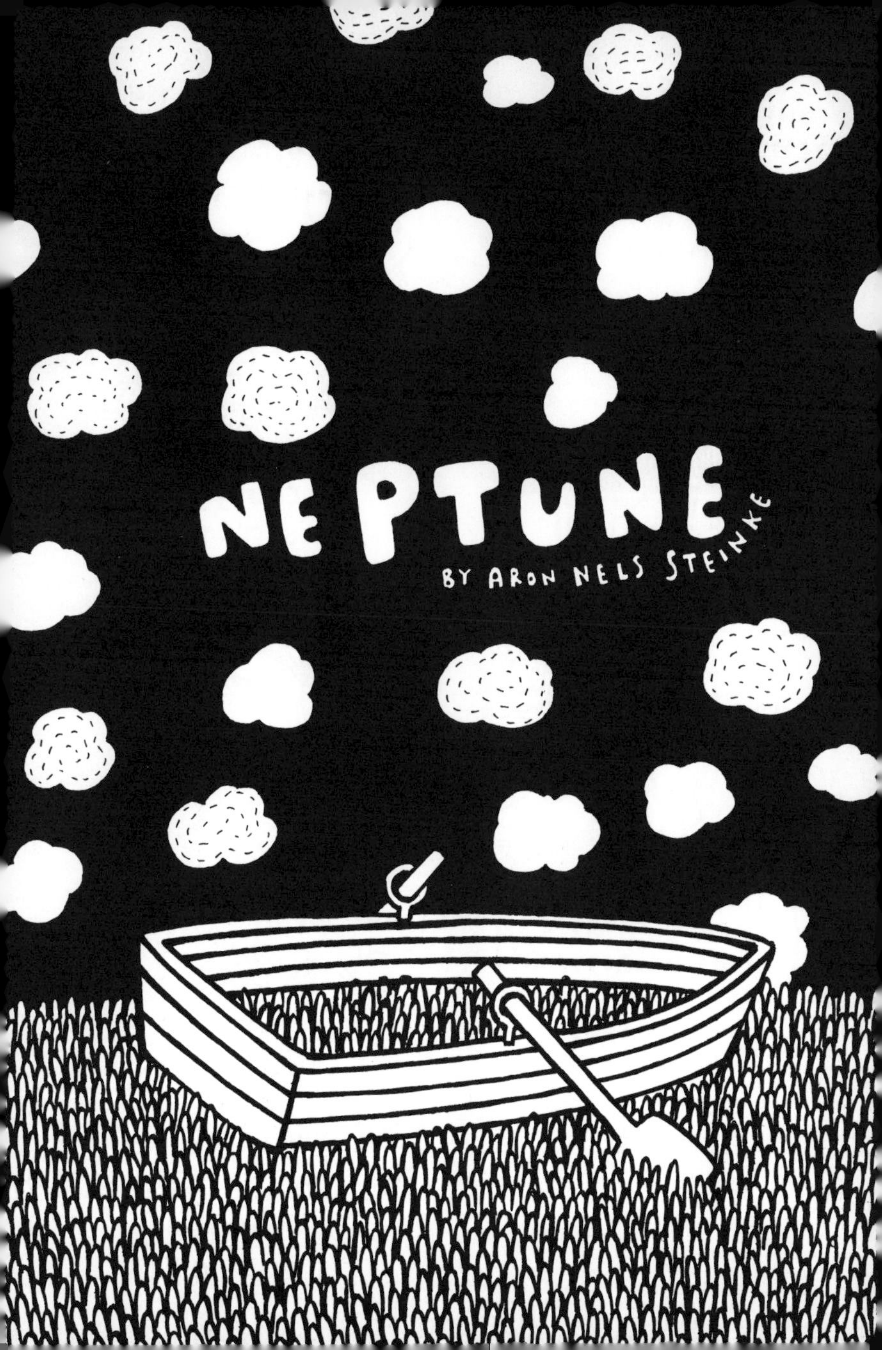
NEPTUNE
BY ARON NELS STEINKE

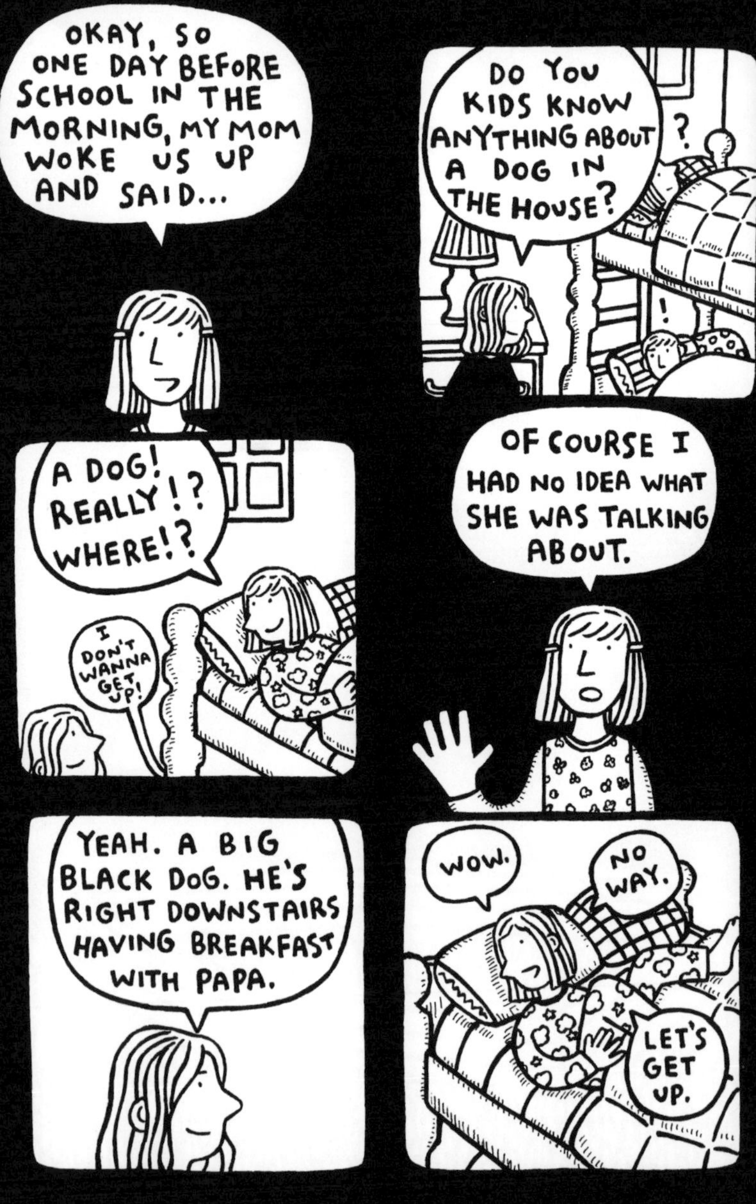
OKAY, SO ONE DAY BEFORE SCHOOL IN THE MORNING, MY MOM WOKE US UP AND SAID...
DO YOU KIDS KNOW ANYTHING ABOUT A DOG IN THE HOUSE?
?
!
A DOG! REALLY!? WHERE!?
I DON'T WANNA GET UP!
OF COURSE I HAD NO IDEA WHAT SHE WAS TALKING ABOUT.
YEAH. A BIG BLACK DOG. HE'S RIGHT DOWNSTAIRS HAVING BREAKFAST WITH PAPA.
WOW.
NO WAY.
LET'S GET UP.

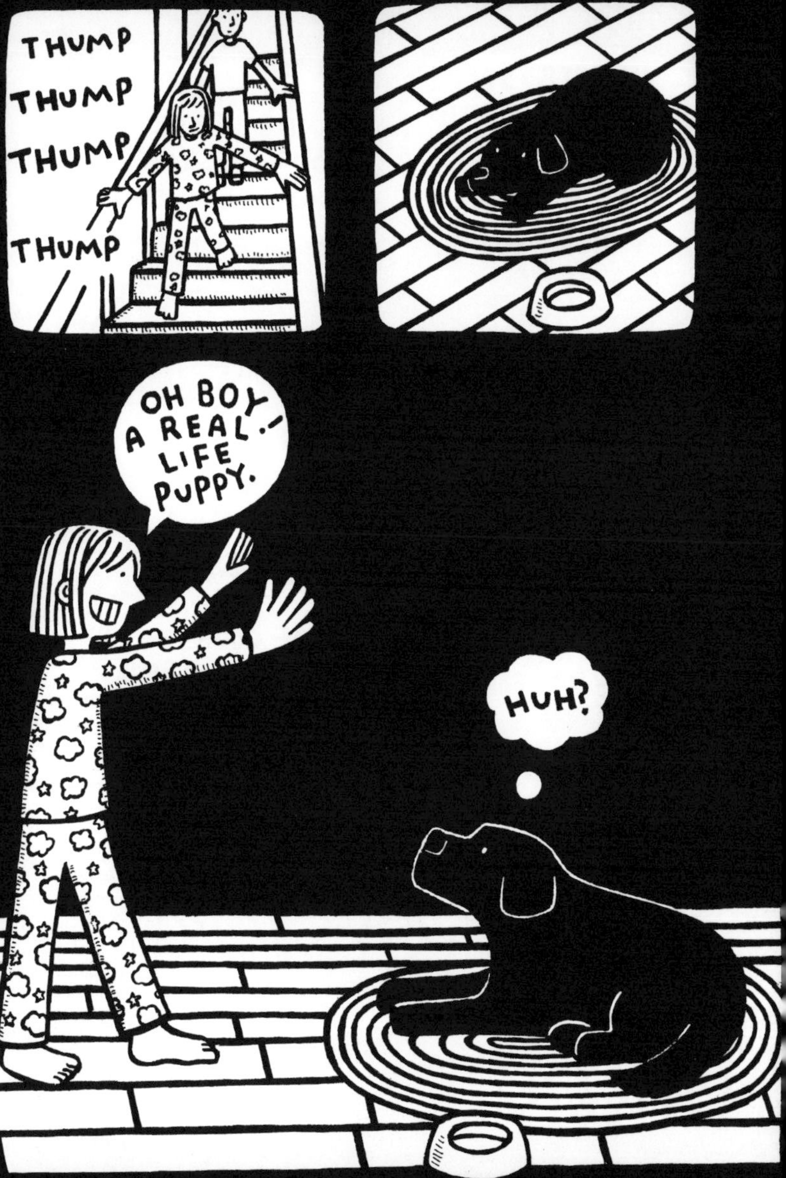
THUMP
THUMP
THUMP
THUMP
OH BOY! A REAL LIFE PUPPY.
HUH?

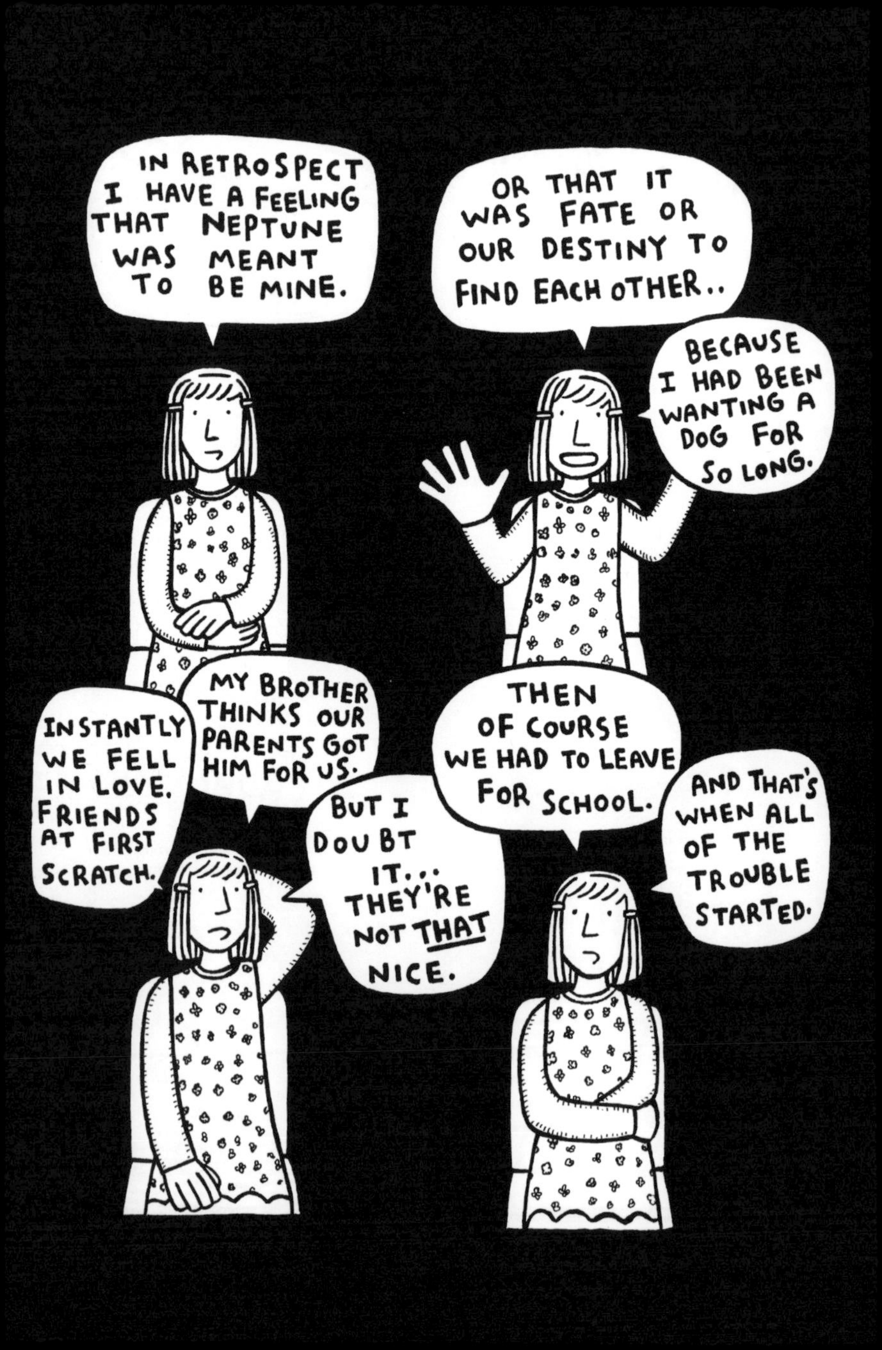
IN RETROSPECT I HAVE A FEELING THAT NEPTUNE WAS MEANT TO BE MINE.
OR THAT IT WAS FATE OR OUR DESTINY TO FIND EACH OTHER..
BECAUSE I HAD BEEN WANTING A DOG FOR SO LONG.
INSTANTLY WE FELL IN LOVE. FRIENDS AT FIRST SCRATCH.
MY BROTHER THINKS OUR PARENTS GOT HIM FOR US.
BUT I DOUBT IT... THEY'RE NOT THAT NICE.
THEN OF COURSE WE HAD TO LEAVE FOR SCHOOL.
AND THAT'S WHEN ALL OF THE TROUBLE STARTED.

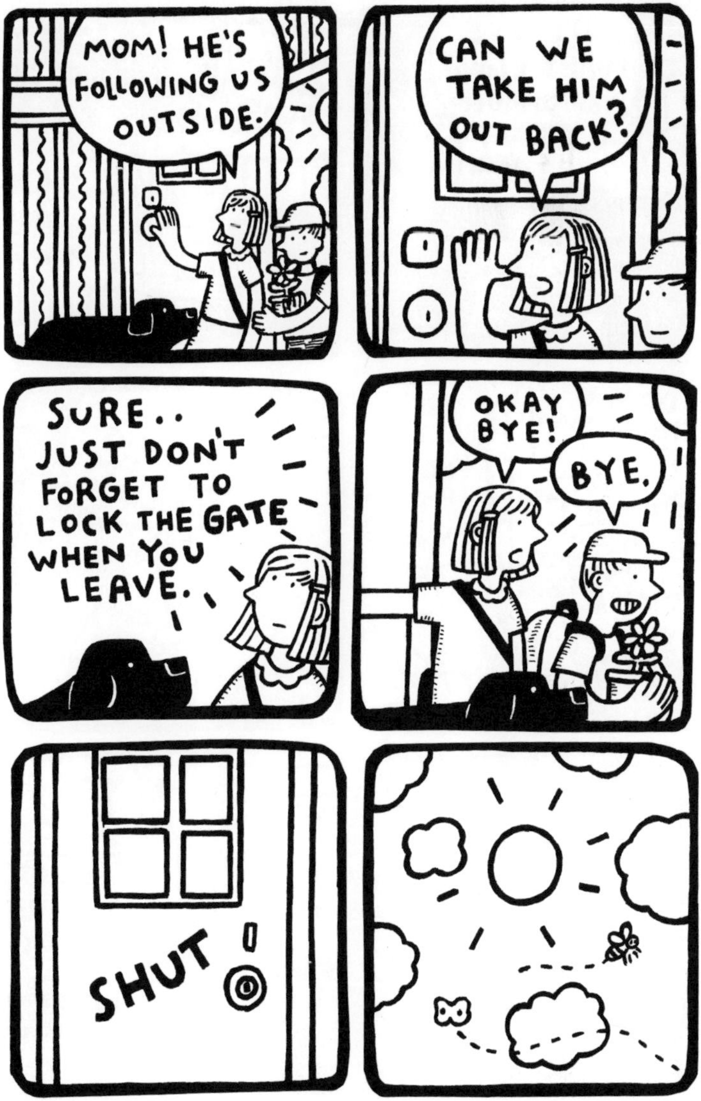
MOM! HE'S FOLLOWING US OUTSIDE.
CAN WE TAKE HIM OUT BACK?
SURE.. JUST DON'T FORGET TO LOCK THE GATE WHEN YOU LEAVE.
OKAY BYE!
BYE.
SHUT!

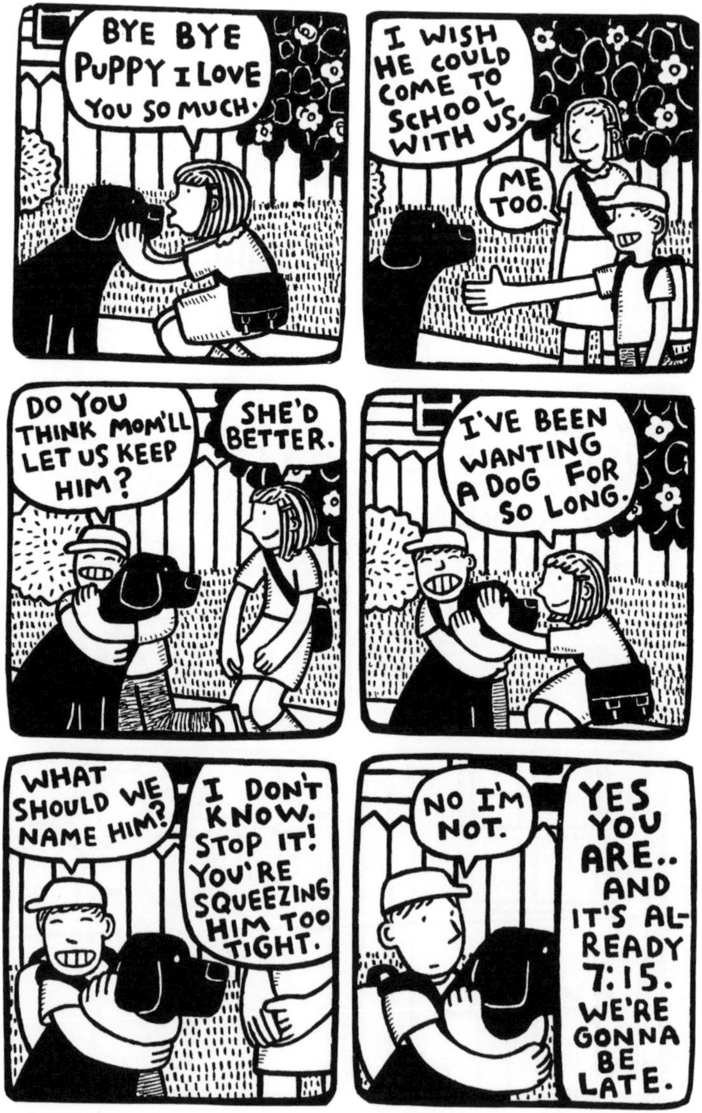
BYE BYE PUPPY I LOVE YOU SO MUCH.
I WISH HE COULD COME TO SCHOOL WITH US.
ME TOO.
DO YOU THINK MOM'LL LET US KEEP HIM?
SHE'D BETTER.
I'VE BEEN WANTING A DOG FOR SO LONG.
WHAT SHOULD WE NAME HIM?
I DON'T KNOW. STOP IT! YOU'RE SQUEEZING HIM TOO TIGHT.
NO I'M NOT.
YES YOU ARE.. AND IT'S AL-READY 7:15. WE'RE GONNA BE LATE.

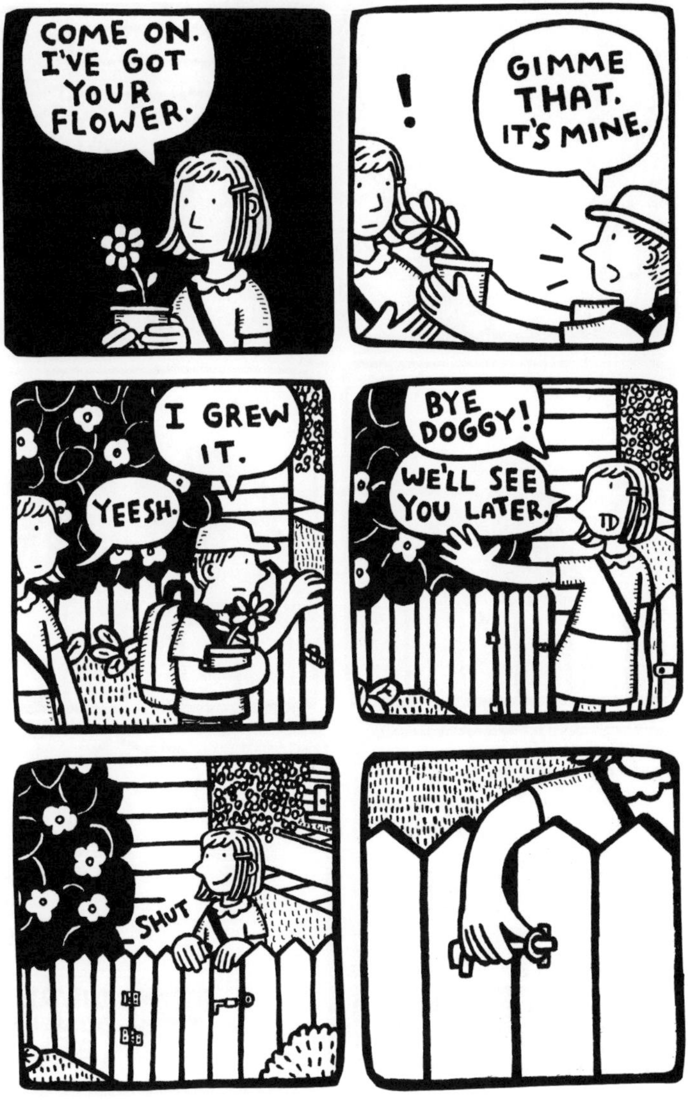
COME ON. I'VE GOT YOUR FLOWER.
!
GIMME THAT. IT'S MINE.
I GREW IT.
YEESH.
BYE DOGGY!
WE'LL SEE YOU LATER.
SHUT

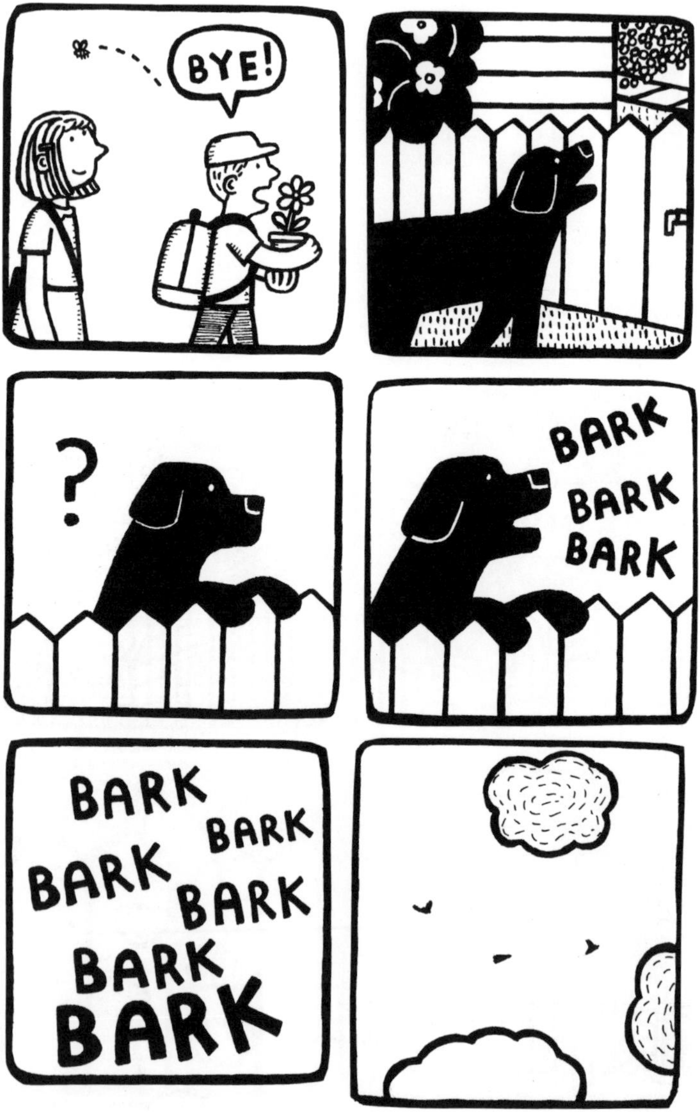
BYE!
?
BARK
BARK
BARK
BARK
BARK
BARK
BARK
BARK
BARK

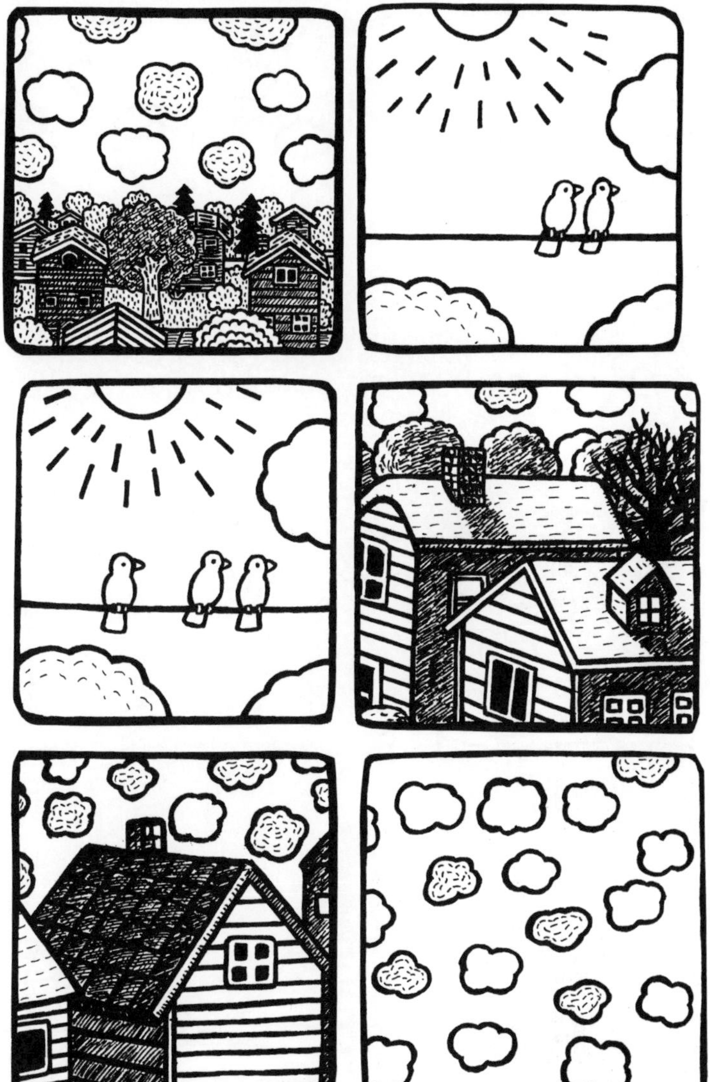

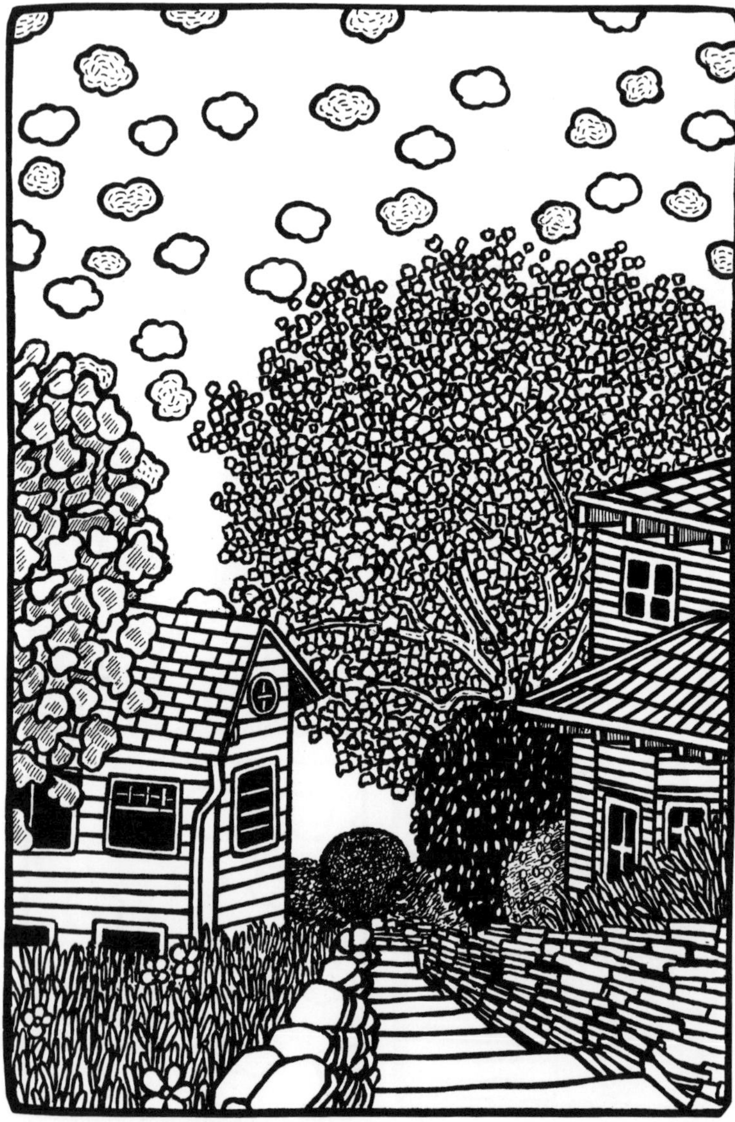

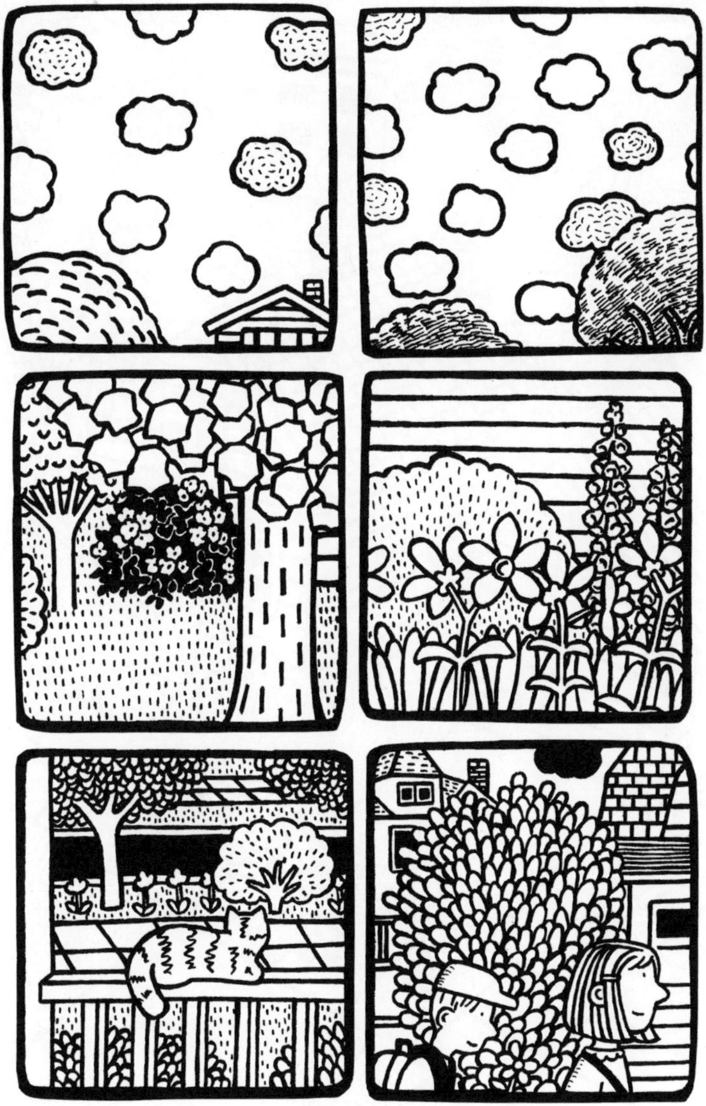

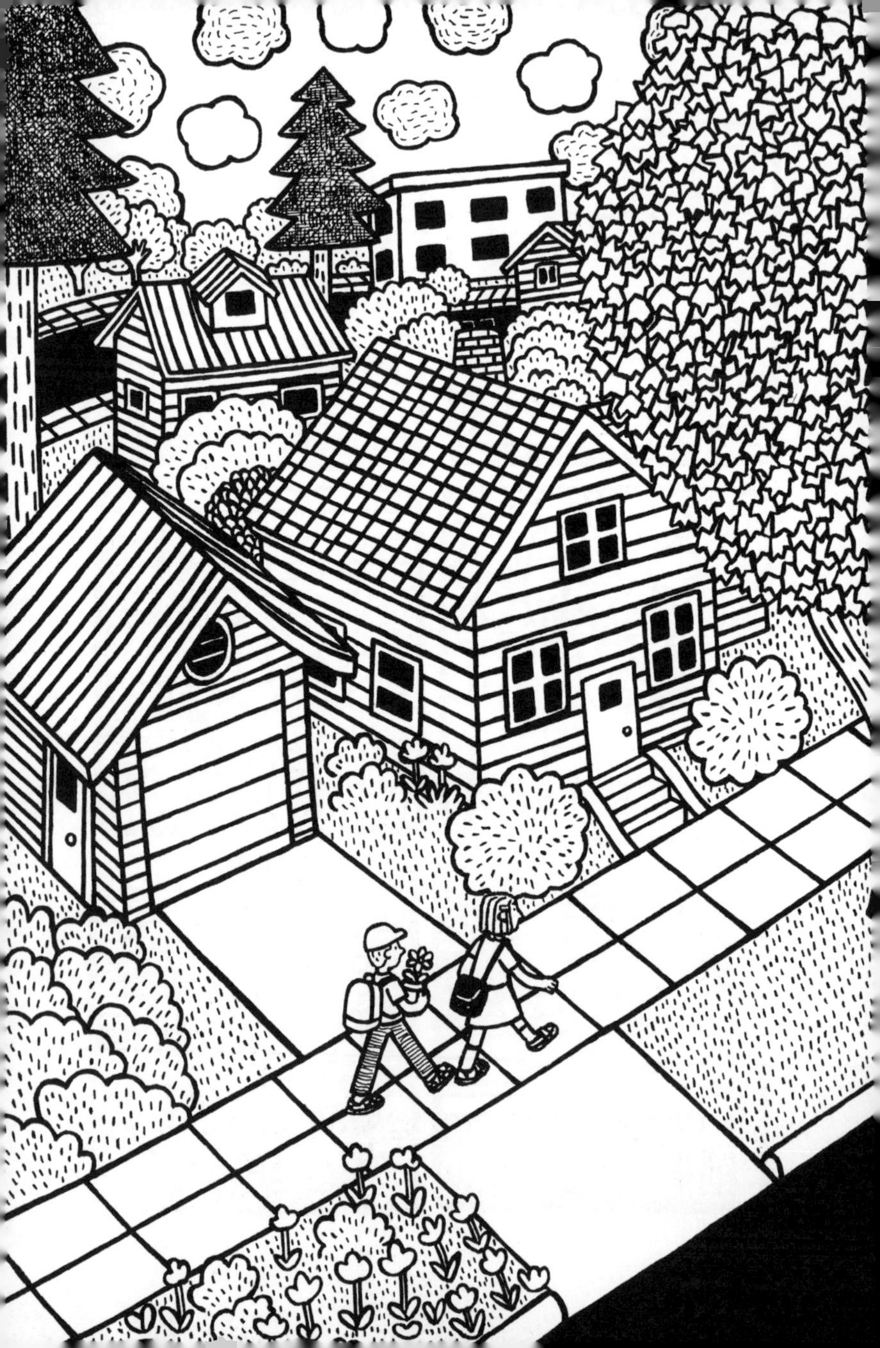

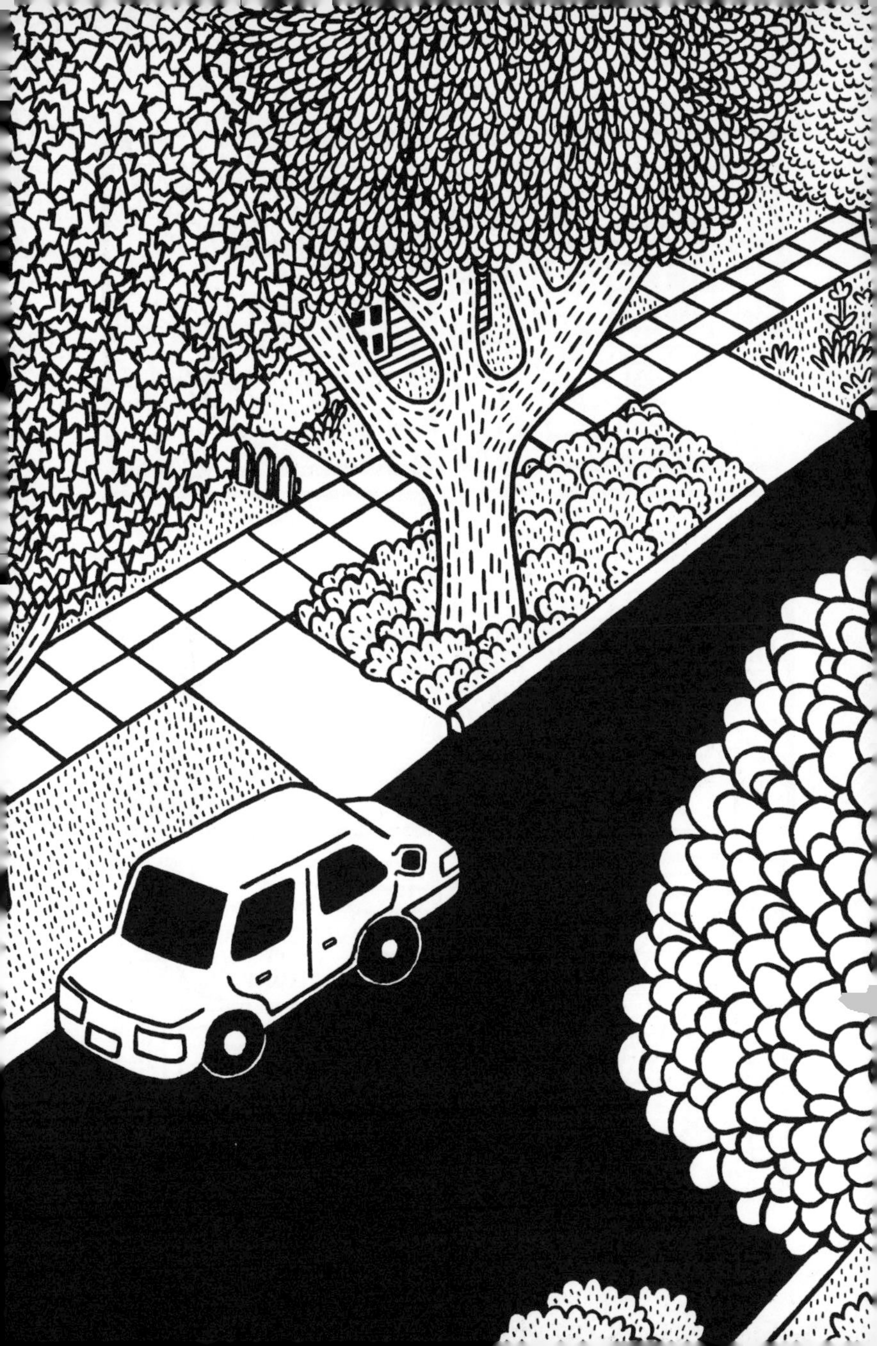

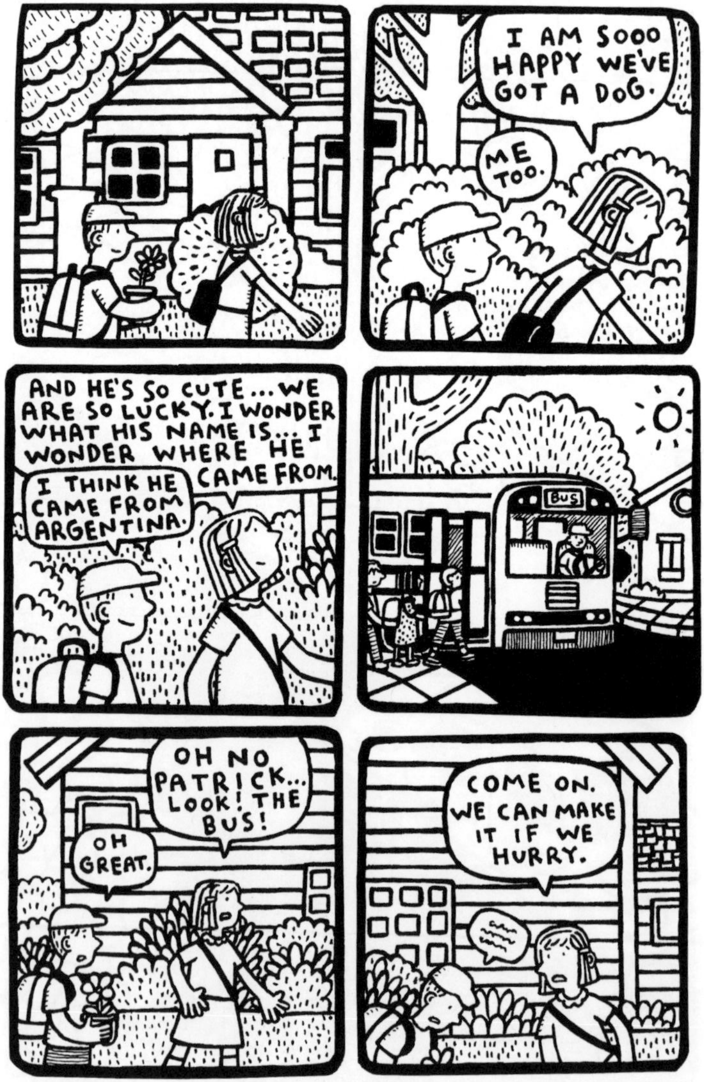
I AM SOOO HAPPY WE'VE GOT A DOG.
ME TOO.
AND HE'S SO CUTE... WE ARE SO LUCKY. I WONDER WHAT HIS NAME IS... I WONDER WHERE HE CAME FROM.
I THINK HE CAME FROM ARGENTINA.
BUS
OH NO PATRICK... LOOK! THE BUS!
OH GREAT.
COME ON. WE CAN MAKE IT IF WE HURRY.

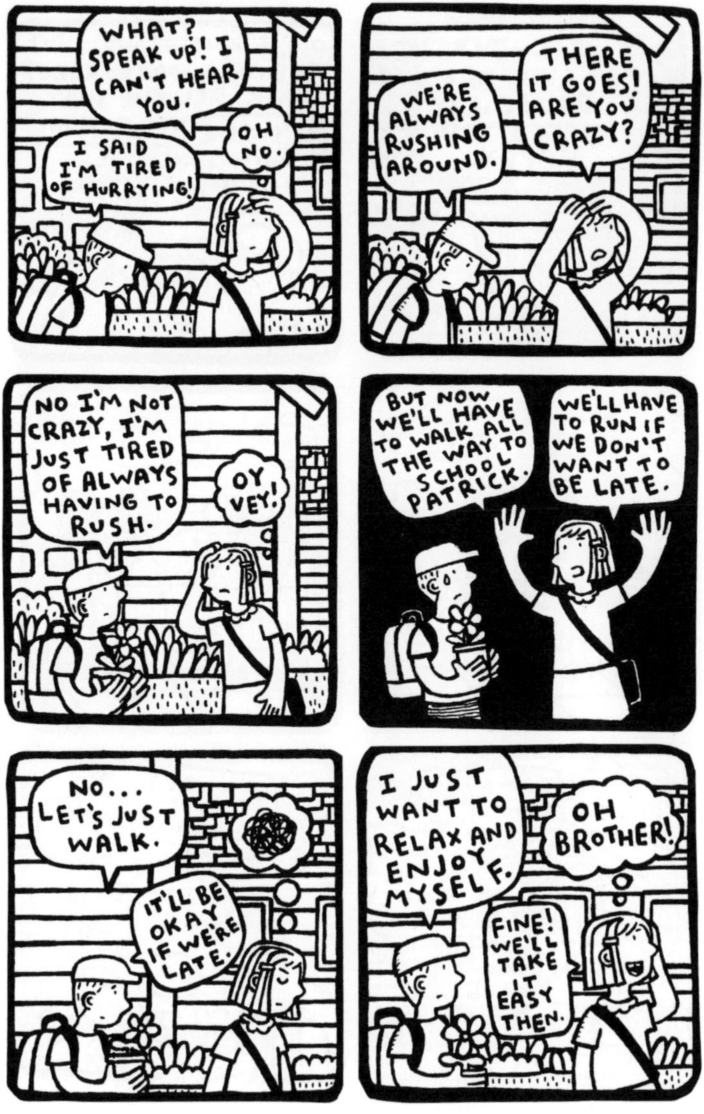
WHAT? SPEAK UP! I CAN'T HEAR YOU.
I SAID I'M TIRED OF HURRYING!
OH NO.
WE'RE ALWAYS RUSHING AROUND.
THERE IT GOES! ARE YOU CRAZY?
NO I'M NOT CRAZY, I'M JUST TIRED OF ALWAYS HAVING TO RUSH.
OY VEY!
BUT NOW WE'LL HAVE TO WALK ALL THE WAY TO SCHOOL PATRICK.
WE'LL HAVE TO RUN IF WE DON'T WANT TO BE LATE.
NO... LET'S JUST WALK.
IT'LL BE OKAY IF WE'RE LATE.
I JUST WANT TO RELAX AND ENJOY MYSELF.
OH BROTHER!
FINE! WE'LL TAKE IT EASY THEN.

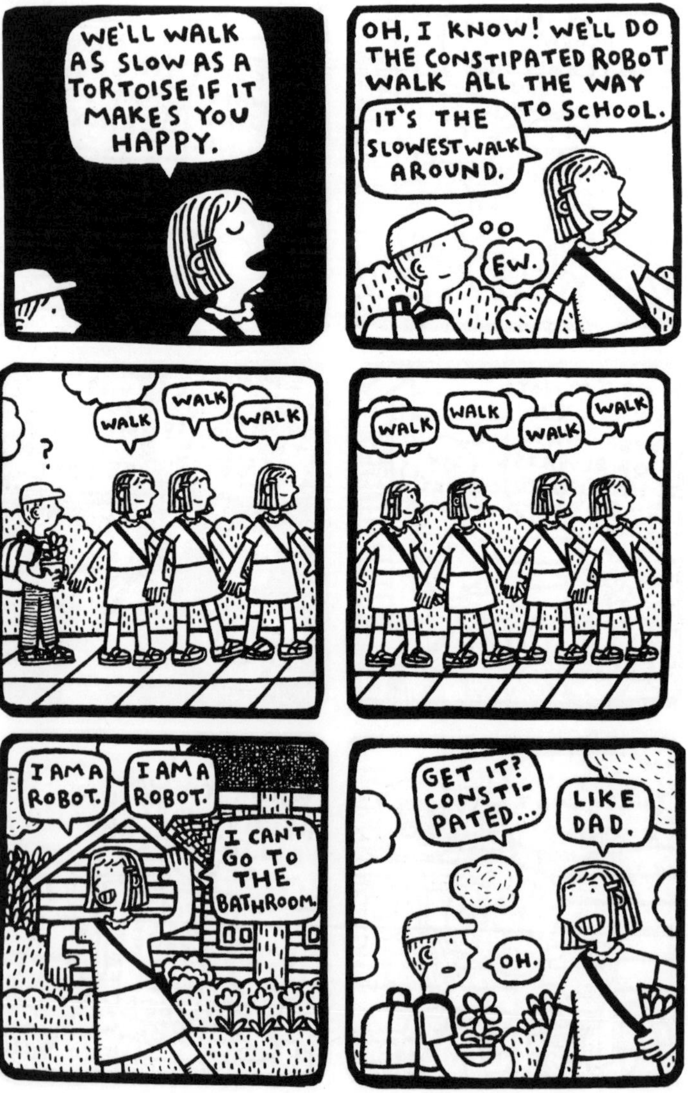
WE'LL WALK AS SLOW AS A TORTOISE IF IT MAKES YOU HAPPY.
OH, I KNOW! WE'LL DO THE CONSTIPATED ROBOT WALK ALL THE WAY TO SCHOOL.
IT'S THE SLOWEST WALK AROUND.
EW.
?
WALK
WALK
WALK
WALK
WALK
WALK
WALK
I AM A ROBOT.
I AM A ROBOT.
I CAN'T GO TO THE BATHROOM.
GET IT? CONSTI-PATED...
LIKE DAD.
OH.

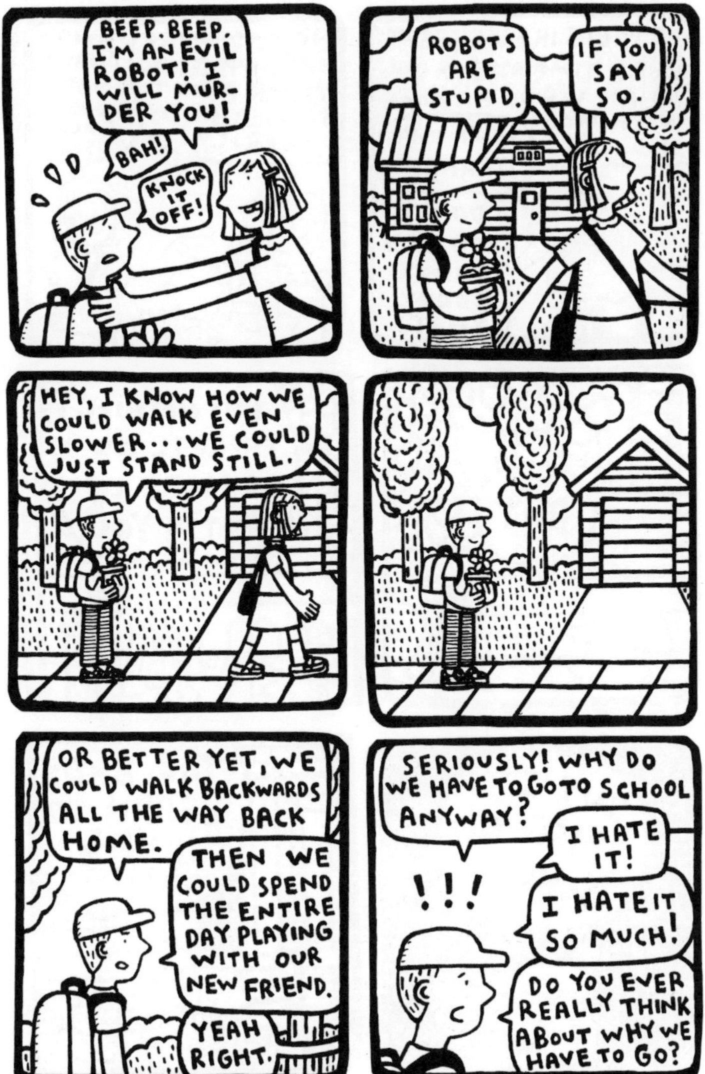
BEEP. BEEP. I'M AN EVIL ROBOT! I WILL MURDER YOU!
BAH!
KNOCK IT OFF!
ROBOTS ARE STUPID.
IF YOU SAY SO.
HEY, I KNOW HOW WE COULD WALK EVEN SLOWER...WE COULD JUST STAND STILL.
OR BETTER YET, WE COULD WALK BACKWARDS ALL THE WAY BACK HOME.
THEN WE COULD SPEND THE ENTIRE DAY PLAYING WITH OUR NEW FRIEND.
YEAH RIGHT.
SERIOUSLY! WHY DO WE HAVE TO GO TO SCHOOL ANYWAY?
I HATE IT!
I HATE IT SO MUCH!
DO YOU EVER REALLY THINK ABOUT WHY WE HAVE TO GO?
!!!

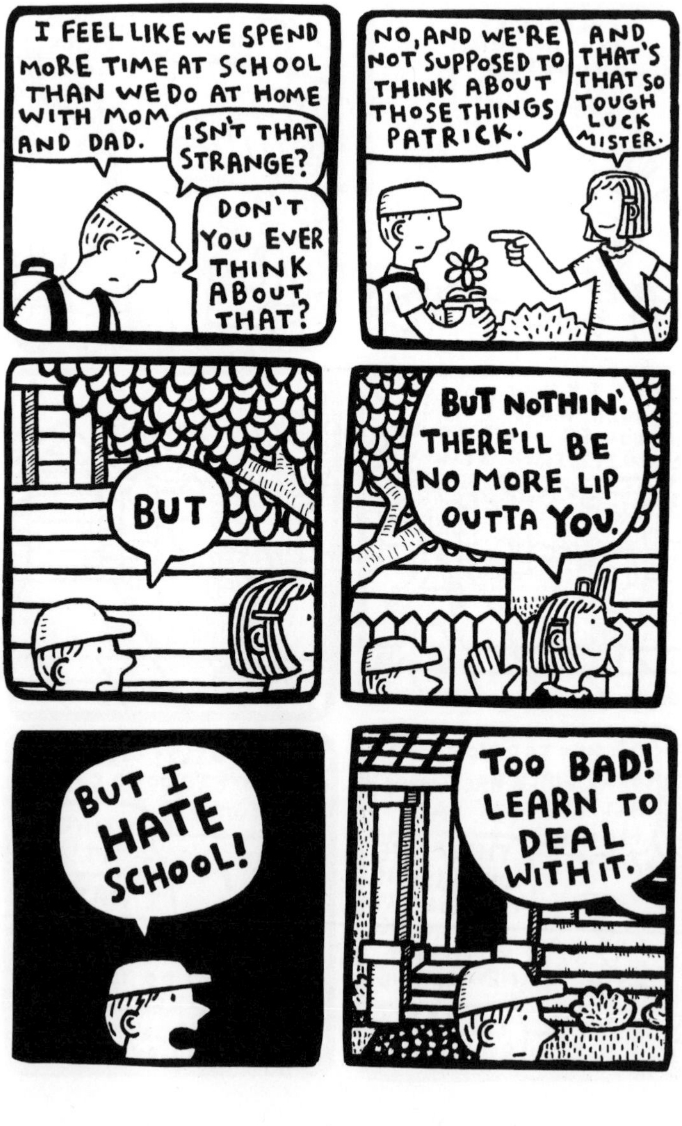
I FEEL LIKE WE SPEND MORE TIME AT SCHOOL THAN WE DO AT HOME WITH MOM AND DAD.
ISN'T THAT STRANGE?
DON'T YOU EVER THINK ABOUT THAT?
NO, AND WE'RE NOT SUPPOSED TO THINK ABOUT THOSE THINGS PATRICK.
AND THAT'S THAT SO TOUGH LUCK MISTER.
BUT
BUT NOTHIN'. THERE'LL BE NO MORE LIP OUTTA YOU.
BUT I HATE SCHOOL!
TOO BAD! LEARN TO DEAL WITH IT.

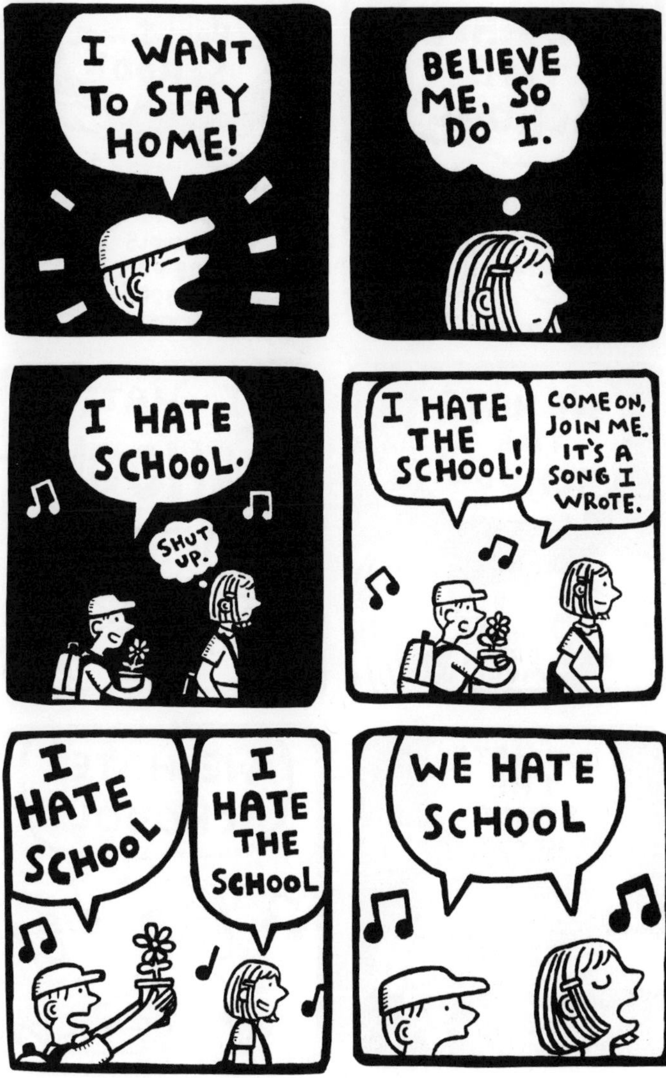
I WANT TO STAY HOME!
BELIEVE ME, SO DO I.
I HATE SCHOOL.
SHUT UP.
I HATE THE SCHOOL!
COME ON, JOIN ME. IT'S A SONG I WROTE.
I HATE SCHOOL
I HATE THE SCHOOL
WE HATE SCHOOL

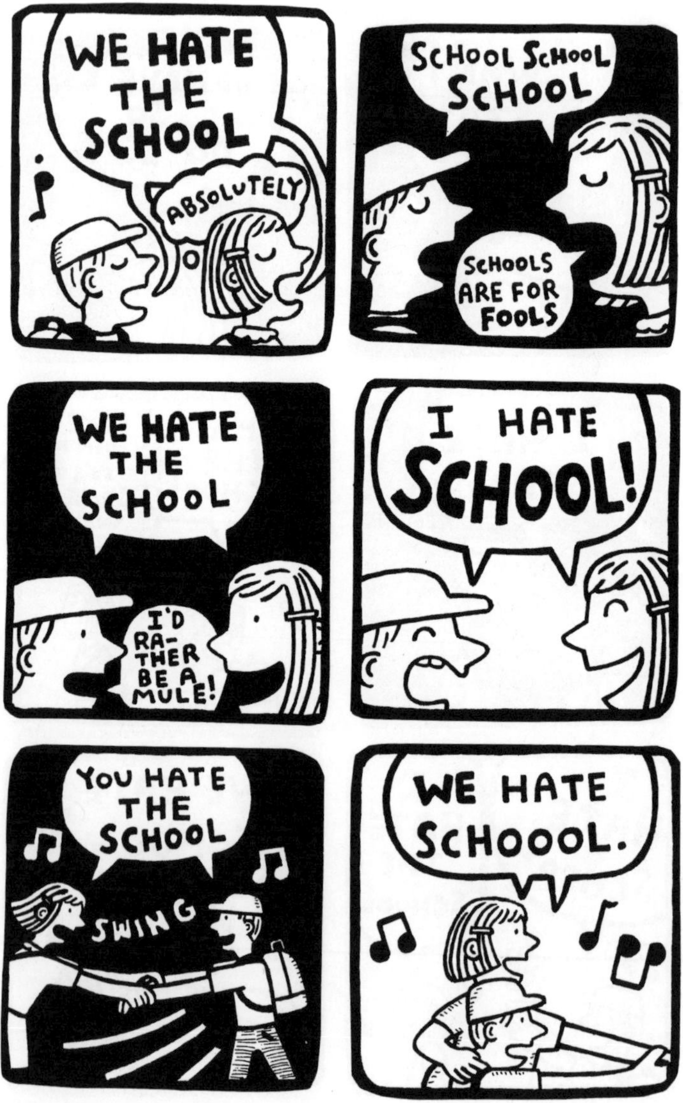
WE HATE THE SCHOOL
ABSOLUTELY
SCHOOL SCHOOL SCHOOL
SCHOOLS ARE FOR FOOLS
WE HATE THE SCHOOL
I'D RA-THER BE A MULE!
I HATE SCHOOL!
YOU HATE THE SCHOOL
SWING
WE HATE SCHOOOL.

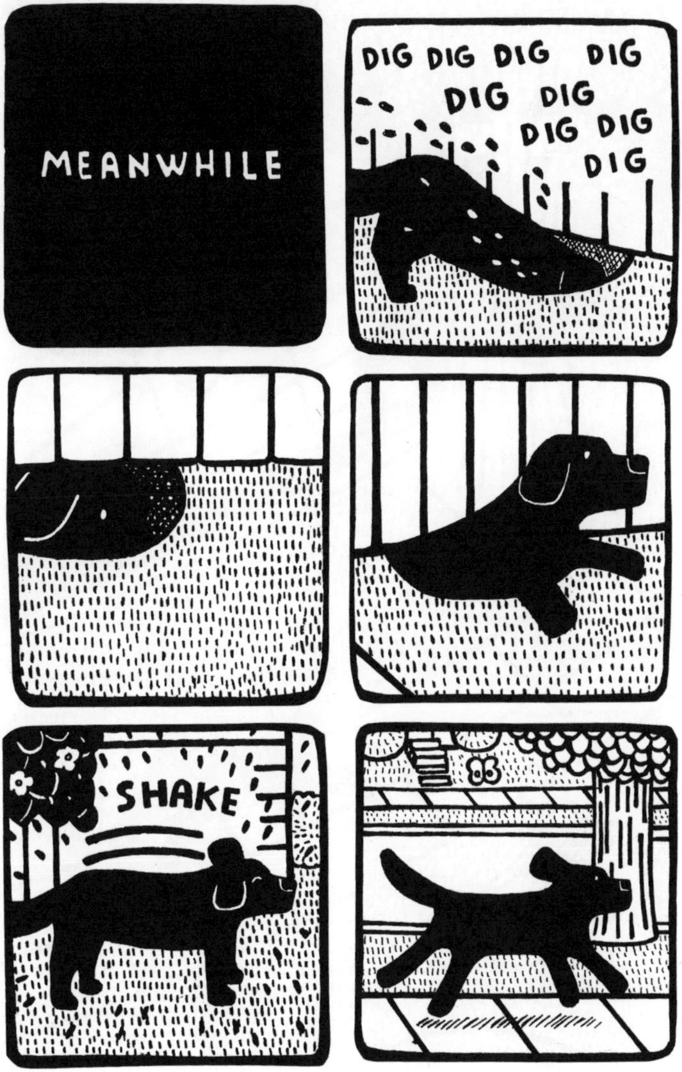
MEANWHILE
DIG DIG DIG DIG
DIG DIG
DIG DIG
DIG
SHAKE
83

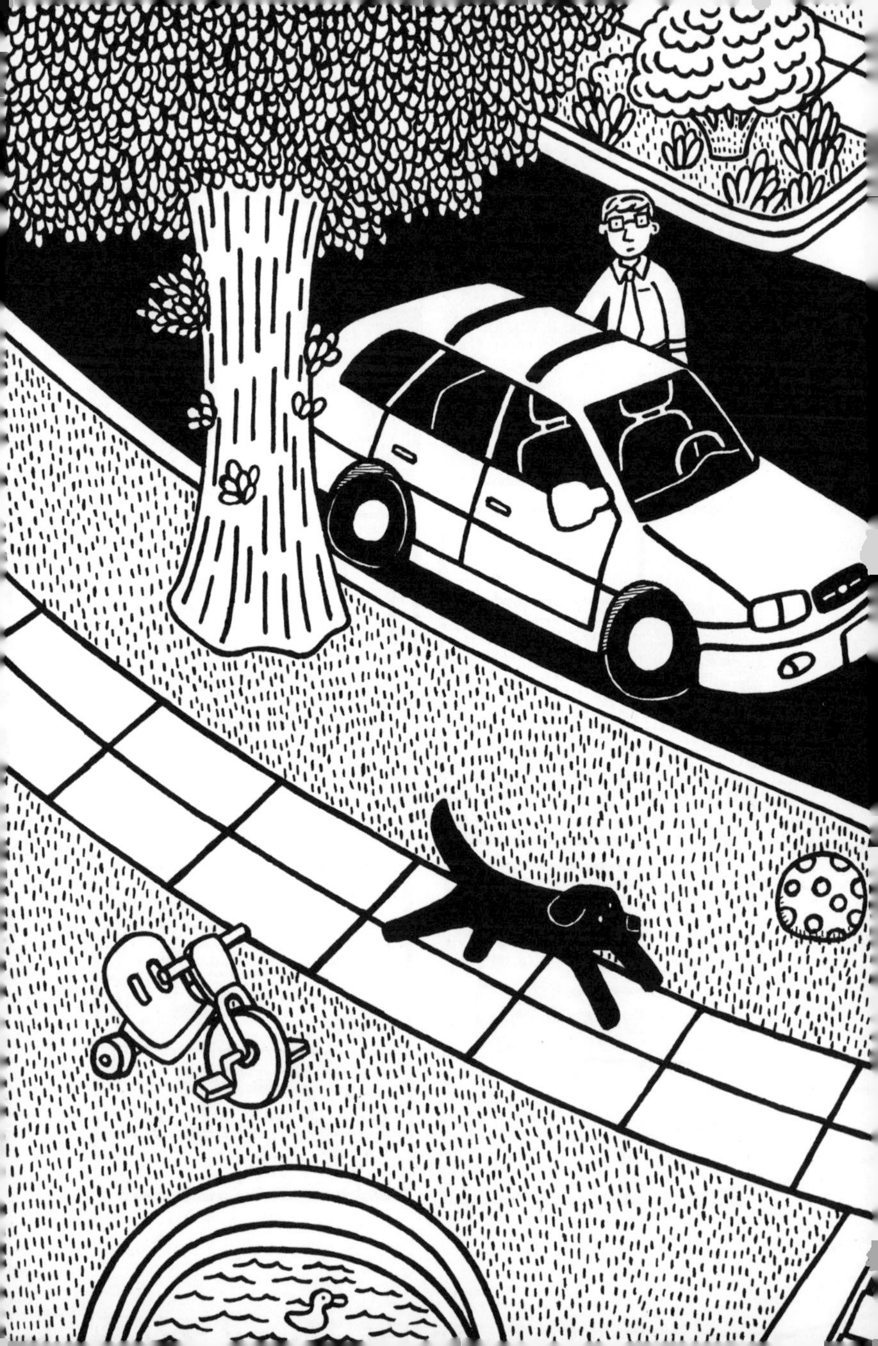

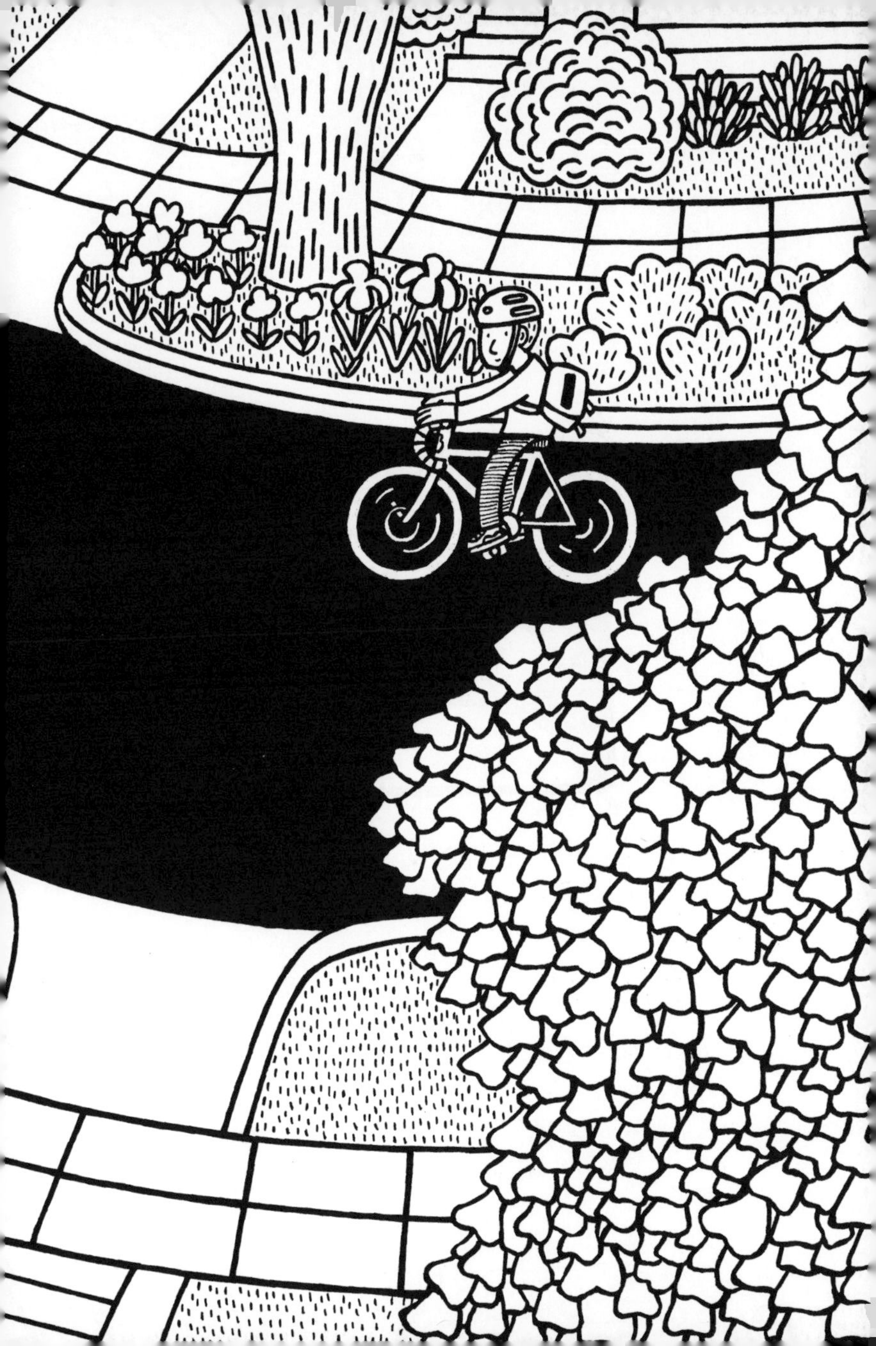

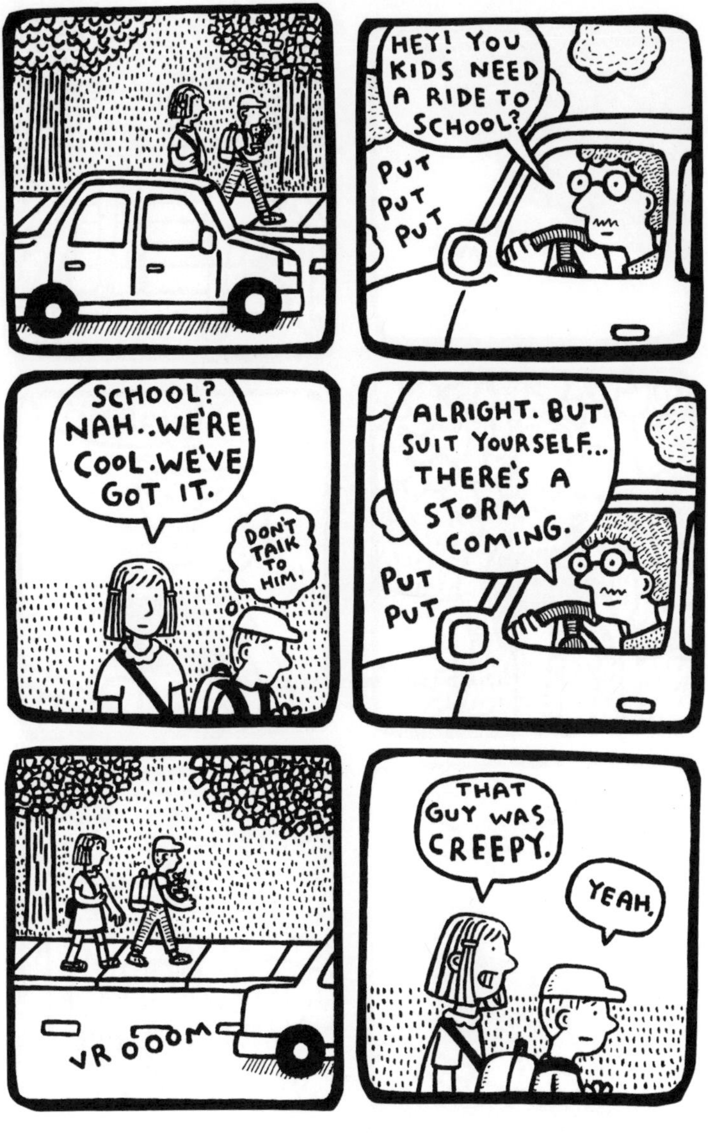
HEY! YOU KIDS NEED A RIDE TO SCHOOL?
PUT PUT PUT
SCHOOL? NAH..WE'RE COOL. WE'VE GOT IT.
DON'T TALK TO HIM.
ALRIGHT. BUT SUIT YOURSELF... THERE'S A STORM COMING.
PUT PUT
VROOOM
THAT GUY WAS CREEPY.
YEAH.

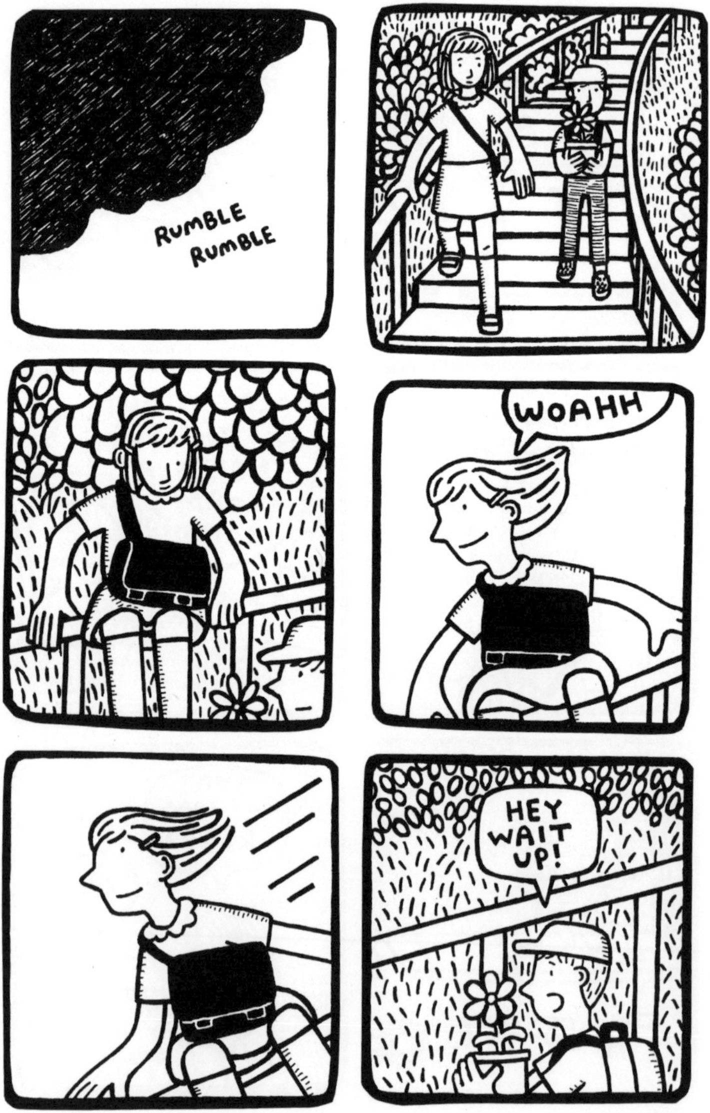
RUMBLE
RUMBLE
WOAHH
HEY WAIT UP!

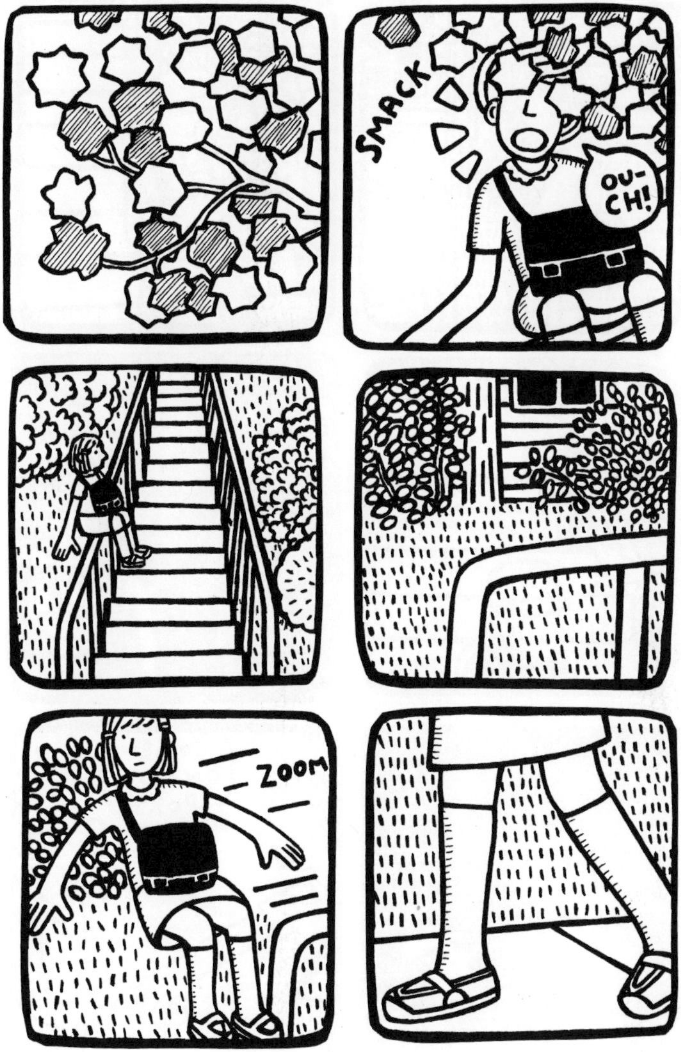
SMACK
OU-CH!
ZOOM

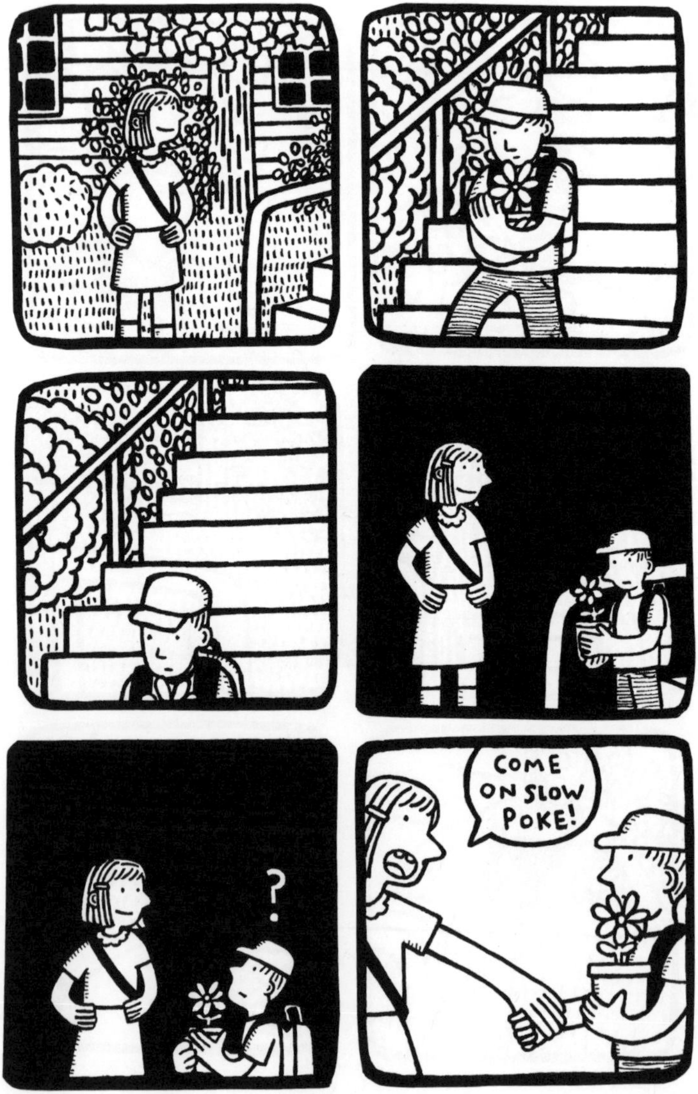
?
COME ON SLOW POKE!

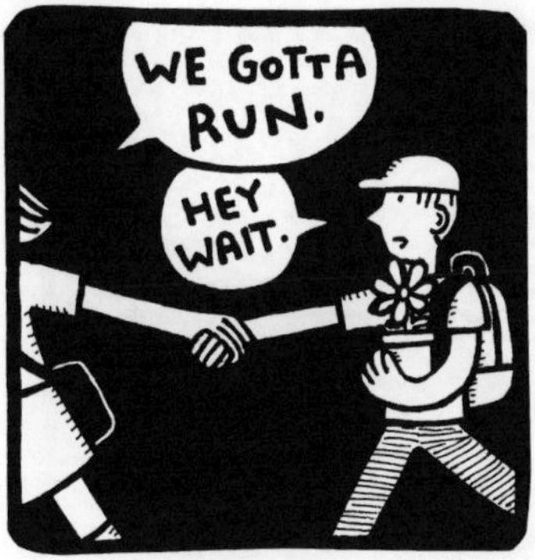
WE GOTTA RUN.
HEY WAIT.

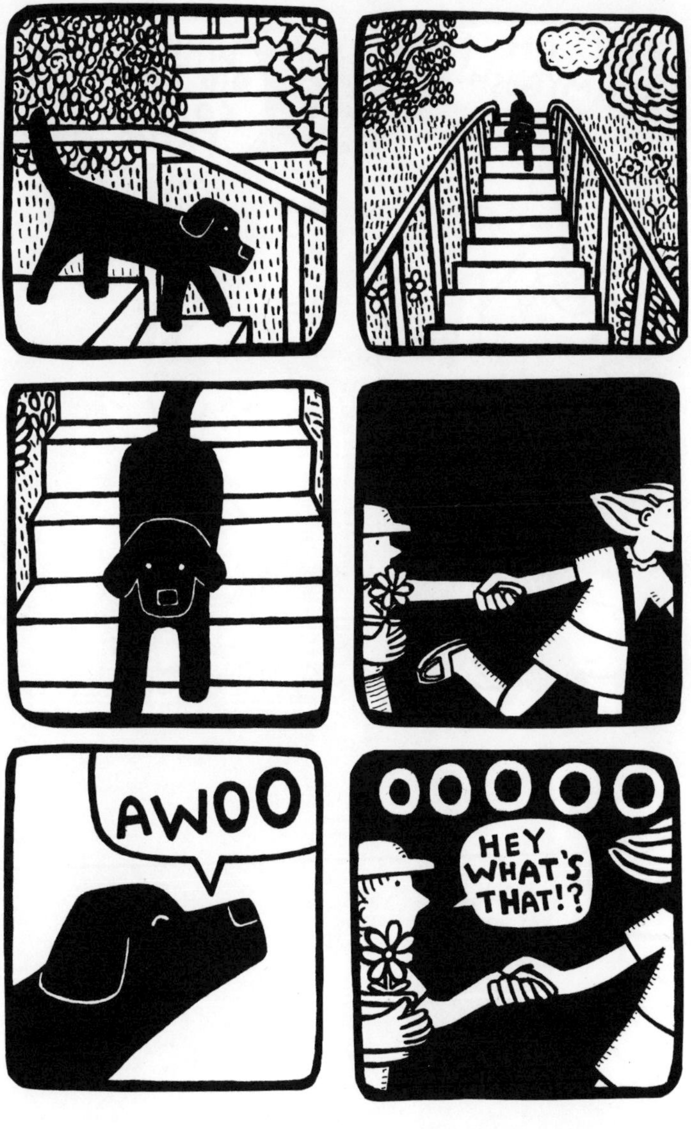
AWOO
OOOOO
HEY WHAT'S THAT!?

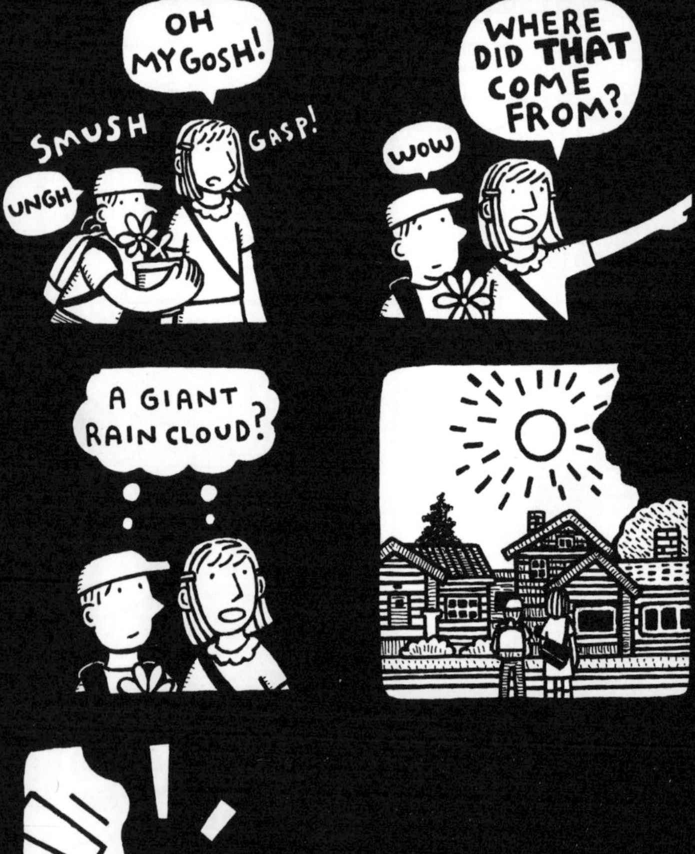
OH MY GOSH!
SMUSH
GASP!
UNGH
WOW
WHERE DID **THAT** COME FROM?
A GIANT RAIN CLOUD?

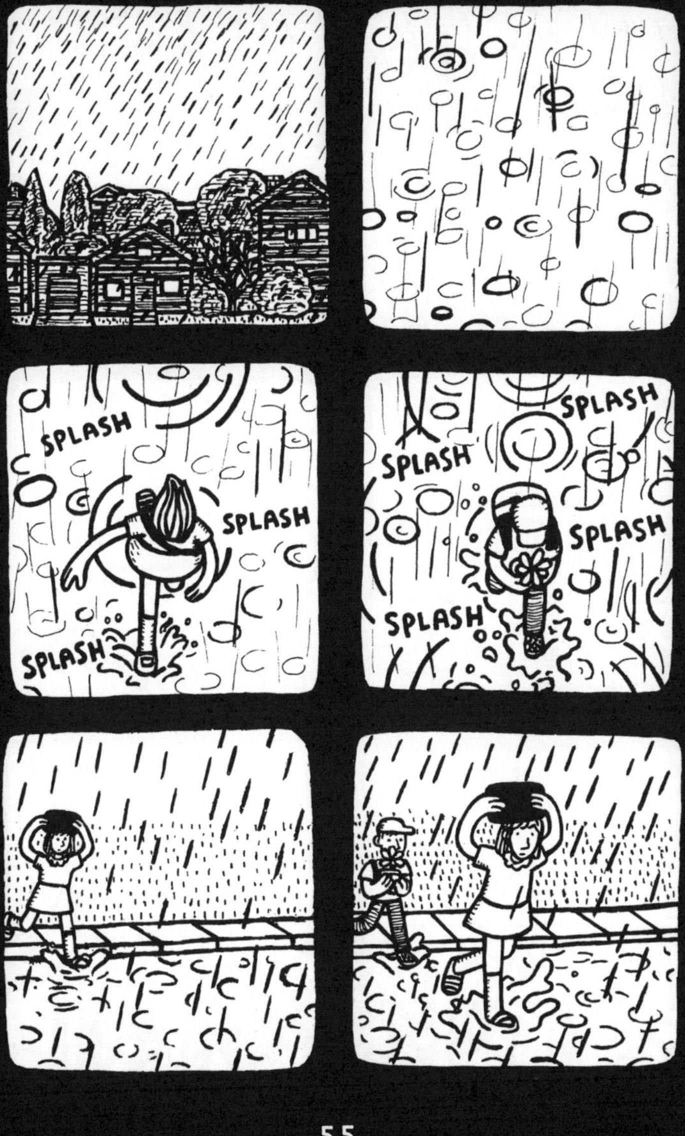
SPLASH
SPLASH
SPLASH
SPLASH
SPLASH
SPLASH
SPLASH

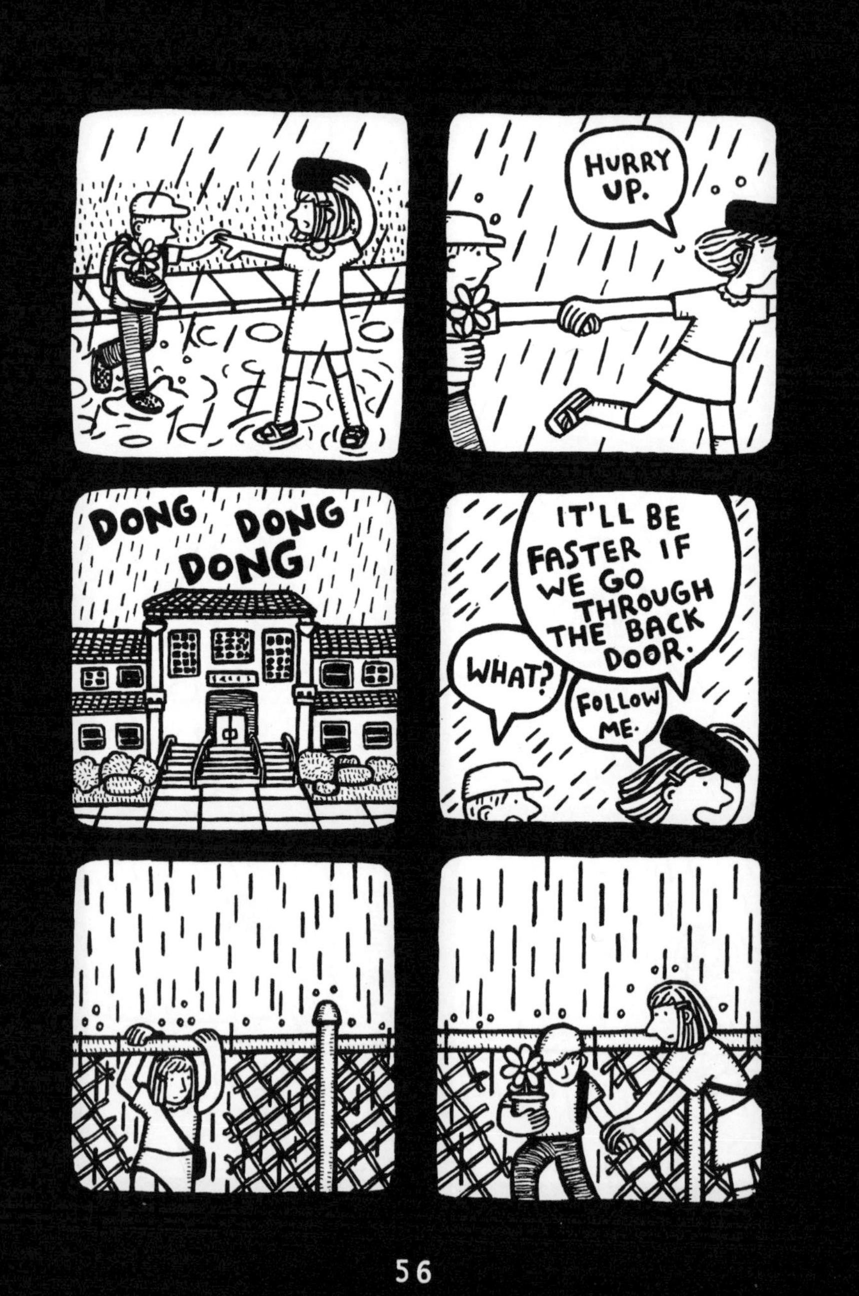
HURRY UP.
DONG DONG DONG
IT'LL BE FASTER IF WE GO THROUGH THE BACK DOOR.
WHAT?
FOLLOW ME.

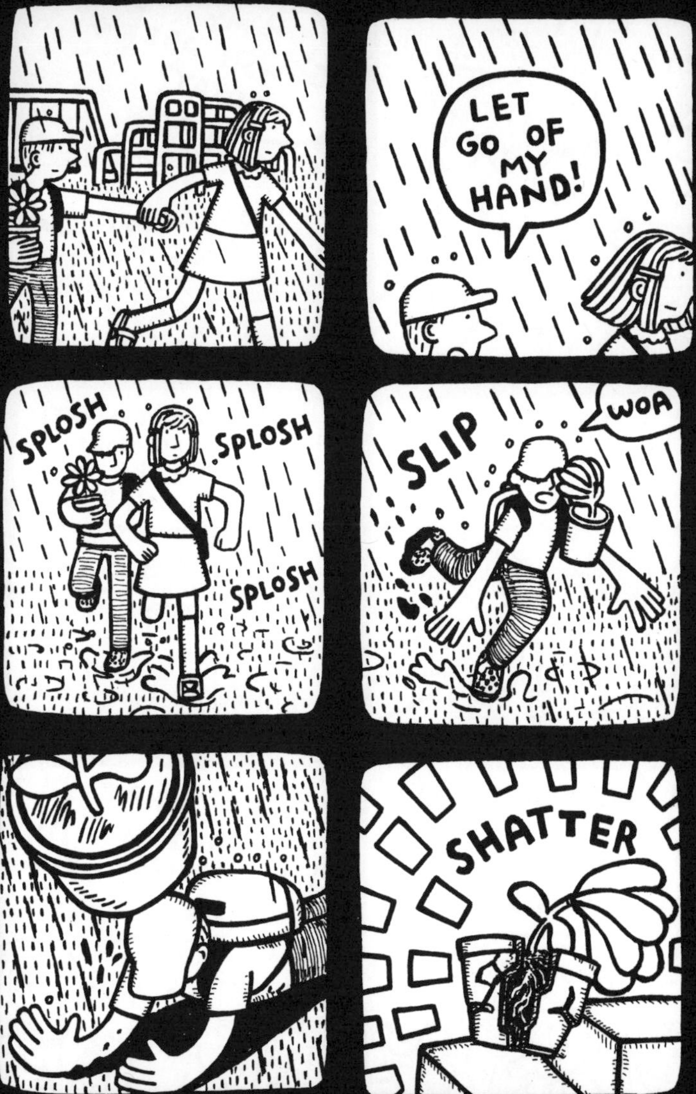
LET GO OF MY HAND!
SPLOSH
SPLOSH
SPLOSH
SLIP
WOA
SHATTER

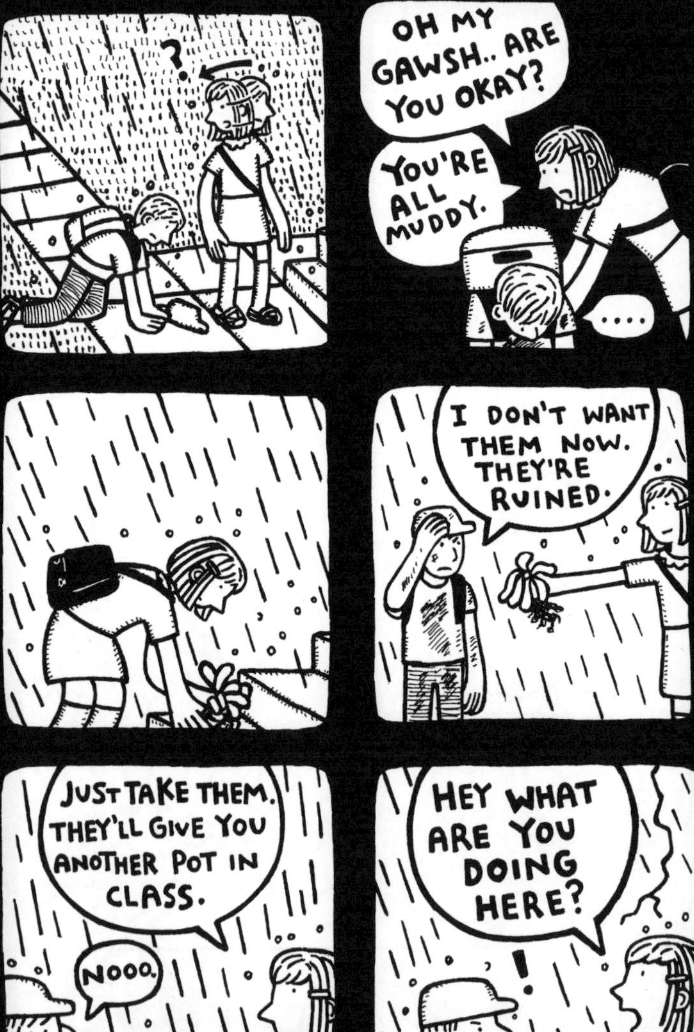
?
OH MY GAWSH.. ARE YOU OKAY?
YOU'RE ALL MUDDY.
....
I DON'T WANT THEM NOW. THEY'RE RUINED.
JUST TAKE THEM. THEY'LL GIVE YOU ANOTHER POT IN CLASS.
NOOO.
HEY WHAT ARE YOU DOING HERE?
!

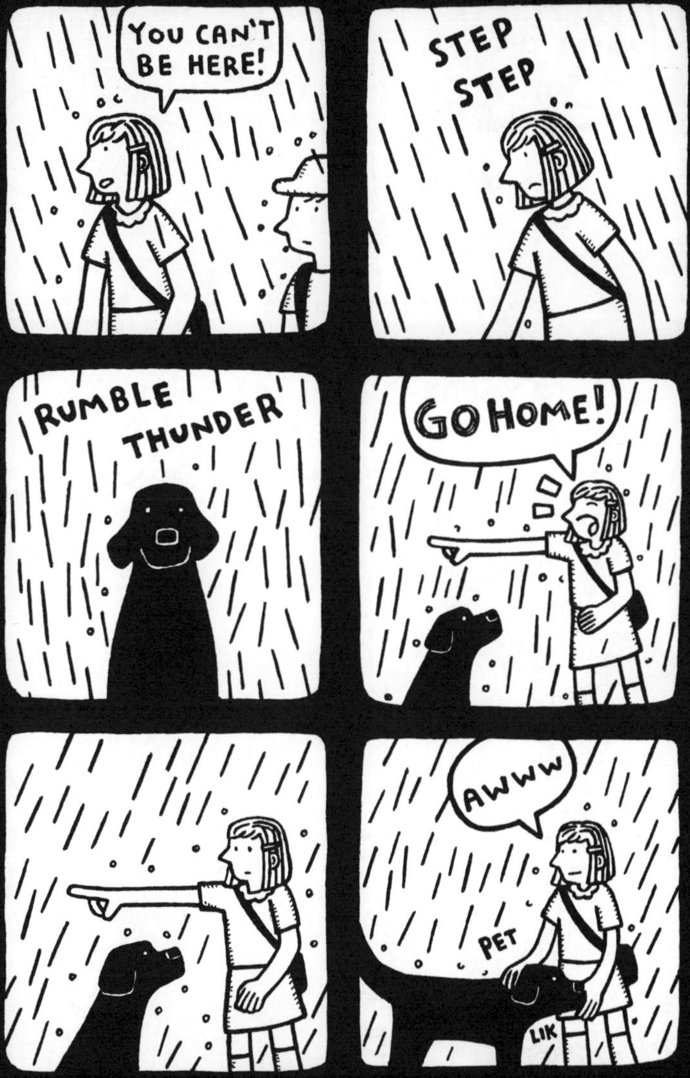
YOU CAN'T BE HERE!
STEP STEP
RUMBLE THUNDER
GO HOME!
AWWW
PET
LIK

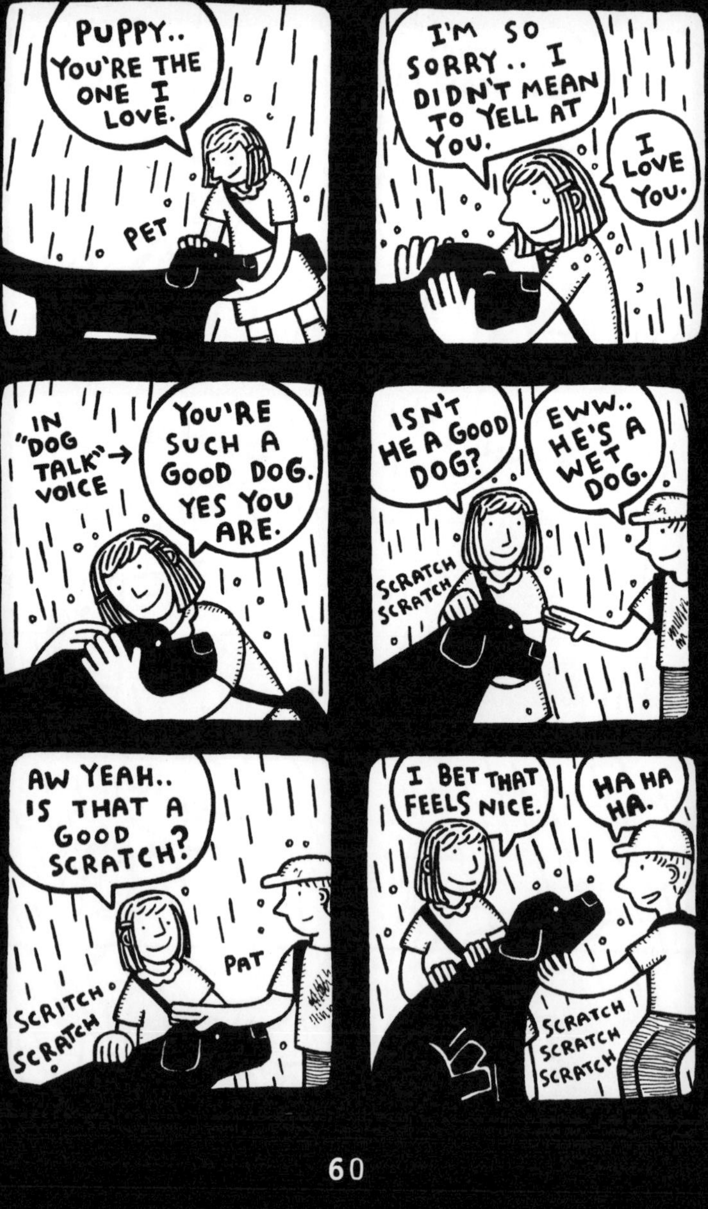
PUPPY.. YOU'RE THE ONE I LOVE.
PET
I'M SO SORRY.. I DIDN'T MEAN TO YELL AT YOU.
I LOVE YOU.
IN "DOG TALK" VOICE
YOU'RE SUCH A GOOD DOG. YES YOU ARE.
ISN'T HE A GOOD DOG?
EWW.. HE'S A WET DOG.
SCRATCH SCRATCH
AW YEAH.. IS THAT A GOOD SCRATCH?
PAT
SCRITCH SCRATCH
I BET THAT FEELS NICE.
HA HA HA.
SCRATCH SCRATCH SCRATCH

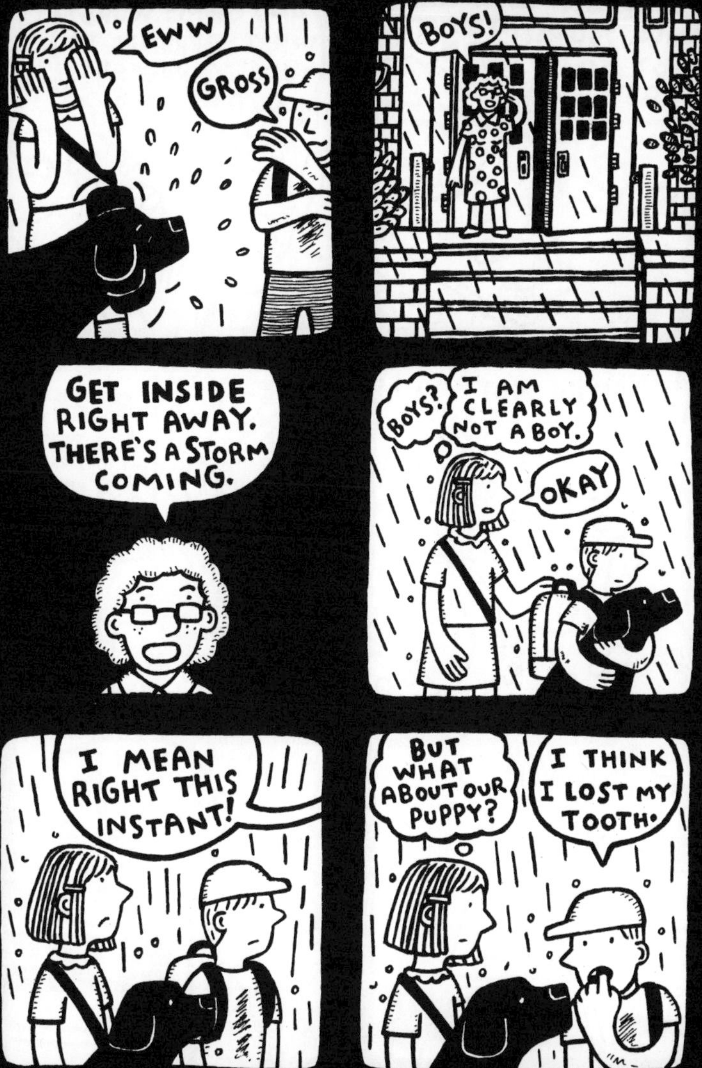
EWW
GROSS
BOYS!
GET INSIDE RIGHT AWAY. THERE'S A STORM COMING.
BOYS?
I AM CLEARLY NOT A BOY.
OKAY
I MEAN RIGHT THIS INSTANT!
BUT WHAT ABOUT OUR PUPPY?
I THINK I LOST MY TOOTH.

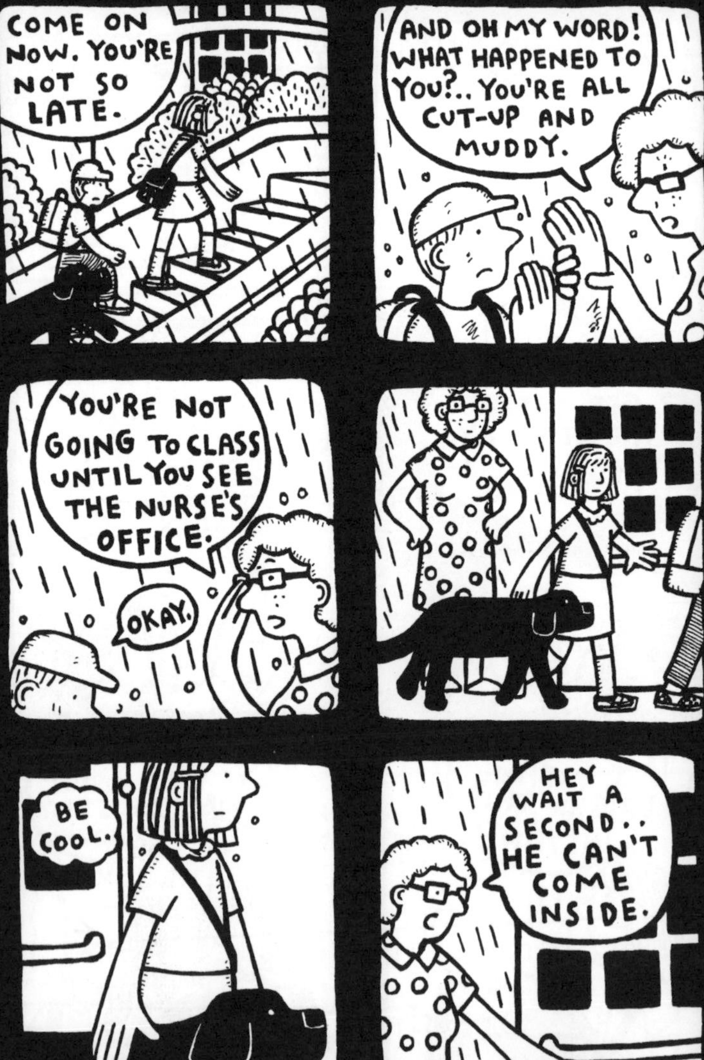
COME ON NOW. YOU'RE NOT SO LATE.
AND OH MY WORD! WHAT HAPPENED TO YOU?.. YOU'RE ALL CUT-UP AND MUDDY.
YOU'RE NOT GOING TO CLASS UNTIL YOU SEE THE NURSE'S OFFICE.
OKAY.
BE COOL.
HEY WAIT A SECOND.. HE CAN'T COME INSIDE.

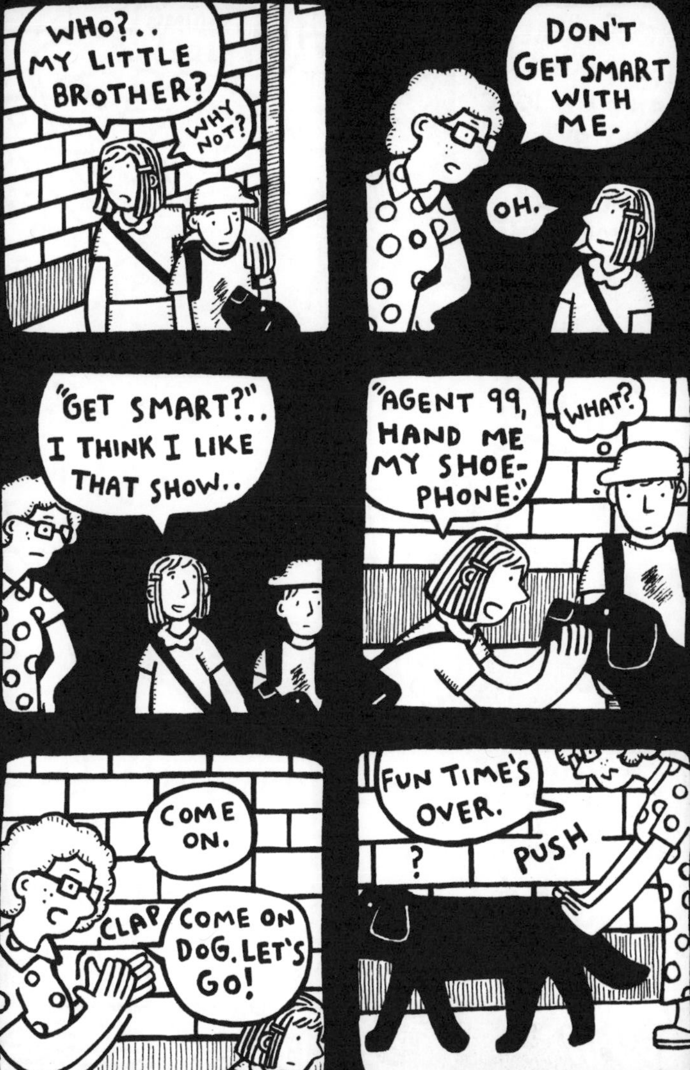
WHO?.. MY LITTLE BROTHER?
WHY NOT?
DON'T GET SMART WITH ME.
OH.
"GET SMART?".. I THINK I LIKE THAT SHOW..
"AGENT 99, HAND ME MY SHOE-PHONE."
WHAT?
COME ON.
CLAP
COME ON DOG. LET'S GO!
FUN TIME'S OVER.
?
PUSH

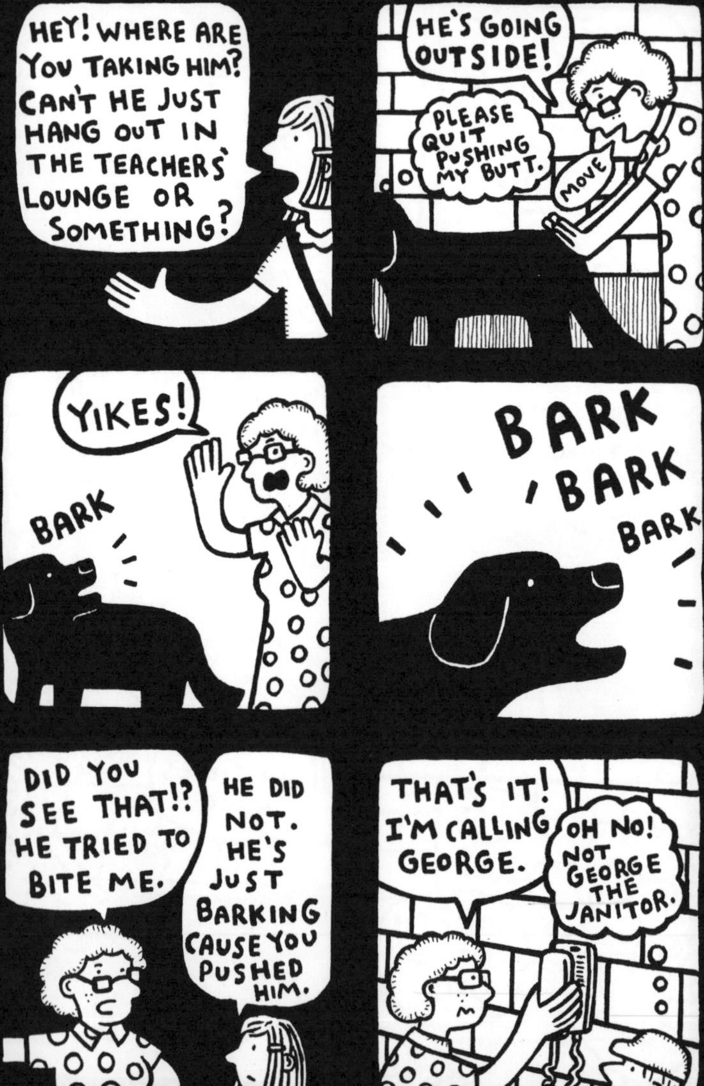
HEY! WHERE ARE YOU TAKING HIM? CAN'T HE JUST HANG OUT IN THE TEACHERS' LOUNGE OR SOMETHING?
HE'S GOING OUTSIDE!
PLEASE QUIT PUSHING MY BUTT.
MOVE
YIKES!
BARK
BARK
BARK
BARK
DID YOU SEE THAT!? HE TRIED TO BITE ME.
HE DID NOT. HE'S JUST BARKING CAUSE YOU PUSHED HIM.
THAT'S IT! I'M CALLING GEORGE.
OH NO! NOT GEORGE THE JANITOR.

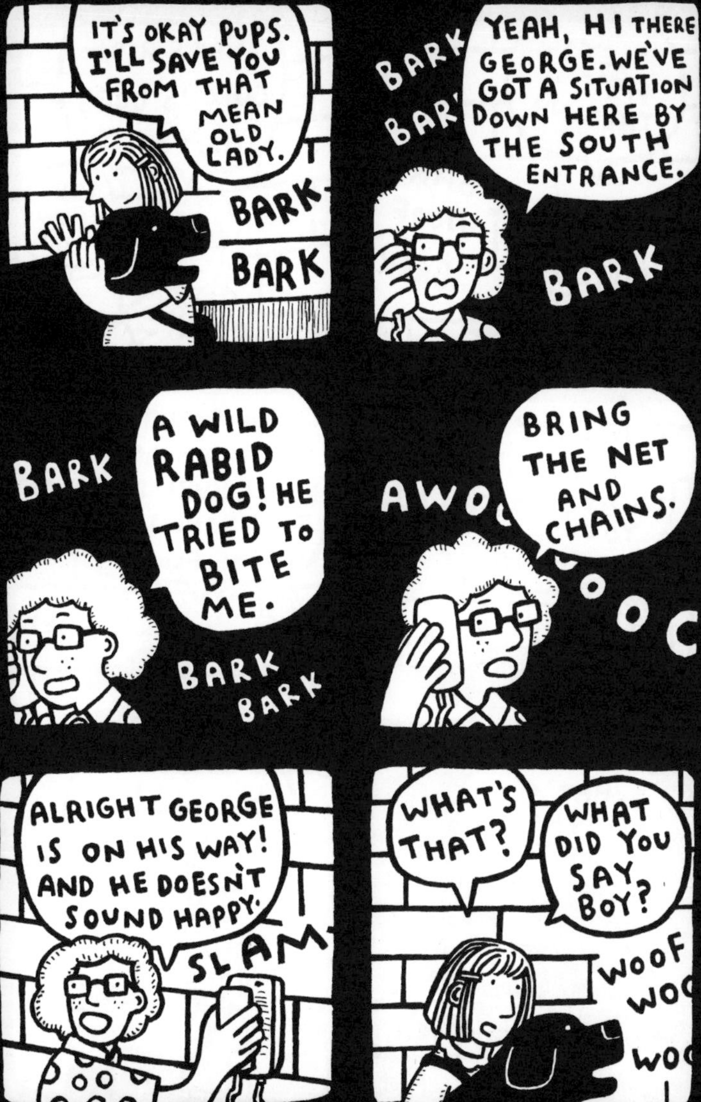
IT'S OKAY PUPS. I'LL SAVE YOU FROM THAT MEAN OLD LADY.
BARK
BARK
BARK
BAR
YEAH, HI THERE GEORGE. WE'VE GOT A SITUATION DOWN HERE BY THE SOUTH ENTRANCE.
BARK
BARK
A WILD RABID DOG! HE TRIED TO BITE ME.
BARK
BARK
BRING THE NET AND CHAINS.
ALRIGHT GEORGE IS ON HIS WAY! AND HE DOESN'T SOUND HAPPY.
SLAM
WHAT'S THAT?
WHAT DID YOU SAY BOY?
WOOF

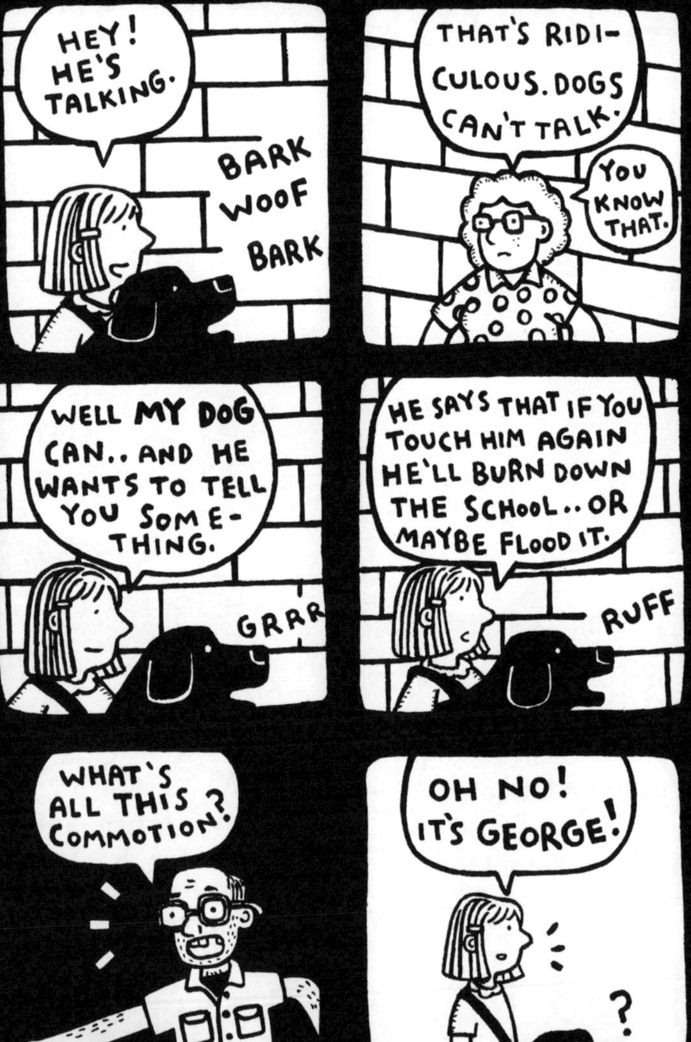
HEY! HE'S TALKING.
BARK WOOF BARK
THAT'S RIDICULOUS. DOGS CAN'T TALK.
YOU KNOW THAT.
WELL MY DOG CAN.. AND HE WANTS TO TELL YOU SOMETHING.
GRRR
HE SAYS THAT IF YOU TOUCH HIM AGAIN HE'LL BURN DOWN THE SCHOOL.. OR MAYBE FLOOD IT.
RUFF
WHAT'S ALL THIS COMMOTION?
OH NO! IT'S GEORGE!
?

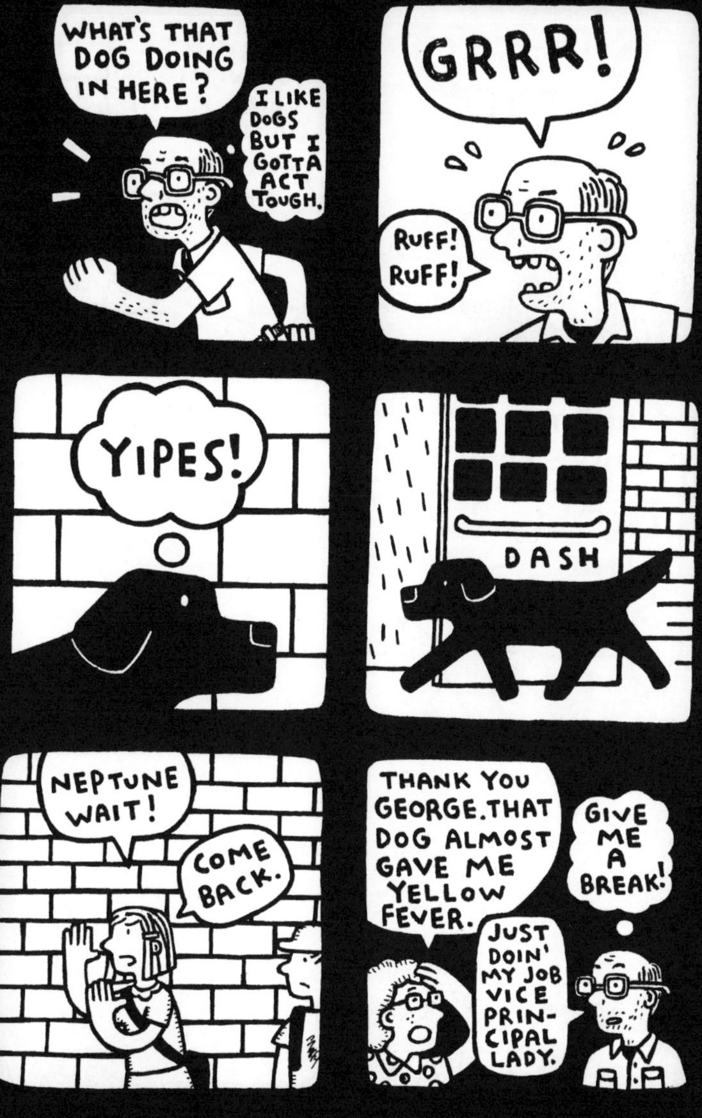
WHAT'S THAT DOG DOING IN HERE?
I LIKE DOGS BUT I GOTTA ACT TOUGH.
GRRRR!
RUFF! RUFF!
YIPES!
DASH
NEPTUNE WAIT!
COME BACK.
THANK YOU GEORGE. THAT DOG ALMOST GAVE ME YELLOW FEVER.
GIVE ME A BREAK!
JUST DOIN' MY JOB VICE PRIN-CIPAL LADY.

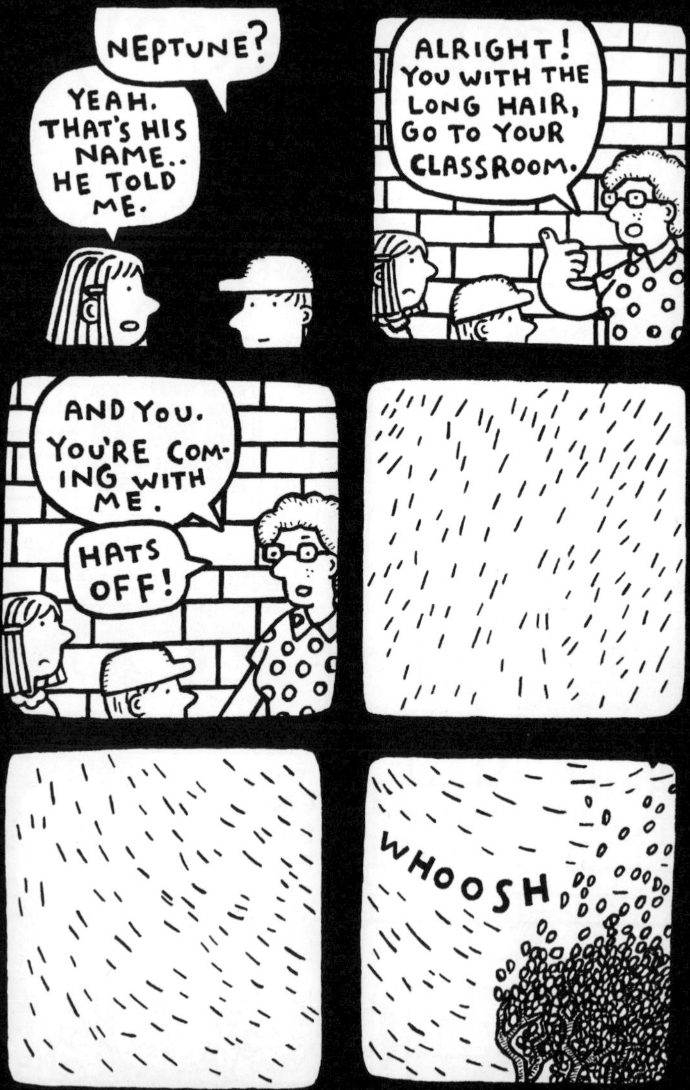
NEPTUNE?
YEAH. THAT'S HIS NAME.. HE TOLD ME.
ALRIGHT! YOU WITH THE LONG HAIR, GO TO YOUR CLASSROOM.
AND YOU. YOU'RE COMING WITH ME.
HATS OFF!
WHOOSH

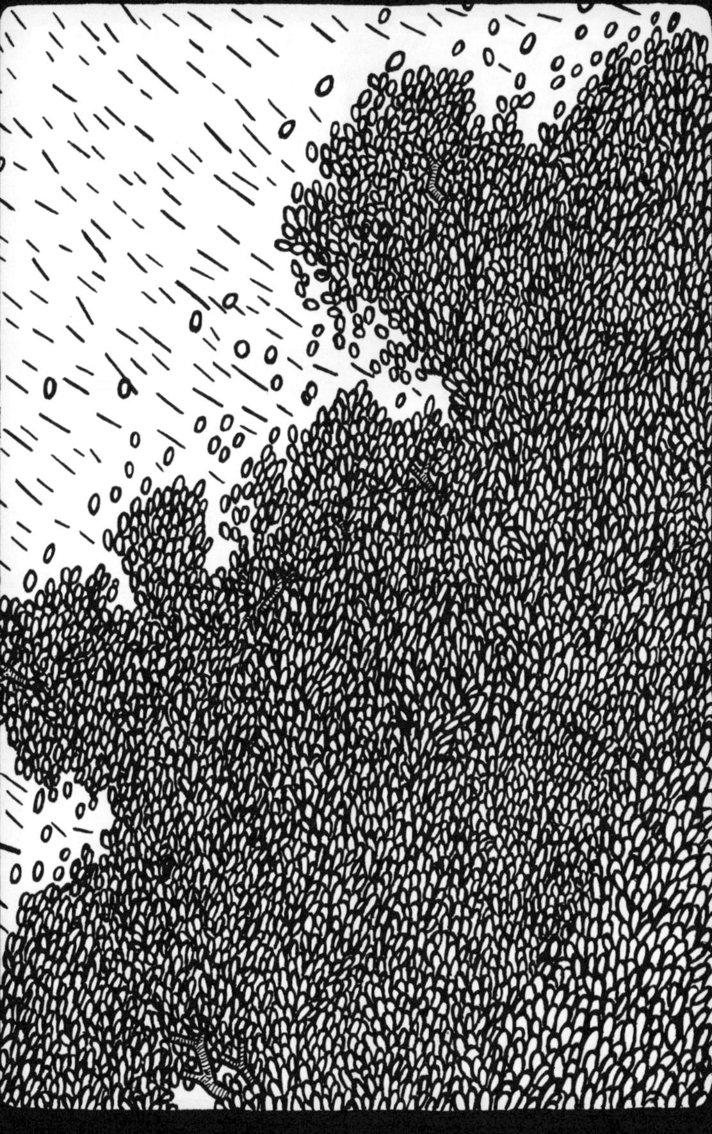

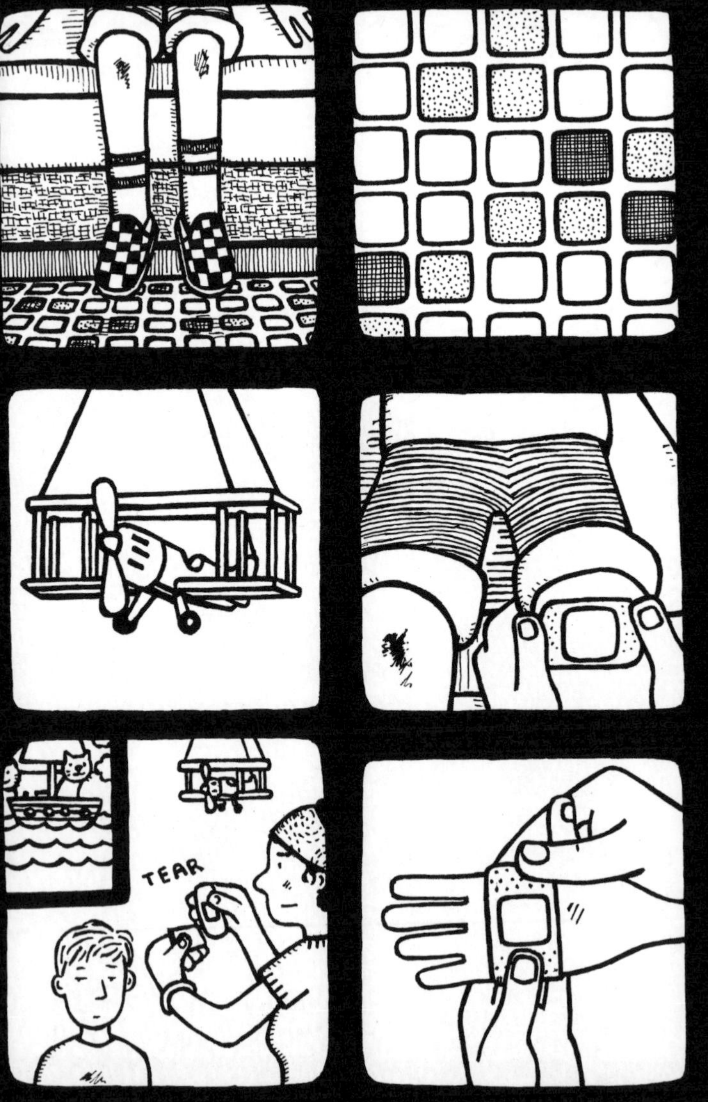
TEAR

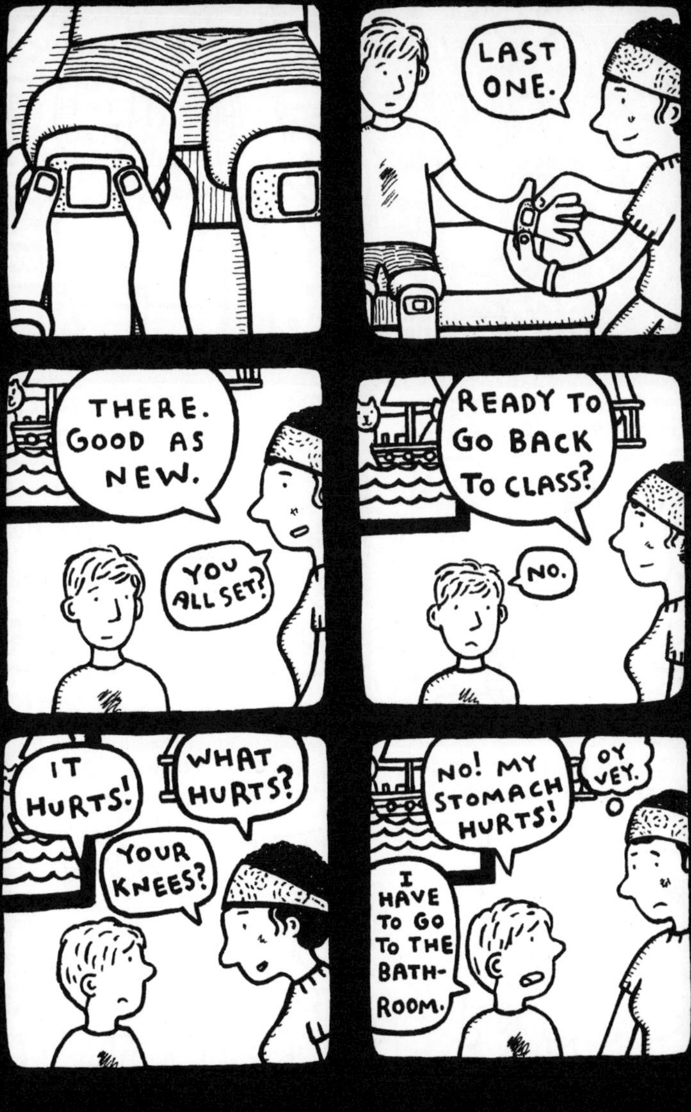
LAST ONE.
THERE. GOOD AS NEW.
YOU ALL SET?
READY TO GO BACK TO CLASS?
NO.
IT HURTS!
WHAT HURTS?
YOUR KNEES?
NO! MY STOMACH HURTS!
OY VEY.
I HAVE TO GO TO THE BATH-ROOM.

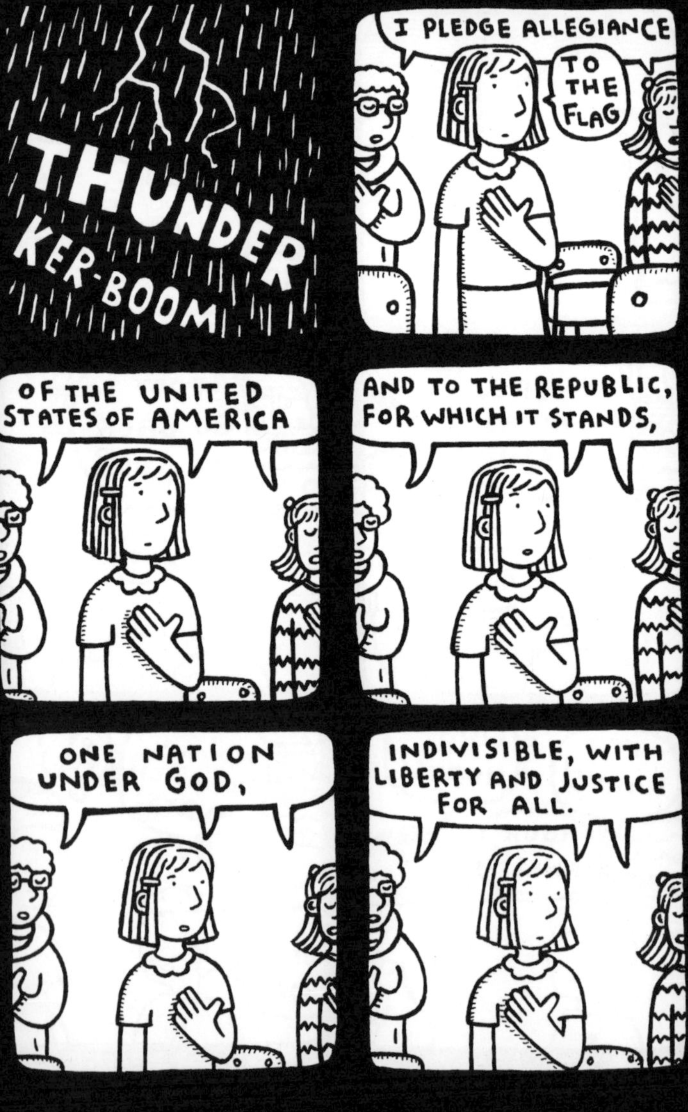
THUNDER
KER-BOOM
I PLEDGE ALLEGIANCE
TO THE FLAG
OF THE UNITED STATES OF AMERICA
AND TO THE REPUBLIC, FOR WHICH IT STANDS,
ONE NATION UNDER GOD,
INDIVISIBLE, WITH LIBERTY AND JUSTICE FOR ALL.

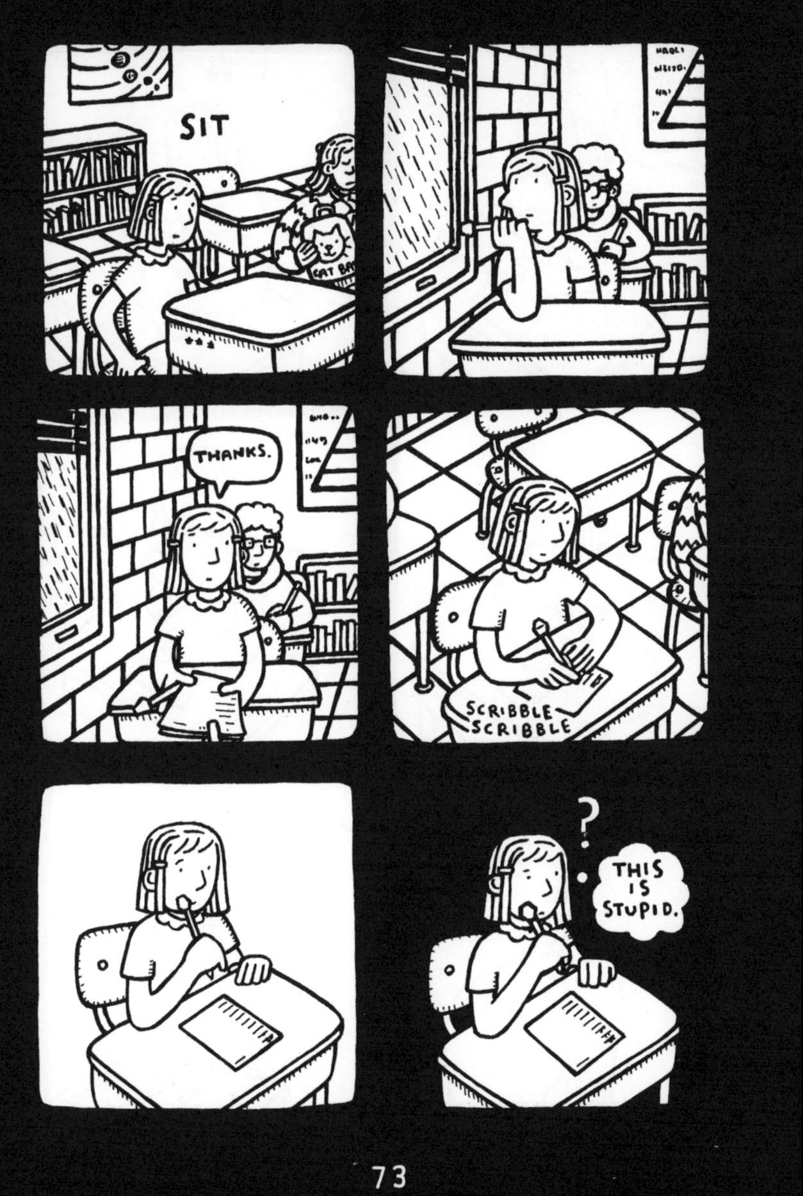
SIT
THANKS.
SCRIBBLE SCRIBBLE
?
THIS IS STUPID.

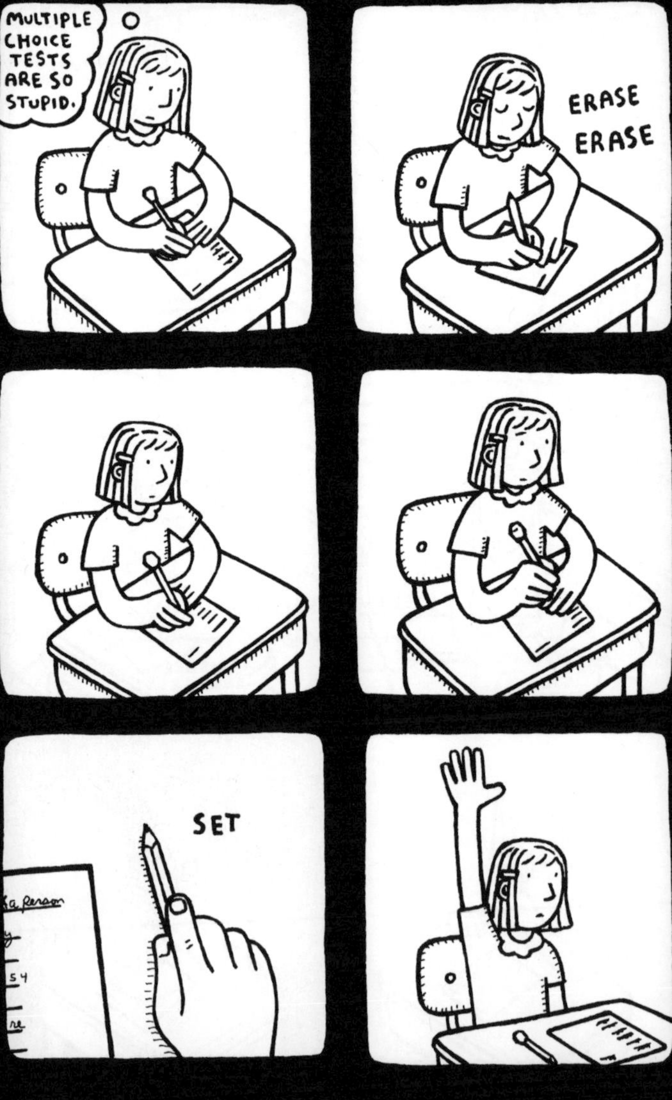
MULTIPLE CHOICE TESTS ARE SO STUPID.
ERASE
ERASE
SET

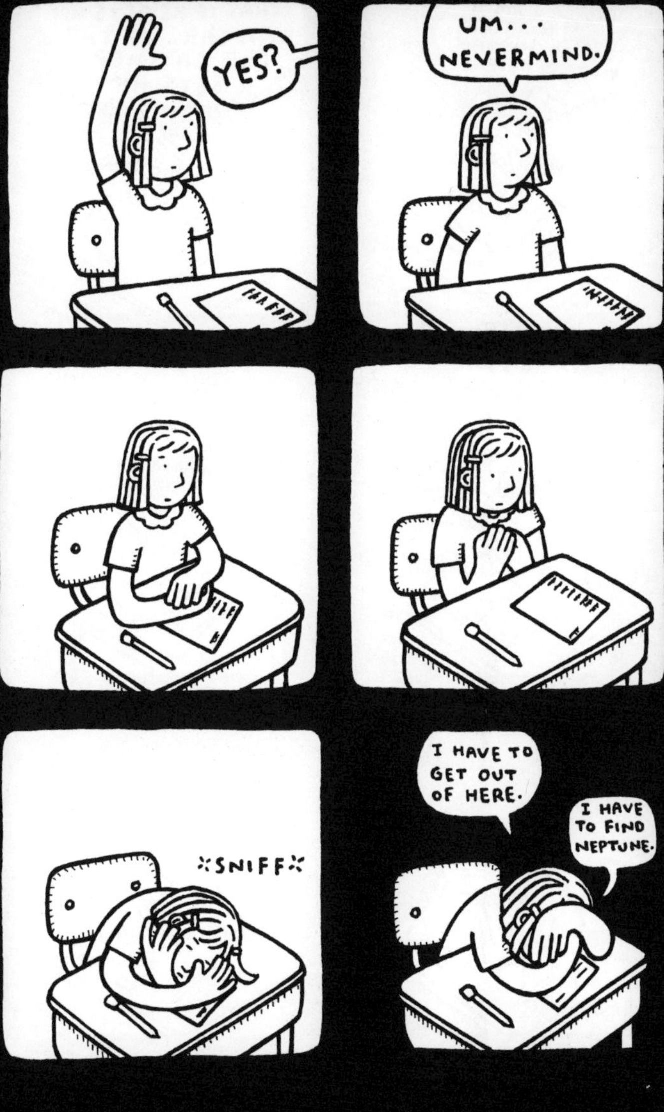
YES?
UM...
NEVERMIND.
SNIFF
I HAVE TO GET OUT OF HERE.
I HAVE TO FIND NEPTUNE.

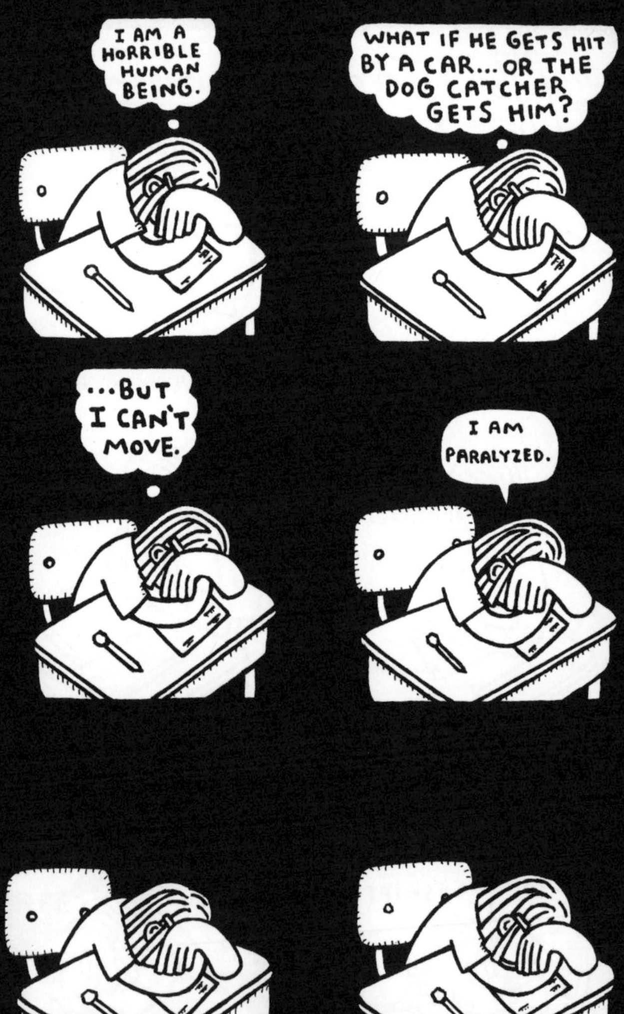
I AM A HORRIBLE HUMAN BEING.
WHAT IF HE GETS HIT BY A CAR... OR THE DOG CATCHER GETS HIM?
...BUT I CAN'T MOVE.
I AM PARALYZED.

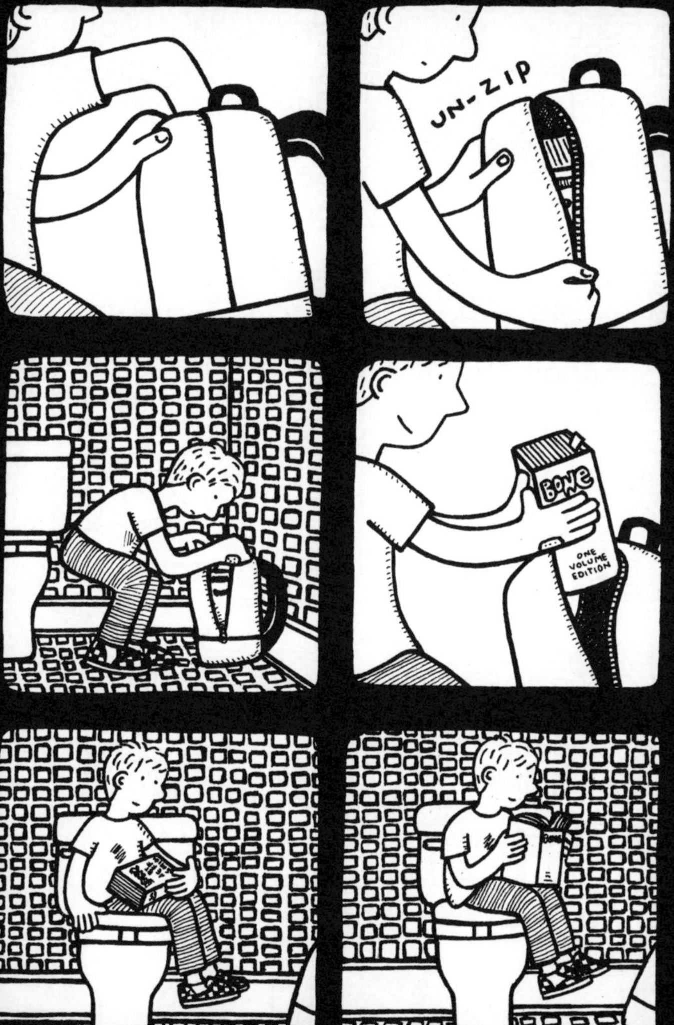
UN-ZIP
BONE
ONE VOLUME EDITION

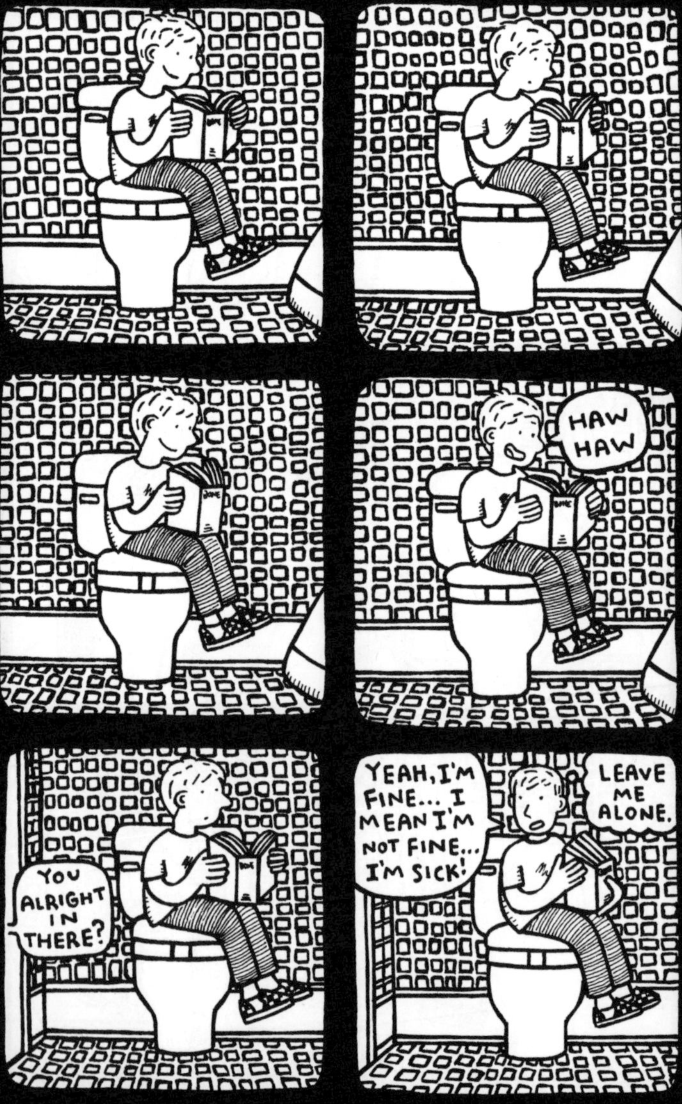
HAW HAW
YOU ALRIGHT IN THERE?
YEAH, I'M FINE... I MEAN I'M NOT FINE... I'M SICK!
LEAVE ME ALONE.

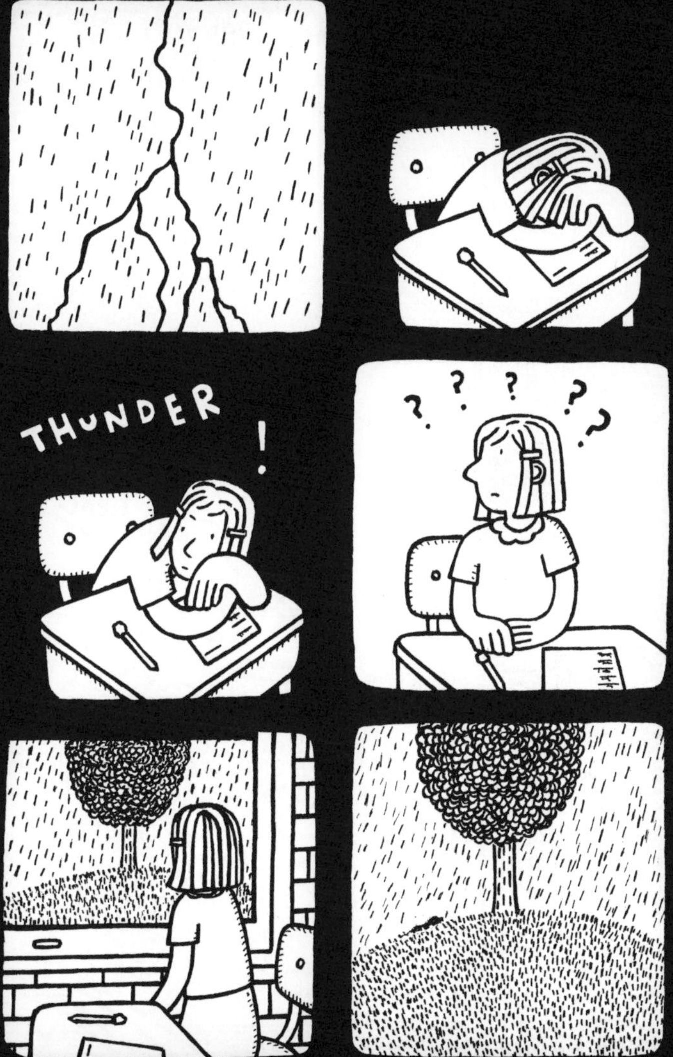
THUNDER
!

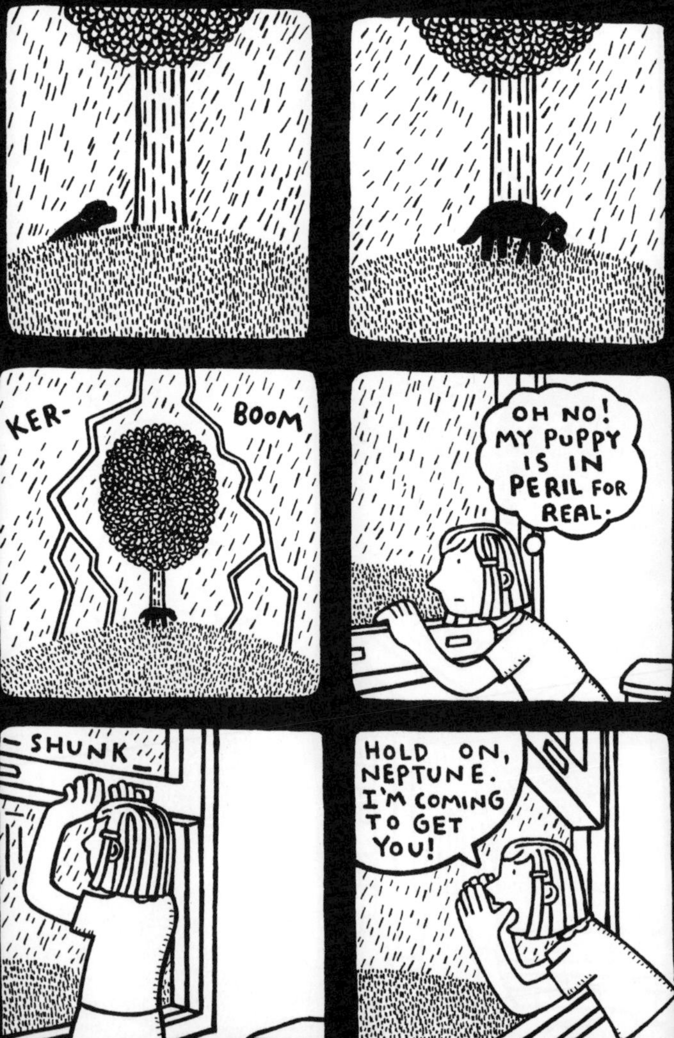
KER-
BOOM
OH NO! MY PUPPY IS IN PERIL FOR REAL.
SHUNK
HOLD ON, NEPTUNE. I'M COMING TO GET YOU!

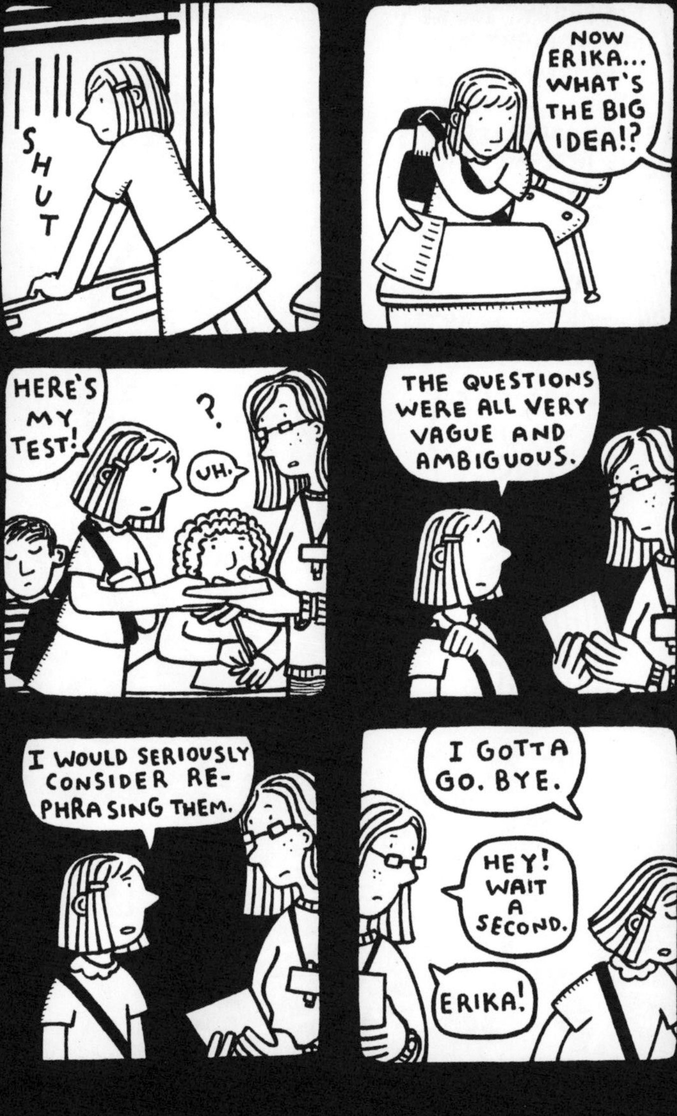
SHUT
NOW ERIKA... WHAT'S THE BIG IDEA!?
HERE'S MY TEST!
?
UH.
THE QUESTIONS WERE ALL VERY VAGUE AND AMBIGUOUS.
I WOULD SERIOUSLY CONSIDER RE-PHRASING THEM.
I GOTTA GO. BYE.
HEY! WAIT A SECOND.
ERIKA!

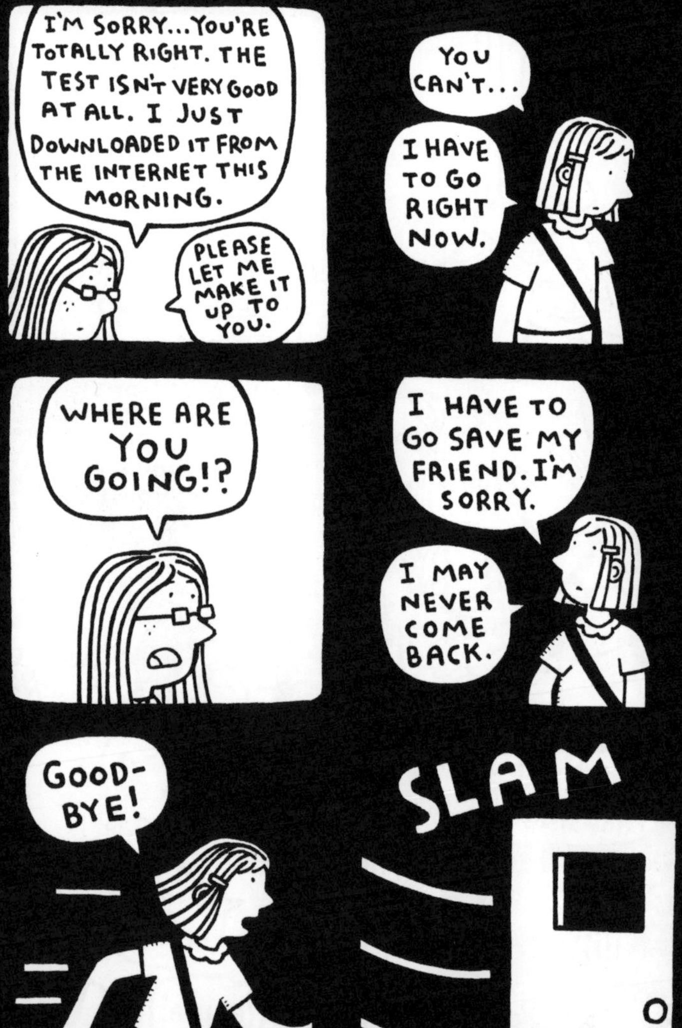
I'M SORRY... YOU'RE TOTALLY RIGHT. THE TEST ISN'T VERY GOOD AT ALL. I JUST DOWNLOADED IT FROM THE INTERNET THIS MORNING.
PLEASE LET ME MAKE IT UP TO YOU.
YOU CAN'T...
I HAVE TO GO RIGHT NOW.
WHERE ARE YOU GOING!?
I HAVE TO GO SAVE MY FRIEND. I'M SORRY.
I MAY NEVER COME BACK.
GOOD-BYE!
SLAM

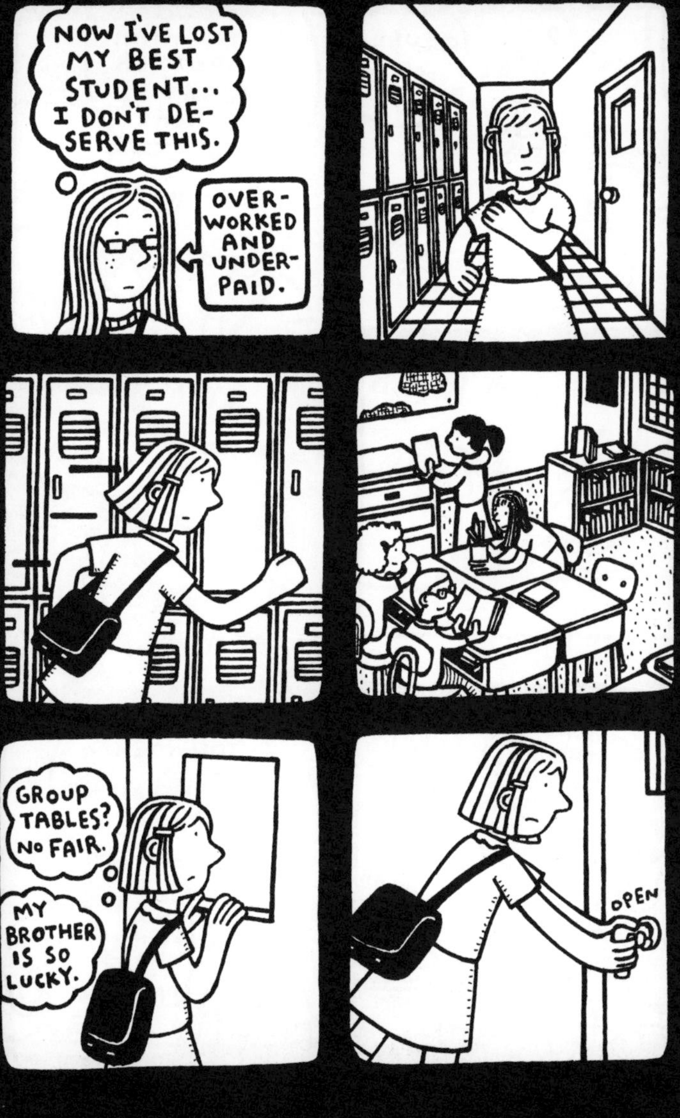
NOW I'VE LOST MY BEST STUDENT... I DON'T DE-SERVE THIS.
OVER-WORKED AND UNDER-PAID.
GROUP TABLES? NO FAIR.
MY BROTHER IS SO LUCKY.
OPEN

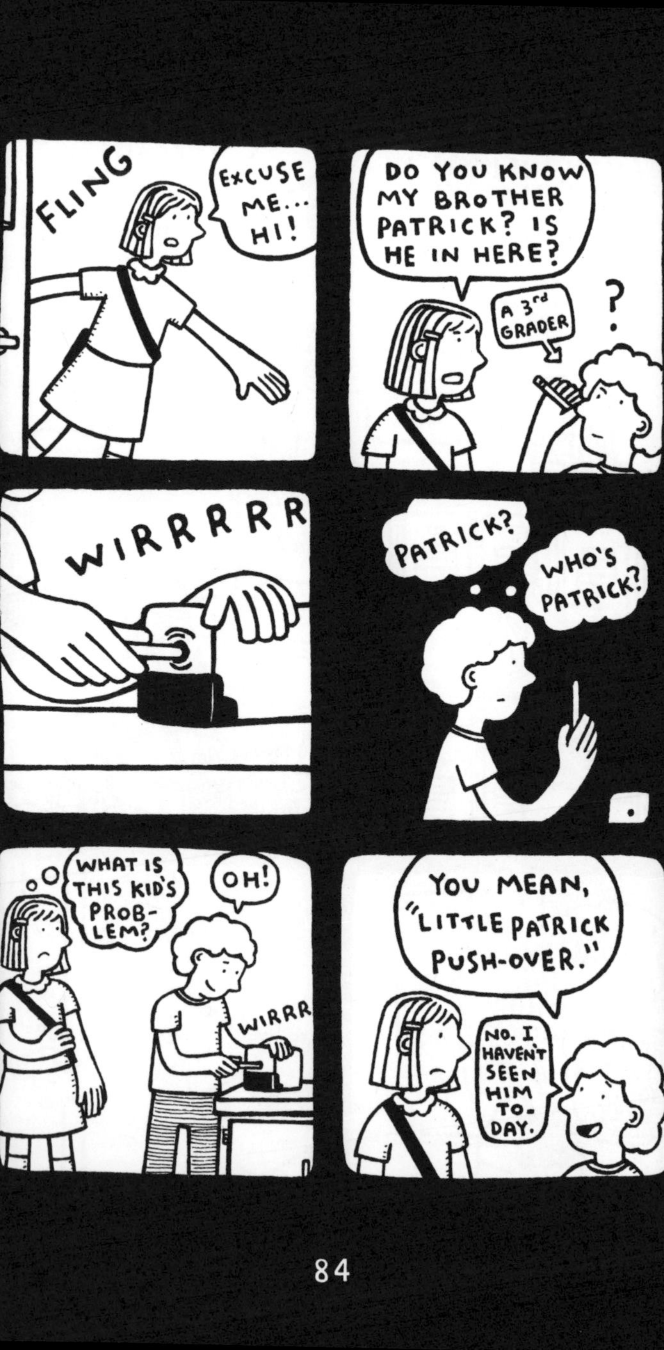
FLING
EXCUSE ME... HI!
DO YOU KNOW MY BROTHER PATRICK? IS HE IN HERE?
A 3rd GRADER
?
WIRRRRRR
PATRICK?
WHO'S PATRICK?
WHAT IS THIS KID'S PROB-LEM?
OH!
WIRRR
YOU MEAN, "LITTLE PATRICK PUSH-OVER."
NO. I HAVEN'T SEEN HIM TO-DAY.

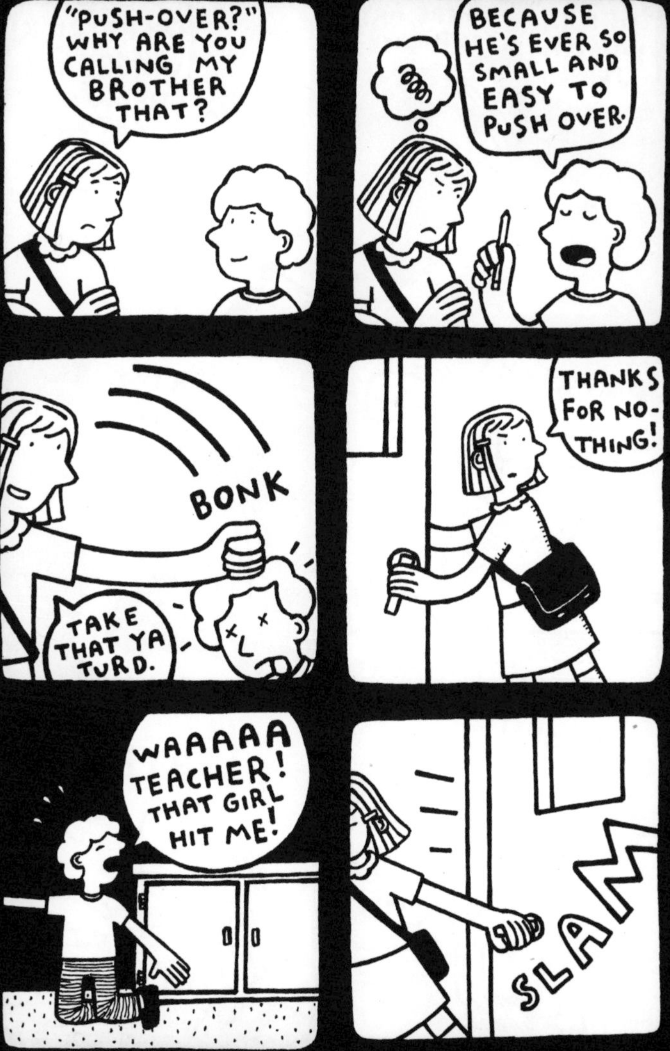
"PUSH-OVER?" WHY ARE YOU CALLING MY BROTHER THAT?
BECAUSE HE'S EVER SO SMALL AND EASY TO PUSH OVER.
BONK
TAKE THAT YA TURD.
THANKS FOR NO-THING!
WAAAAA TEACHER! THAT GIRL HIT ME!
SLAM

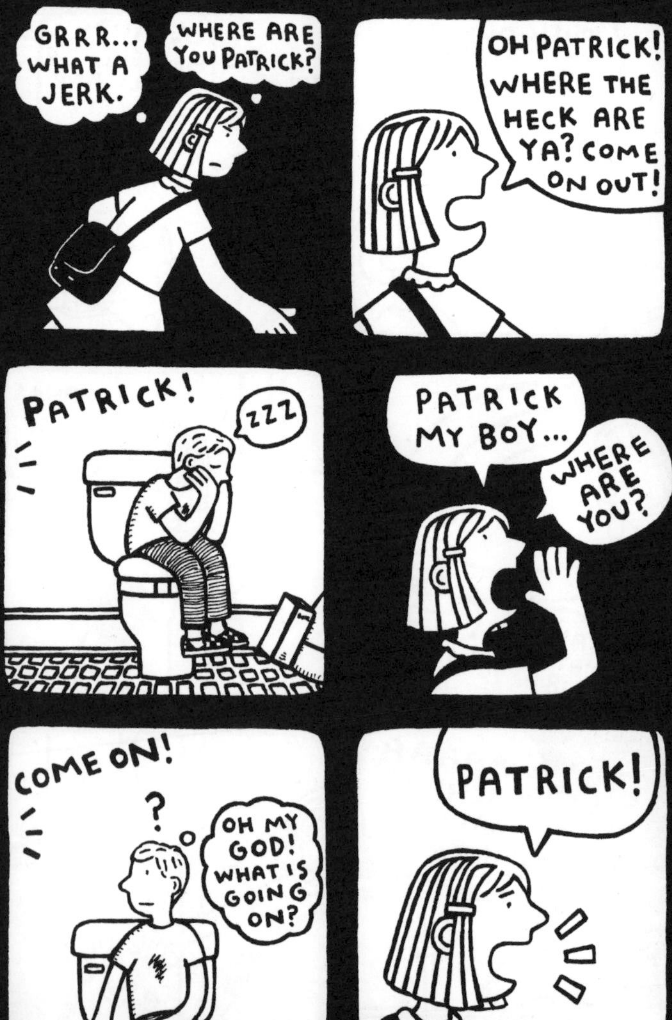
GRRR... WHAT A JERK.
WHERE ARE YOU PATRICK?
OH PATRICK! WHERE THE HECK ARE YA? COME ON OUT!
PATRICK!
ZZZ
PATRICK MY BOY...
WHERE ARE YOU?
COME ON!
?
OH MY GOD! WHAT IS GOING ON?
PATRICK!

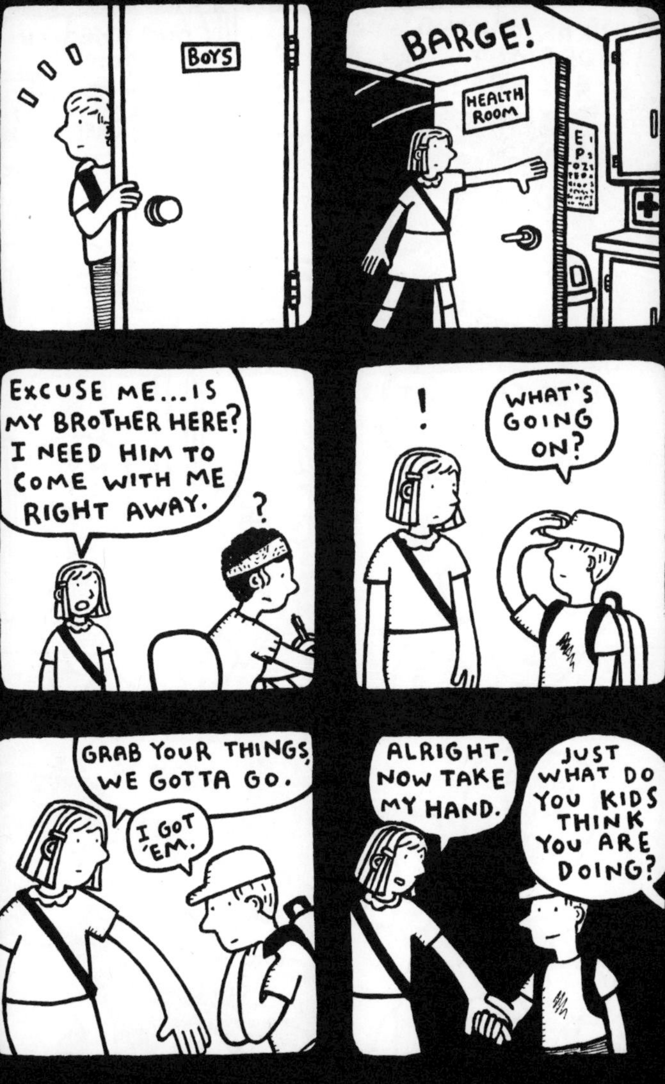
BOYS
BARGE!
HEALTH ROOM
EXCUSE ME...IS MY BROTHER HERE? I NEED HIM TO COME WITH ME RIGHT AWAY.
?
!
WHAT'S GOING ON?
GRAB YOUR THINGS, WE GOTTA GO.
I GOT 'EM.
ALRIGHT. NOW TAKE MY HAND.
JUST WHAT DO YOU KIDS THINK YOU ARE DOING?

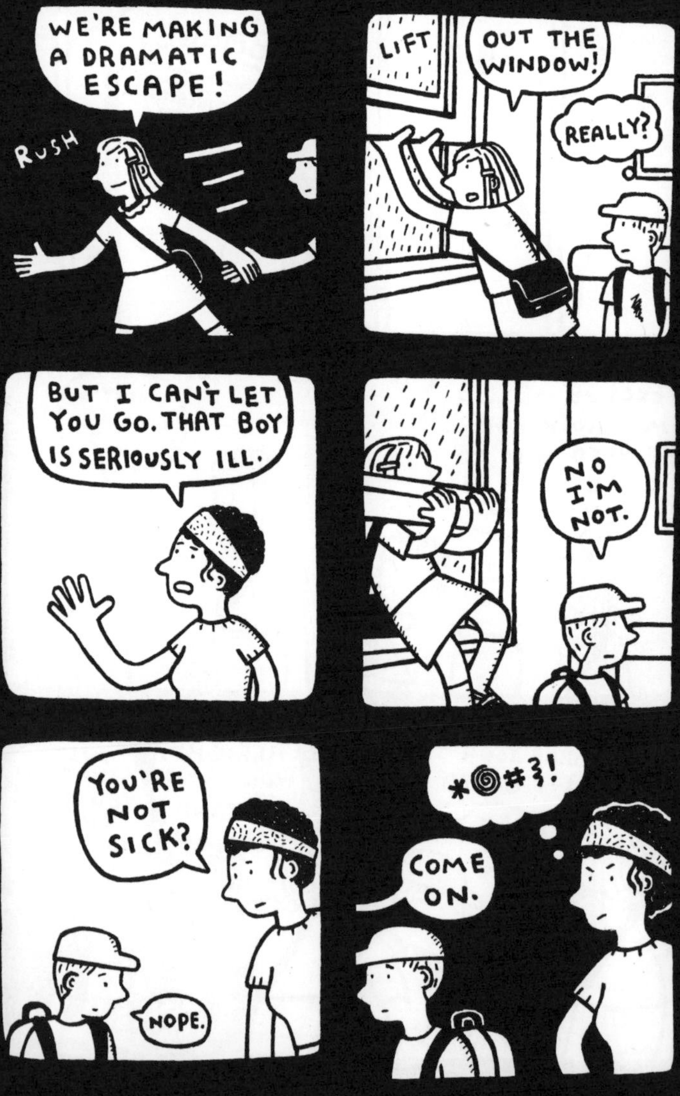
WE'RE MAKING A DRAMATIC ESCAPE!
RUSH
LIFT
OUT THE WINDOW!
REALLY?
BUT I CAN'T LET YOU GO. THAT BOY IS SERIOUSLY ILL.
NO I'M NOT.
YOU'RE NOT SICK?
NOPE.
*@#3!
COME ON.

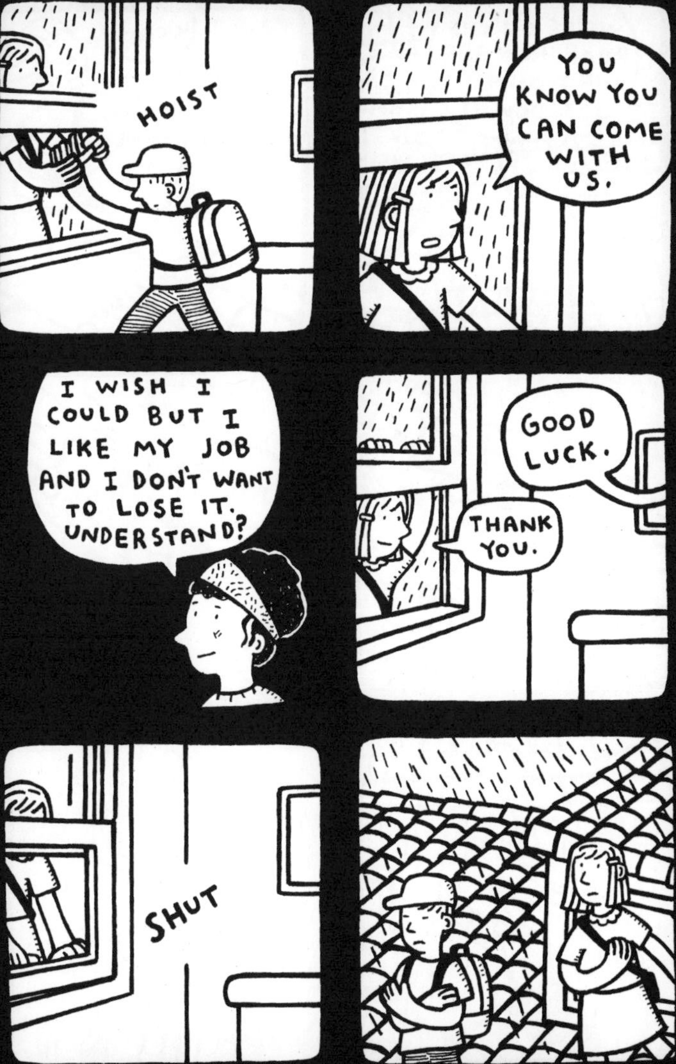
HOIST
YOU KNOW YOU CAN COME WITH US.
I WISH I COULD BUT I LIKE MY JOB AND I DON'T WANT TO LOSE IT. UNDERSTAND?
GOOD LUCK.
THANK YOU.
SHUT

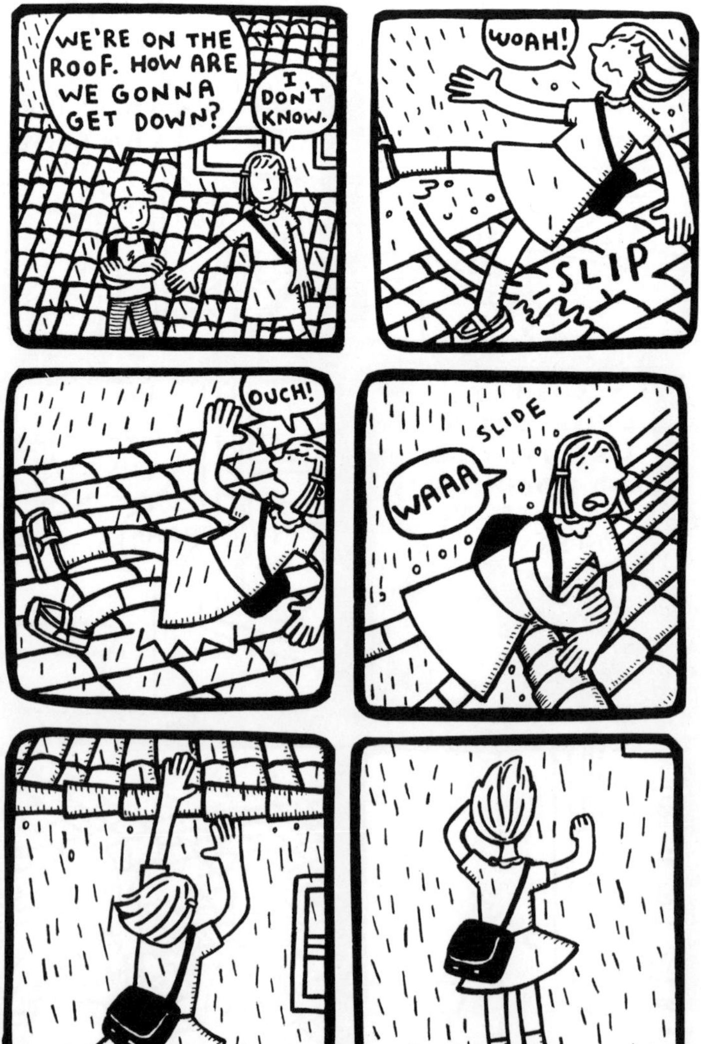
WE'RE ON THE ROOF. HOW ARE WE GONNA GET DOWN?
I DON'T KNOW.
WOAH!
SLIP
OUCH!
SLIDE
WAAA

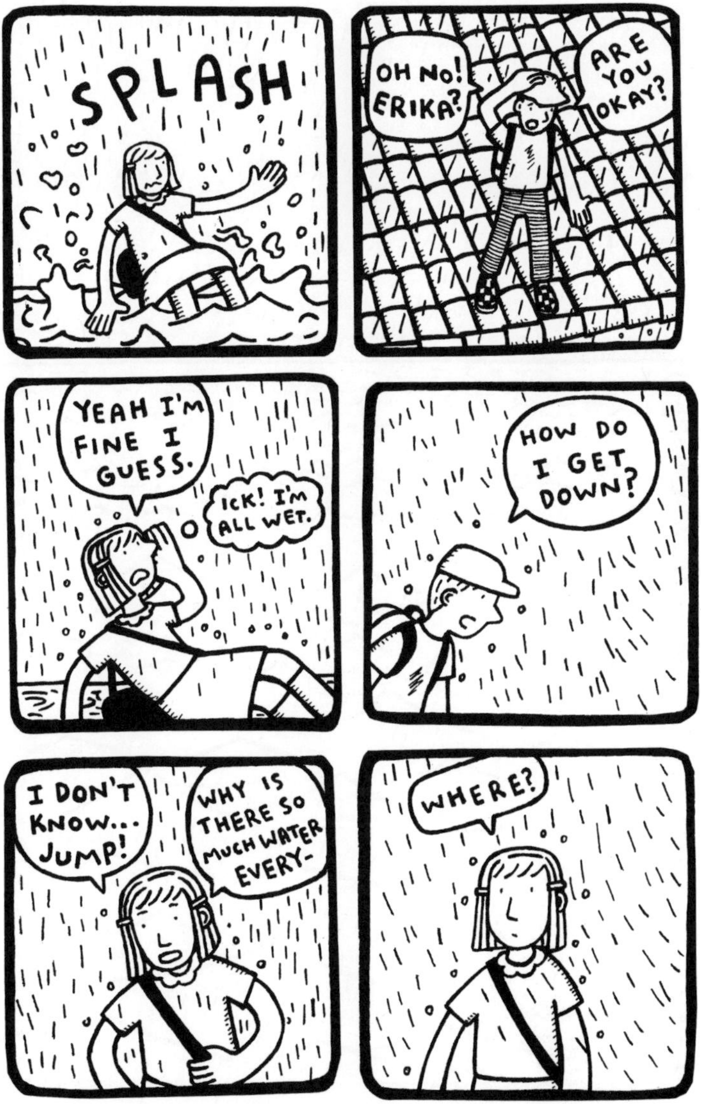
SPLASH
OH NO! ERIKA?
ARE YOU OKAY?
YEAH I'M FINE I GUESS.
ICK! I'M ALL WET.
HOW DO I GET DOWN?
I DON'T KNOW... JUMP!
WHY IS THERE SO MUCH WATER EVERY-
WHERE?

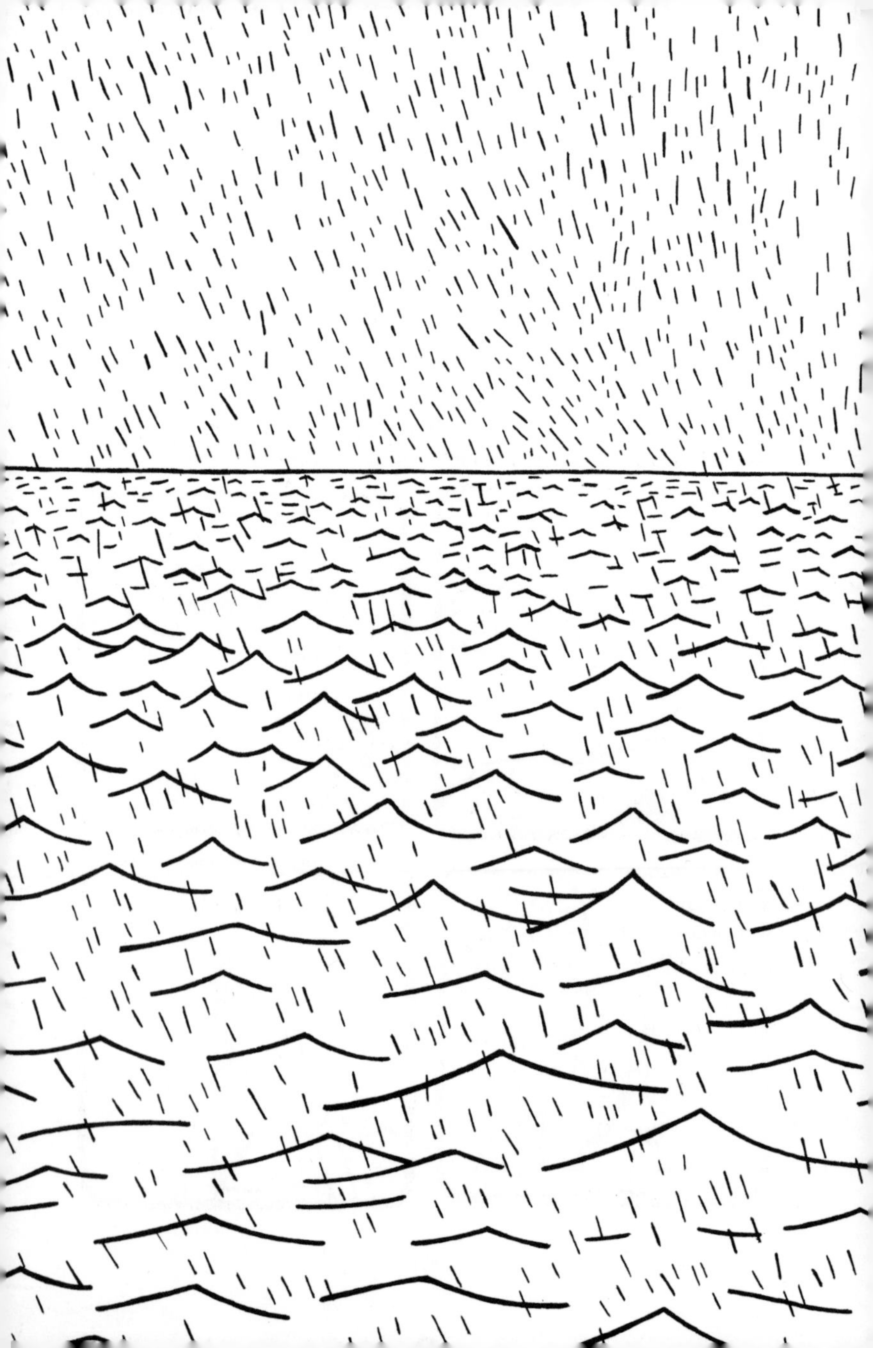

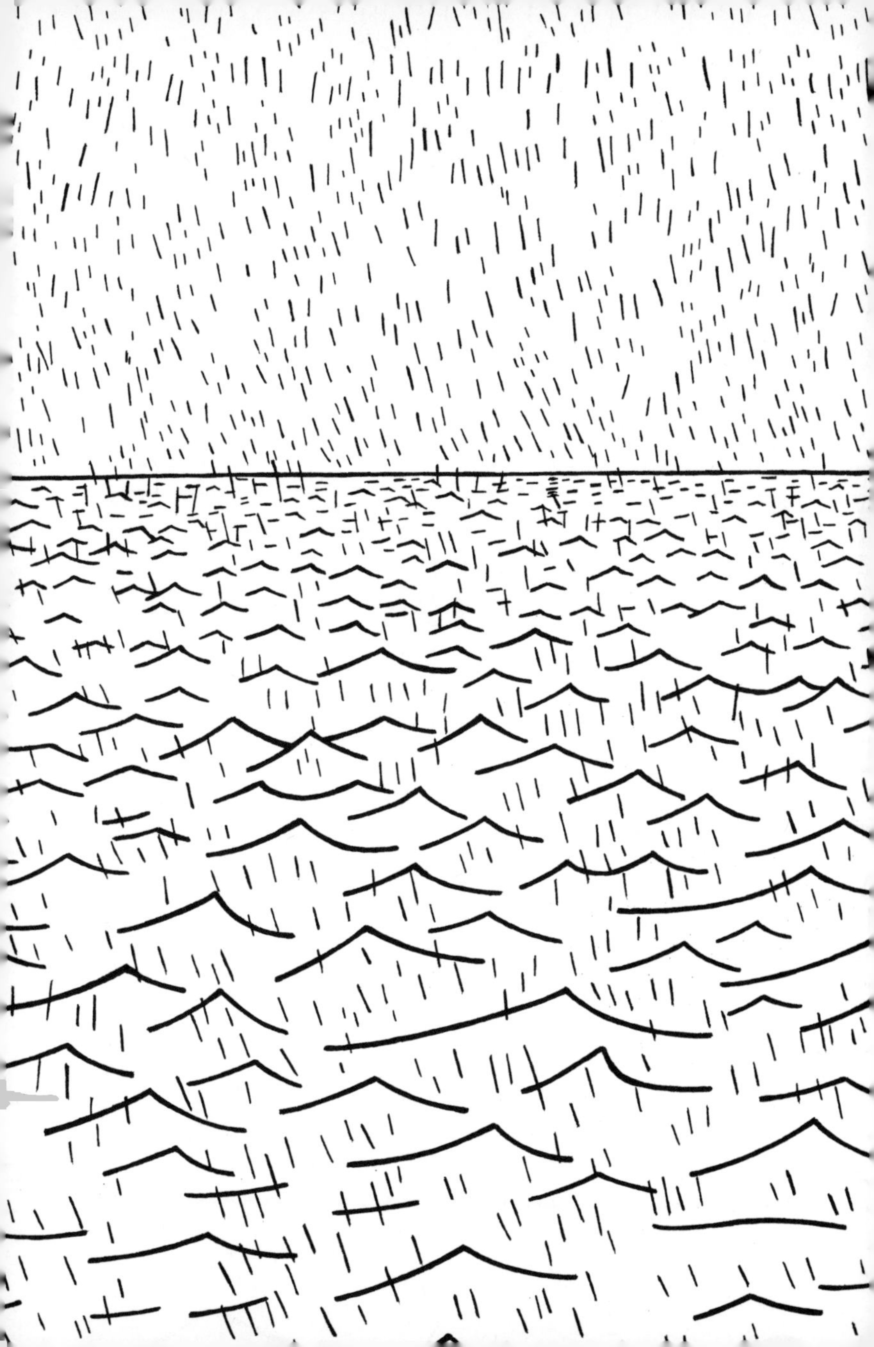

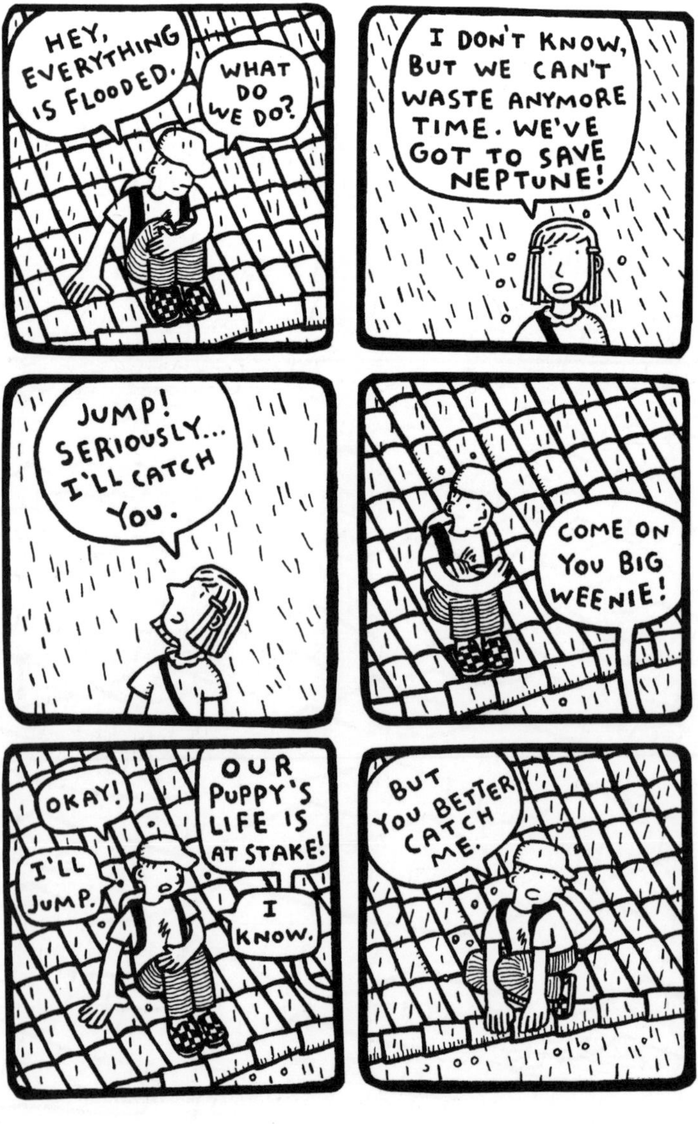
HEY, EVERYTHING IS FLOODED.
WHAT DO WE DO?
I DON'T KNOW, BUT WE CAN'T WASTE ANYMORE TIME. WE'VE GOT TO SAVE NEPTUNE!
JUMP! SERIOUSLY... I'LL CATCH YOU.
COME ON YOU BIG WEENIE!
OKAY!
I'LL JUMP.
OUR PUPPY'S LIFE IS AT STAKE!
I KNOW.
BUT YOU BETTER CATCH ME.

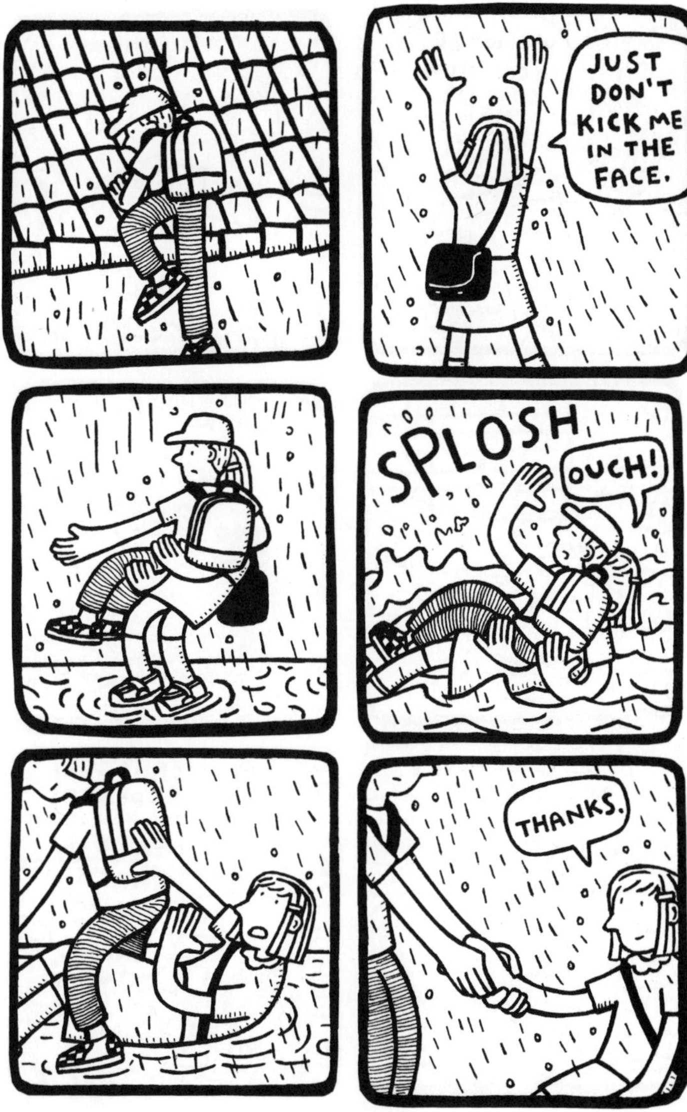
JUST DON'T KICK ME IN THE FACE.
SPLOSH
OUCH!
THANKS.

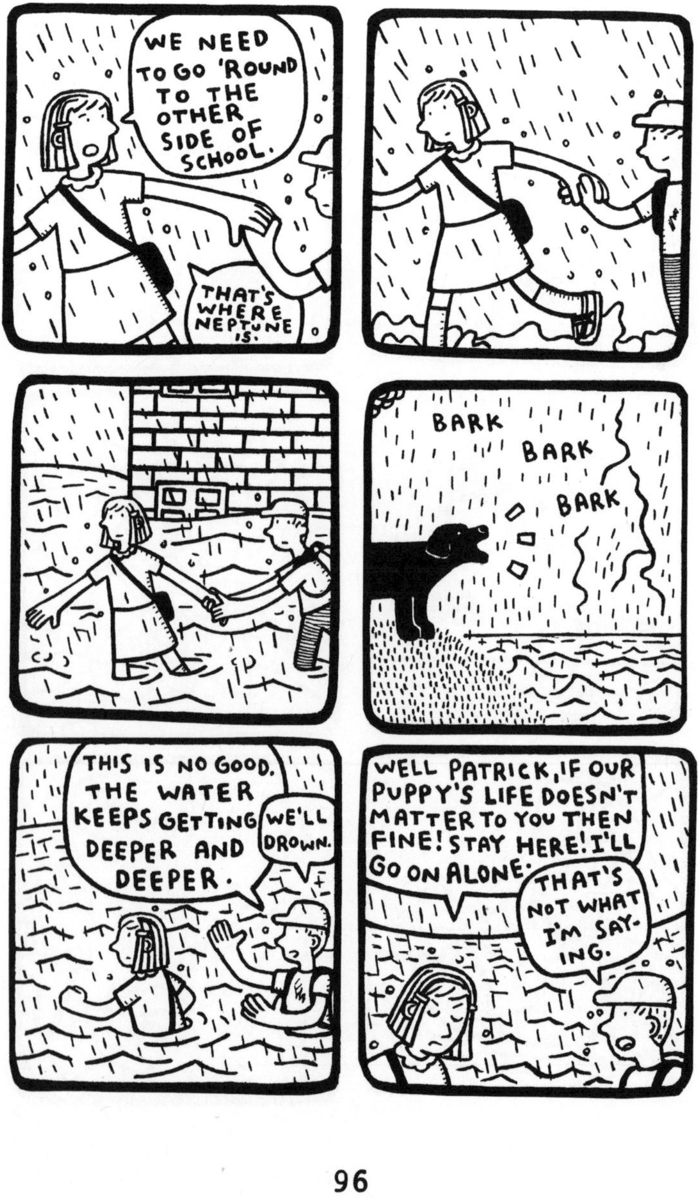
WE NEED TO GO 'ROUND TO THE OTHER SIDE OF SCHOOL.
THAT'S WHERE NEPTUNE IS.
BARK
BARK
BARK
THIS IS NO GOOD. THE WATER KEEPS GETTING DEEPER AND DEEPER.
WE'LL DROWN.
WELL PATRICK, IF OUR PUPPY'S LIFE DOESN'T MATTER TO YOU THEN FINE! STAY HERE! I'LL GO ON ALONE.
THAT'S NOT WHAT I'M SAY-ING.

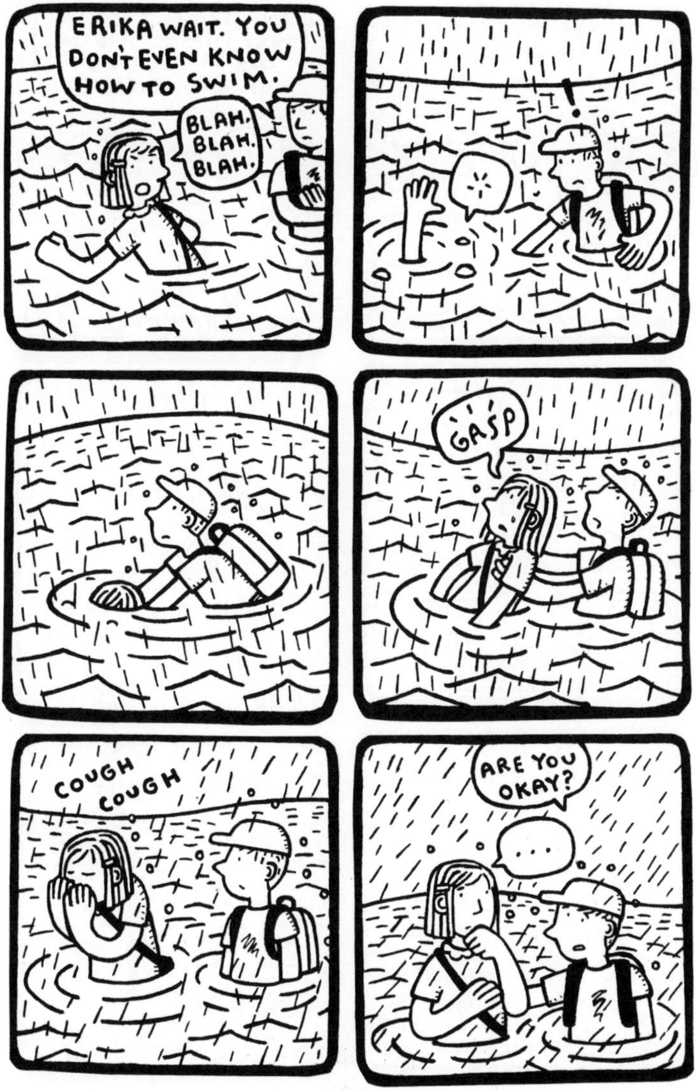
ERIKA WAIT. YOU DON'T EVEN KNOW HOW TO SWIM.
BLAH. BLAH. BLAH.
!
GASP
COUGH COUGH
ARE YOU OKAY?
...

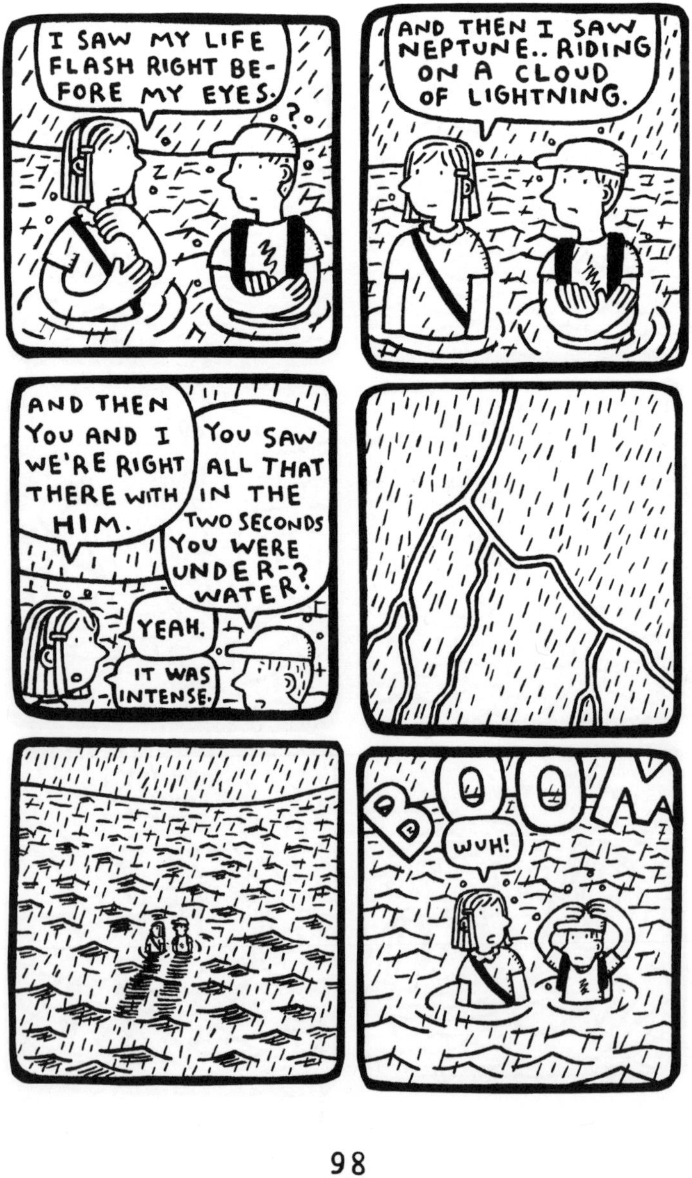
I SAW MY LIFE FLASH RIGHT BEFORE MY EYES.
?
AND THEN I SAW NEPTUNE.. RIDING ON A CLOUD OF LIGHTNING.
AND THEN YOU AND I WE'RE RIGHT THERE WITH HIM.
YOU SAW ALL THAT IN THE TWO SECONDS YOU WERE UNDER-WATER?
YEAH.
IT WAS INTENSE.
BOOM
WUH!

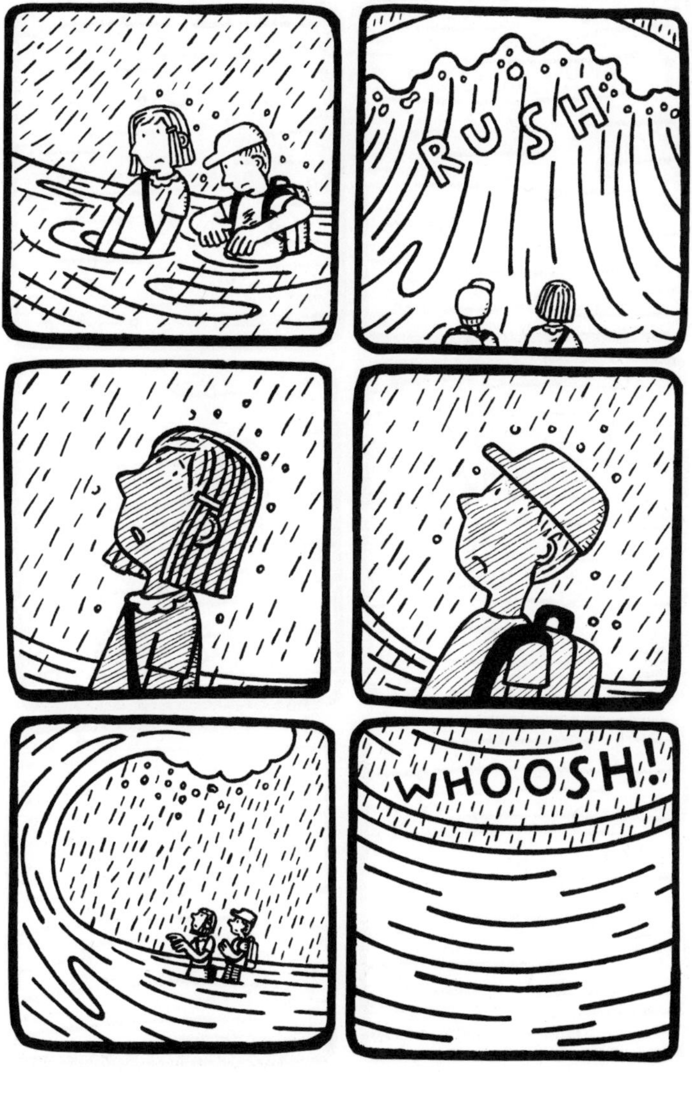
RUSH
WHOOSH!

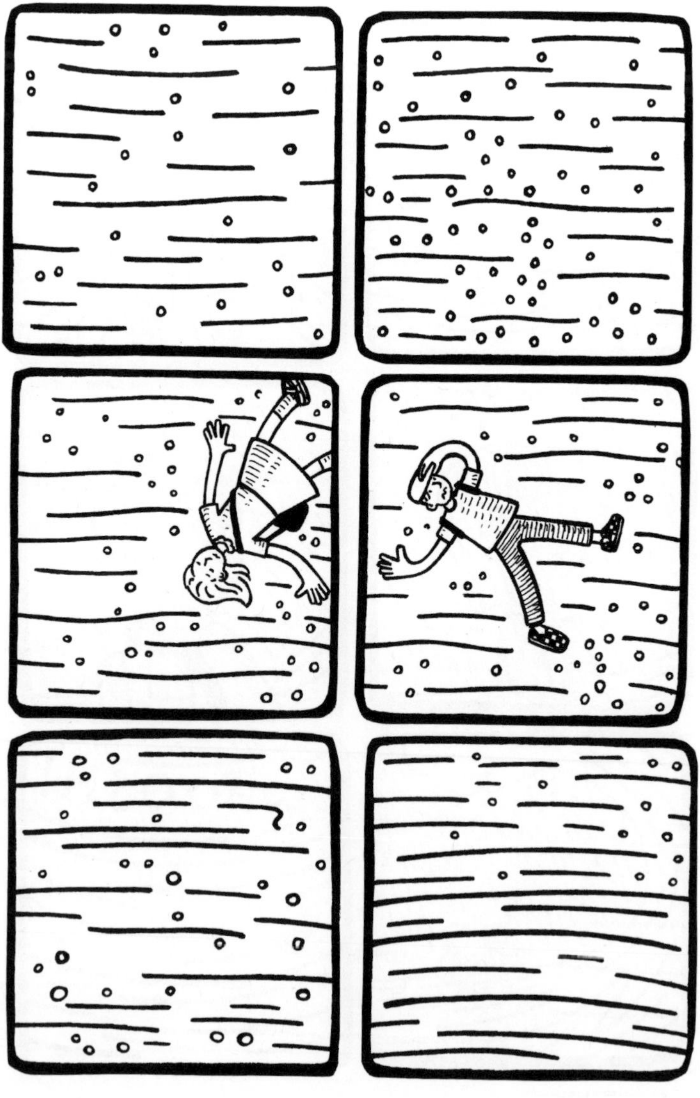

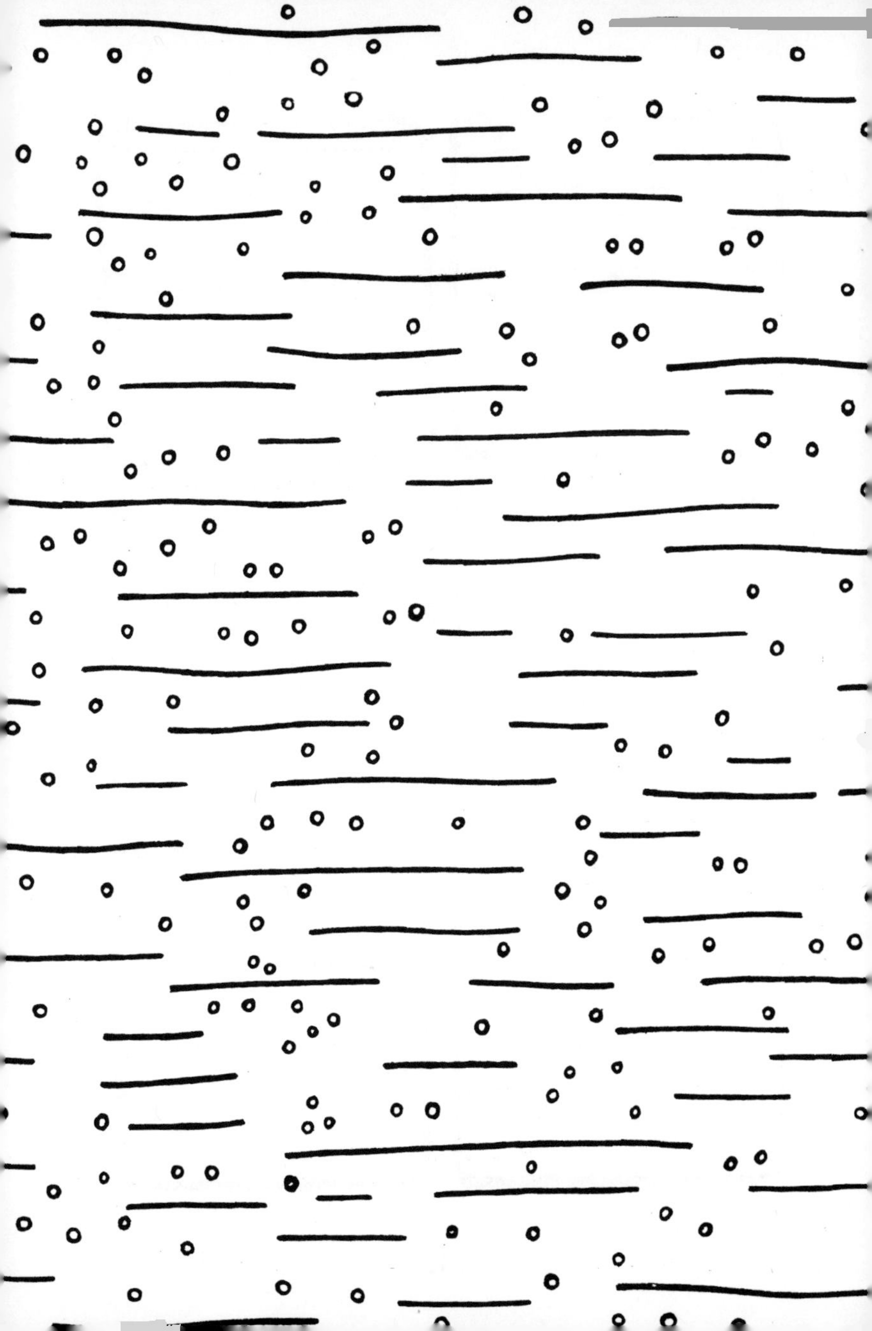

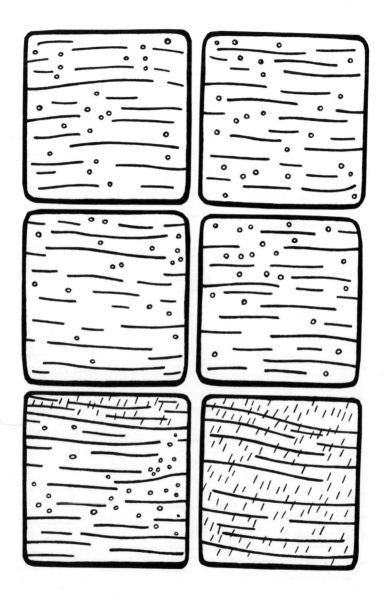

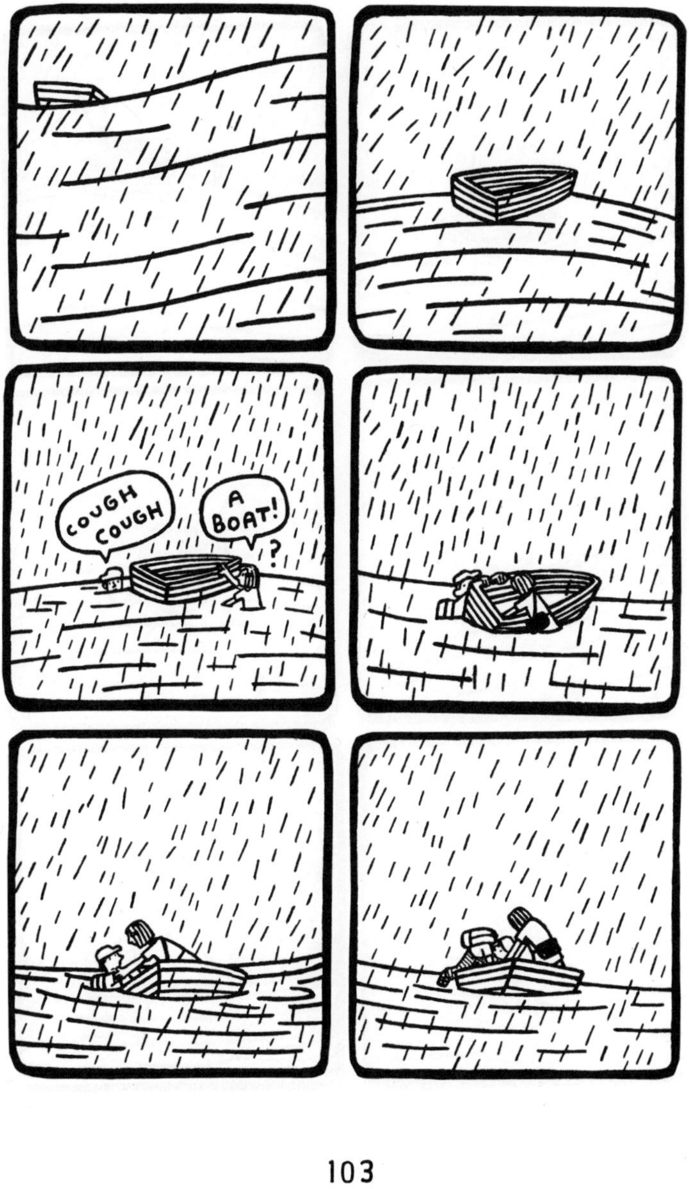
COUGH COUGH
A BOAT!
?

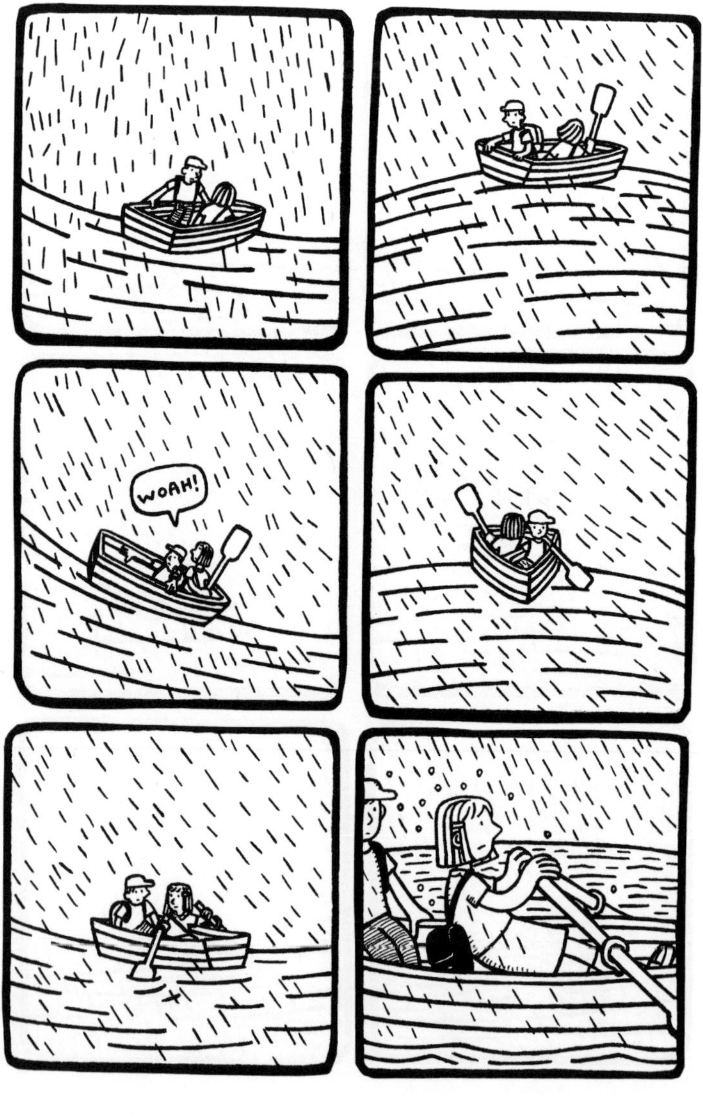
WOAH!

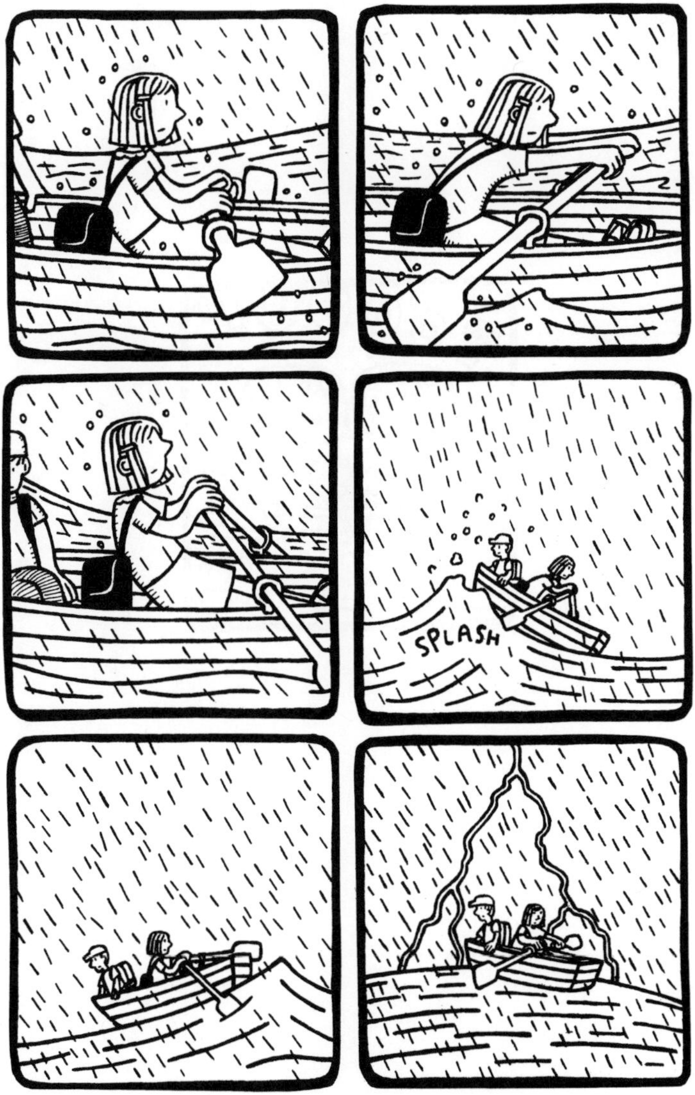
SPLASH

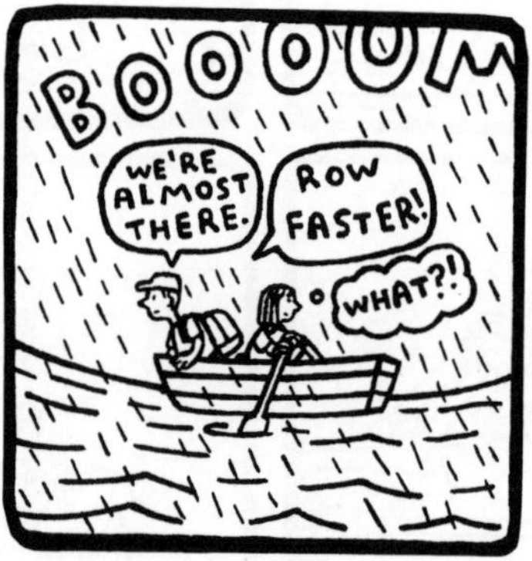
BOOOOM
WE'RE ALMOST THERE.
ROW FASTER!
WHAT?!

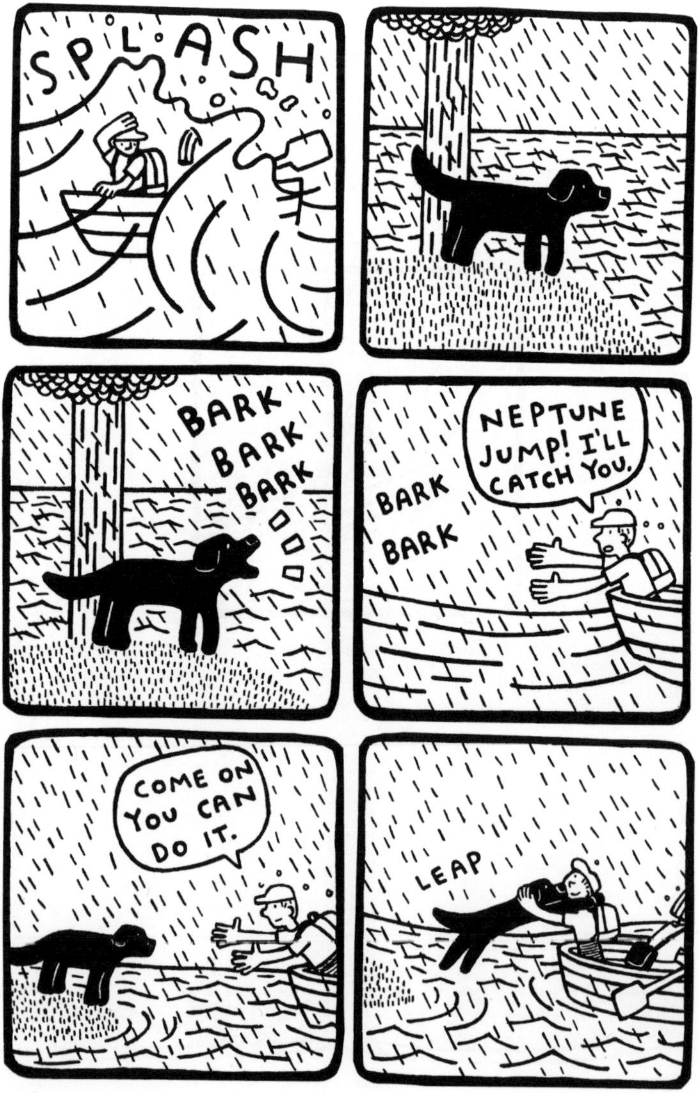
SPLASH
BARK
BARK
BARK
BARK
BARK
NEPTUNE JUMP! I'LL CATCH YOU.
COME ON YOU CAN DO IT.
LEAP

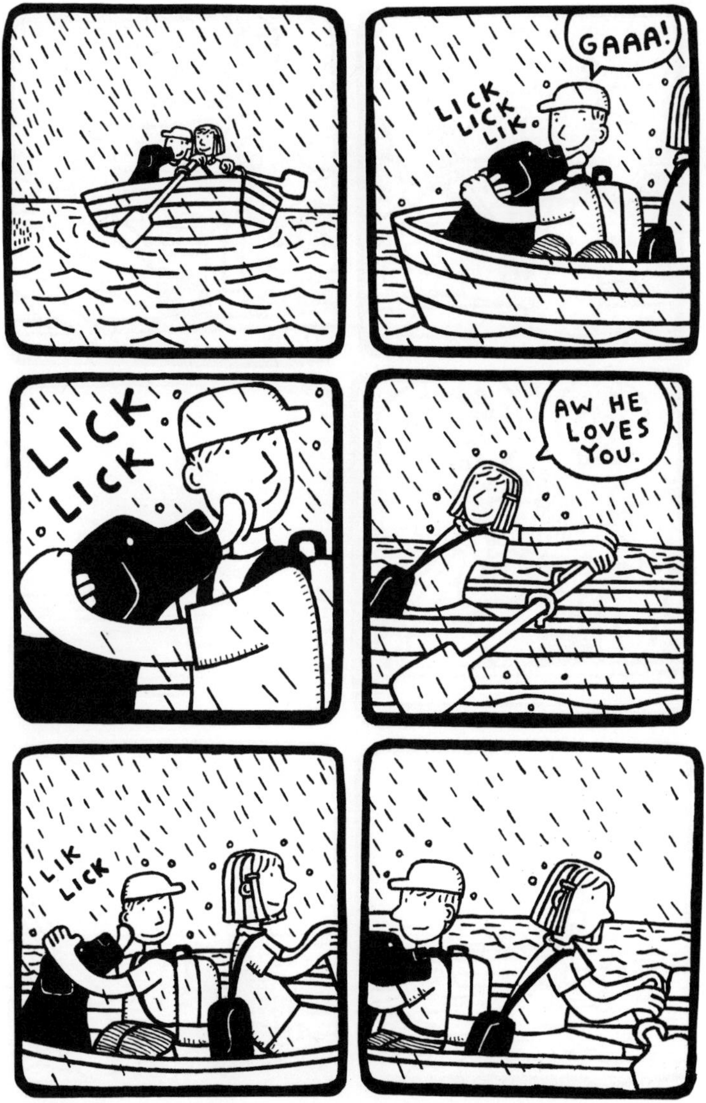
GAAA!
LICK LICK LIK
LICK LICK
AW HE LOVES YOU.
LIK LICK

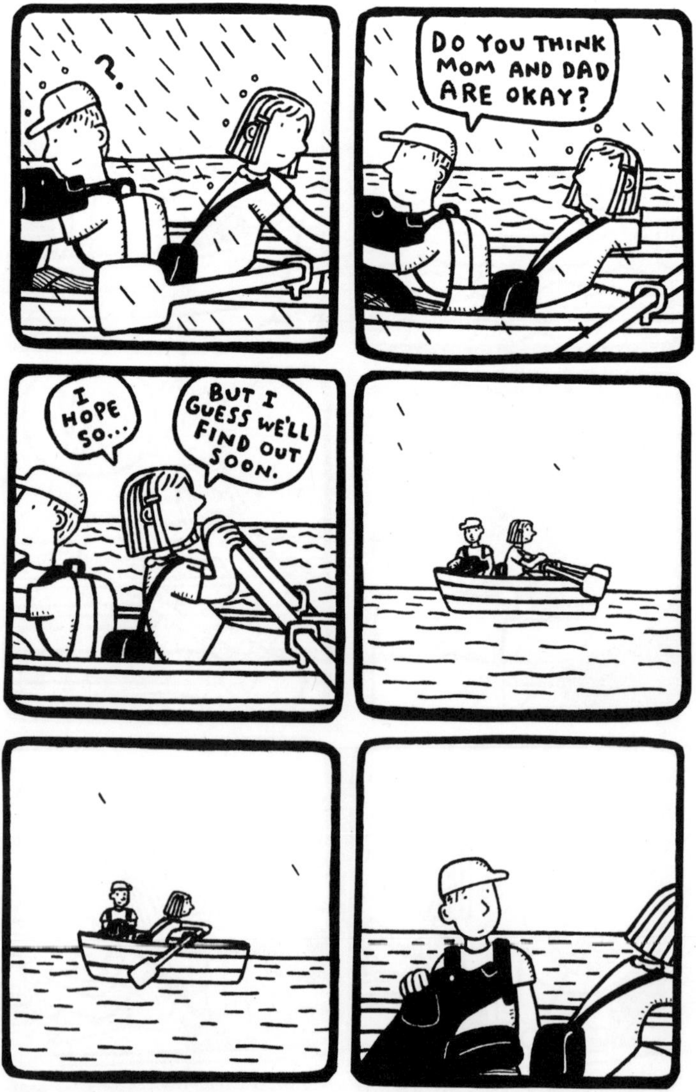
?
DO YOU THINK MOM AND DAD ARE OKAY?
I HOPE SO...
BUT I GUESS WE'LL FIND OUT SOON.

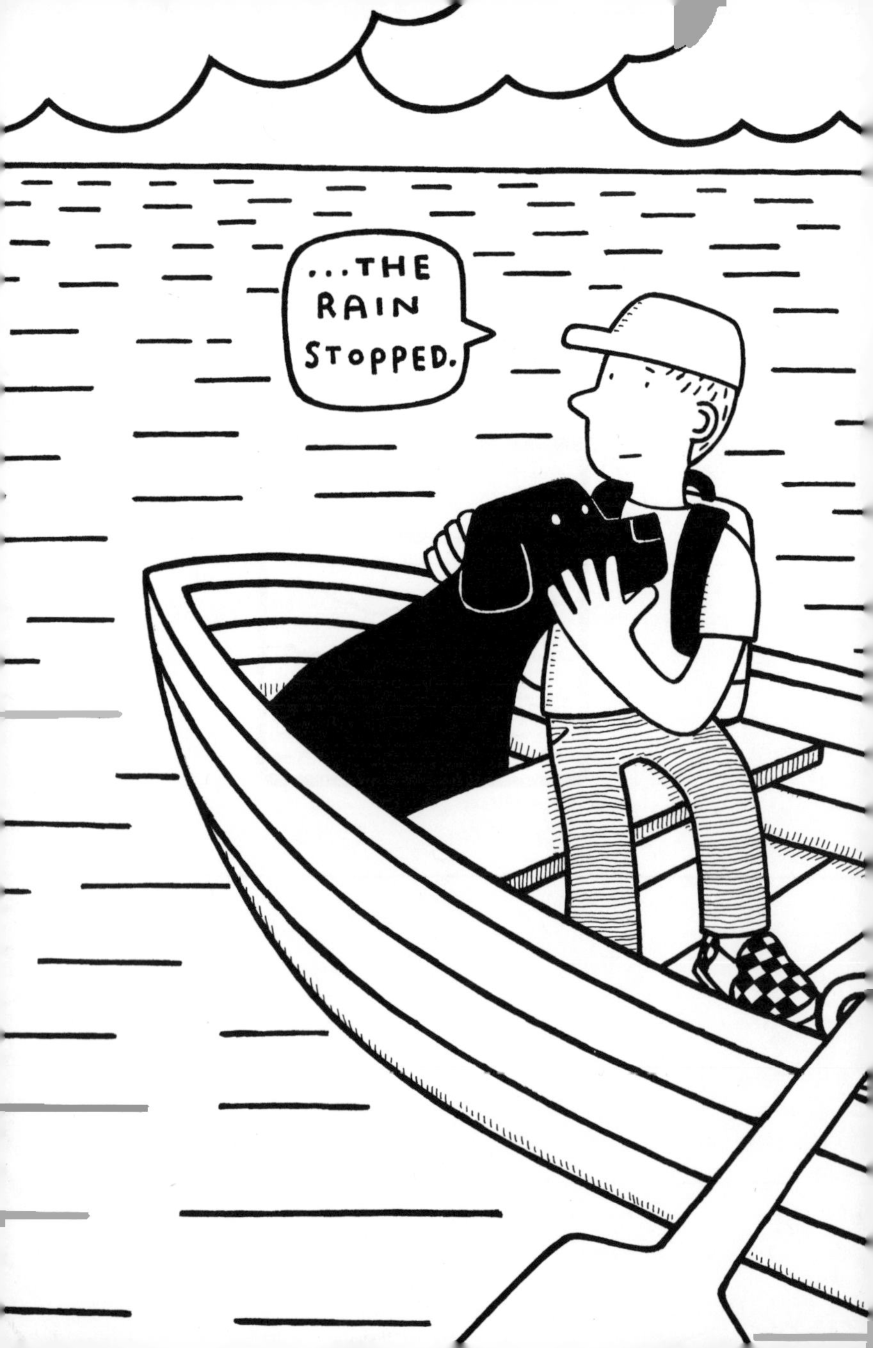
...THE RAIN STOPPED.

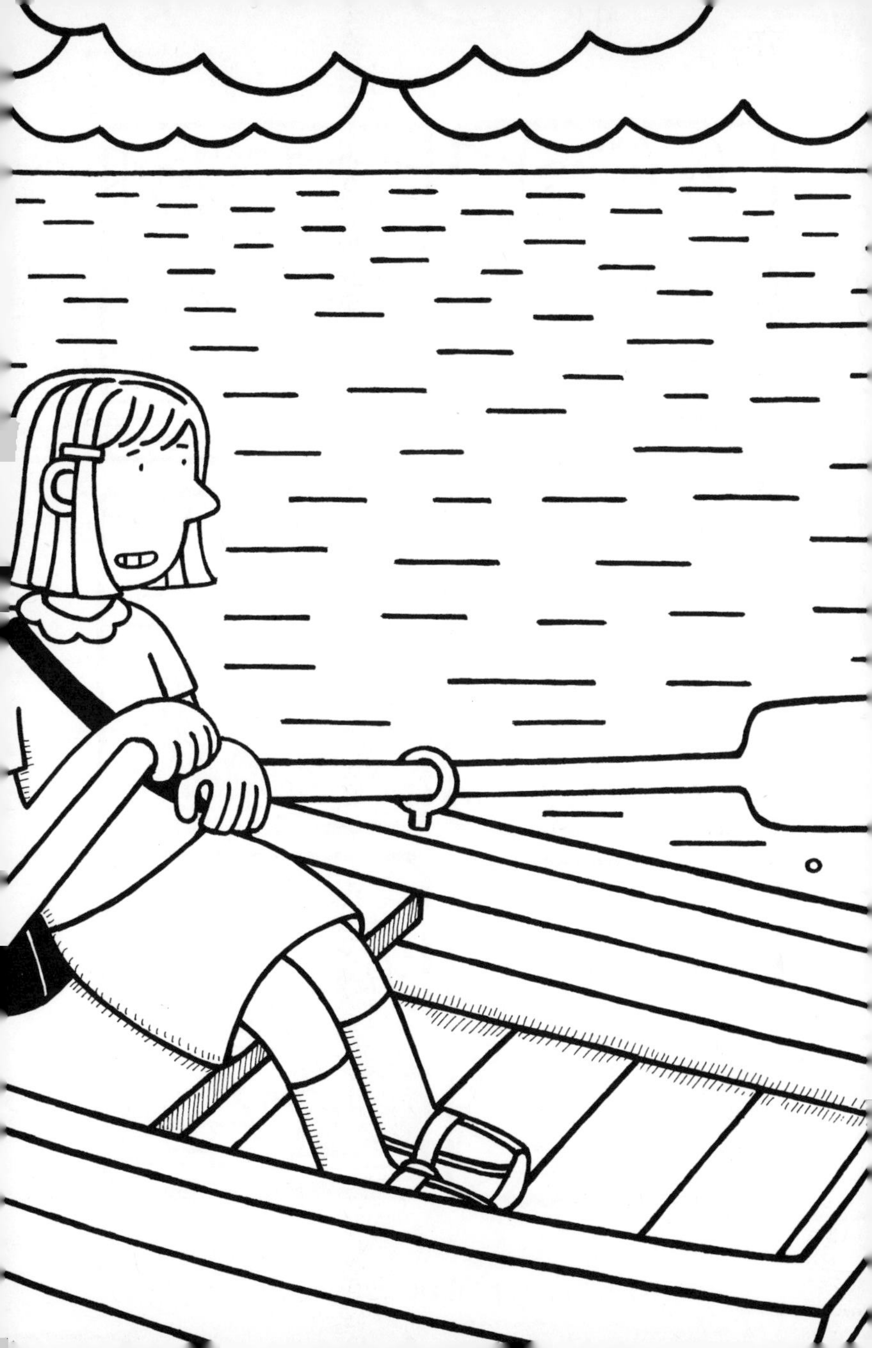

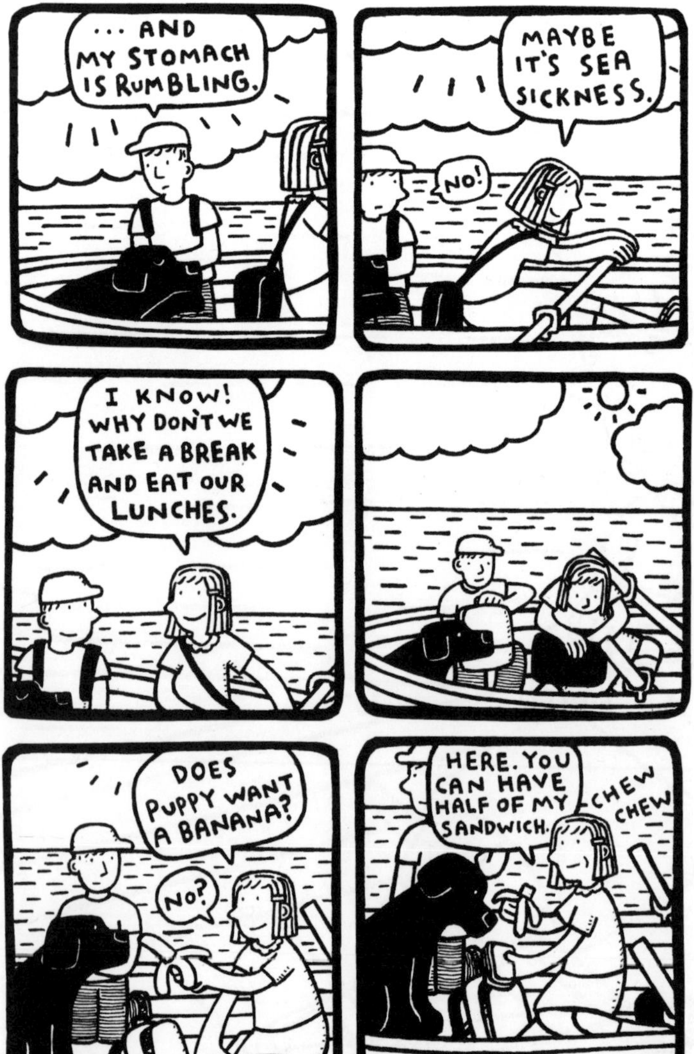
... AND MY STOMACH IS RUMBLING.
MAYBE IT'S SEA SICKNESS.
NO!
I KNOW! WHY DON'T WE TAKE A BREAK AND EAT OUR LUNCHES.
DOES PUPPY WANT A BANANA?
NO?
HERE. YOU CAN HAVE HALF OF MY SANDWICH.
CHEW CHEW

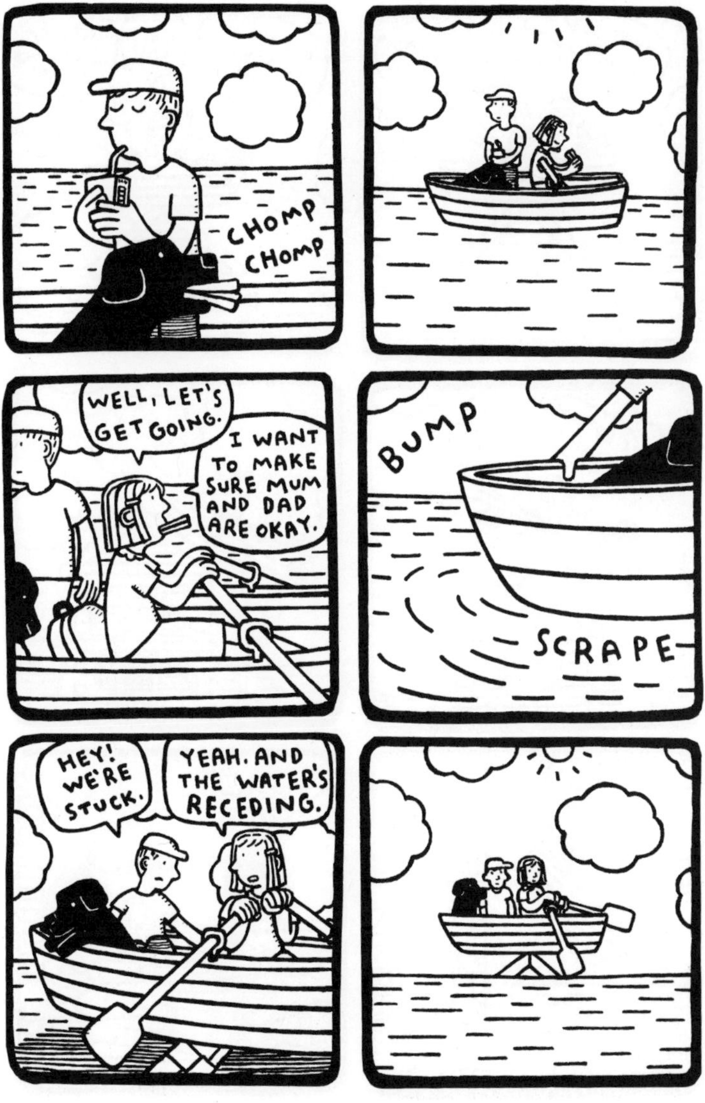
CHOMP
CHOMP
WELL, LET'S GET GOING.
I WANT TO MAKE SURE MUM AND DAD ARE OKAY.
BUMP
SCRAPE
HEY! WE'RE STUCK.
YEAH. AND THE WATER'S RECEDING.

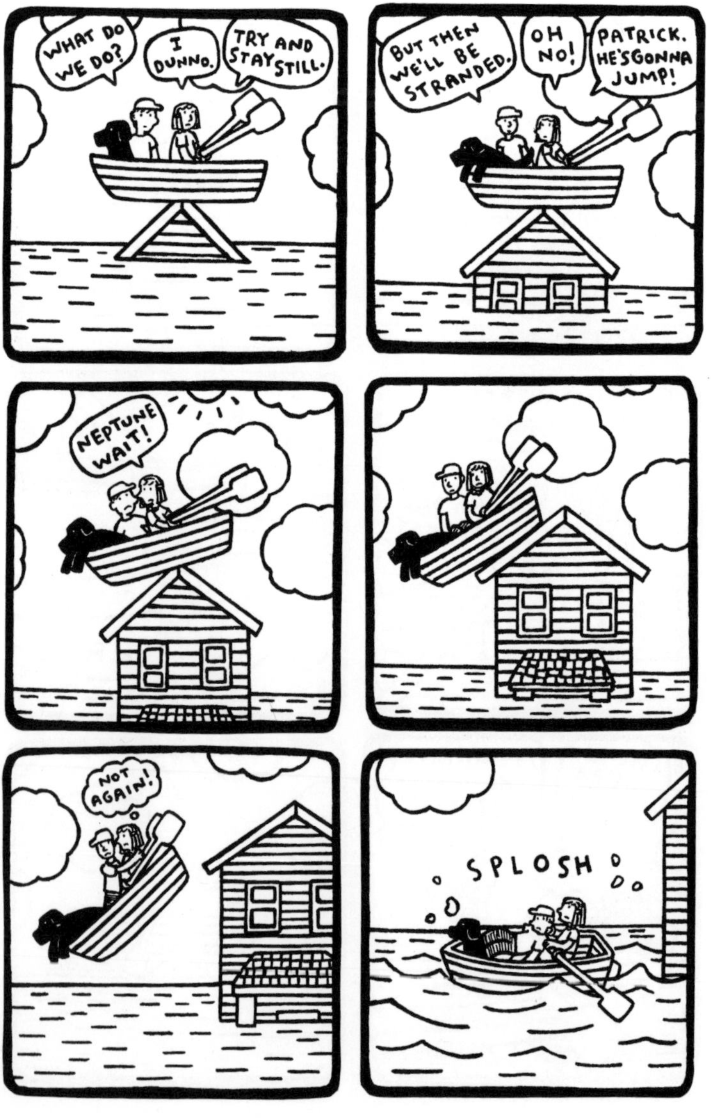
WHAT DO WE DO?
I DUNNO.
TRY AND STAY STILL.
BUT THEN WE'LL BE STRANDED.
OH NO!
PATRICK. HE'S GONNA JUMP!
NEPTUNE WAIT!
NOT AGAIN!
SPLOSH

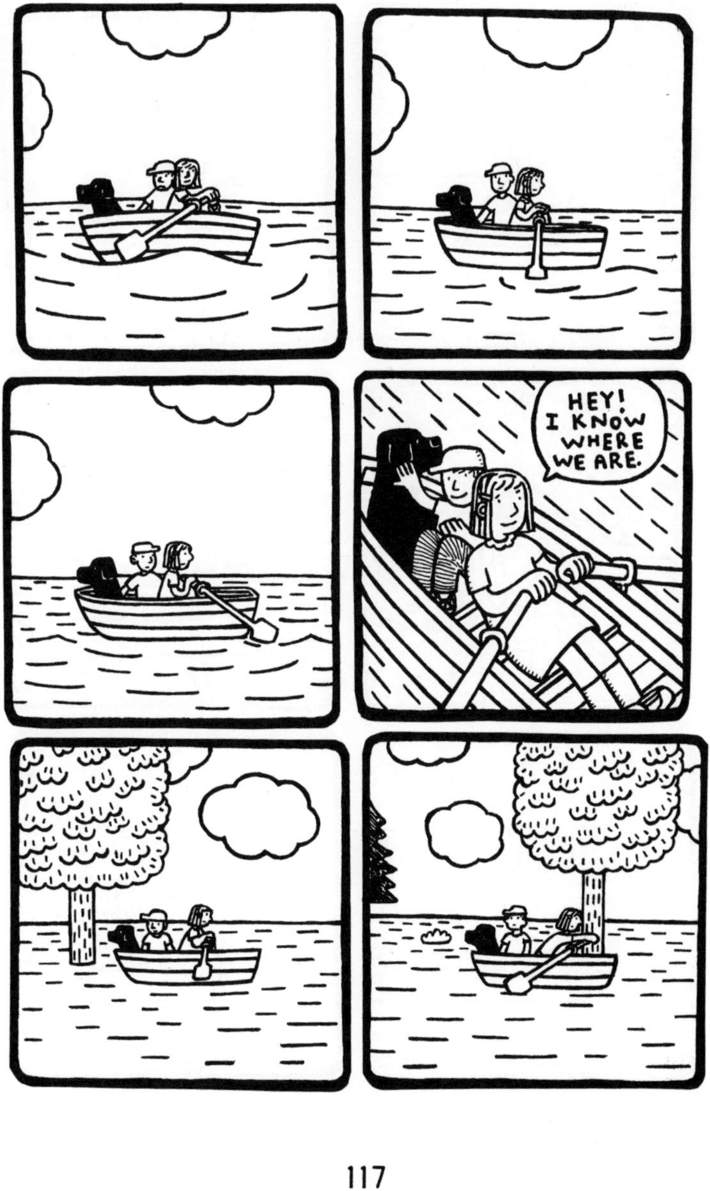
HEY! I KNOW WHERE WE ARE.

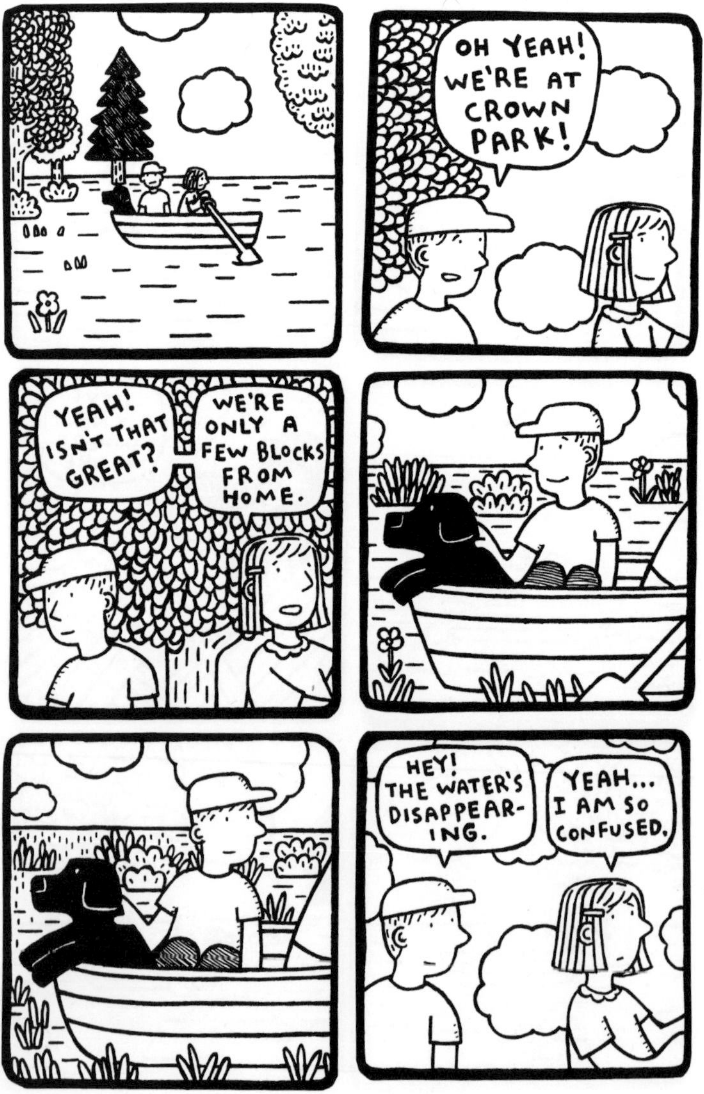
OH YEAH! WE'RE AT CROWN PARK!
YEAH! ISN'T THAT GREAT?
WE'RE ONLY A FEW BLOCKS FROM HOME.
HEY! THE WATER'S DISAPPEAR-ING.
YEAH... I AM SO CONFUSED.

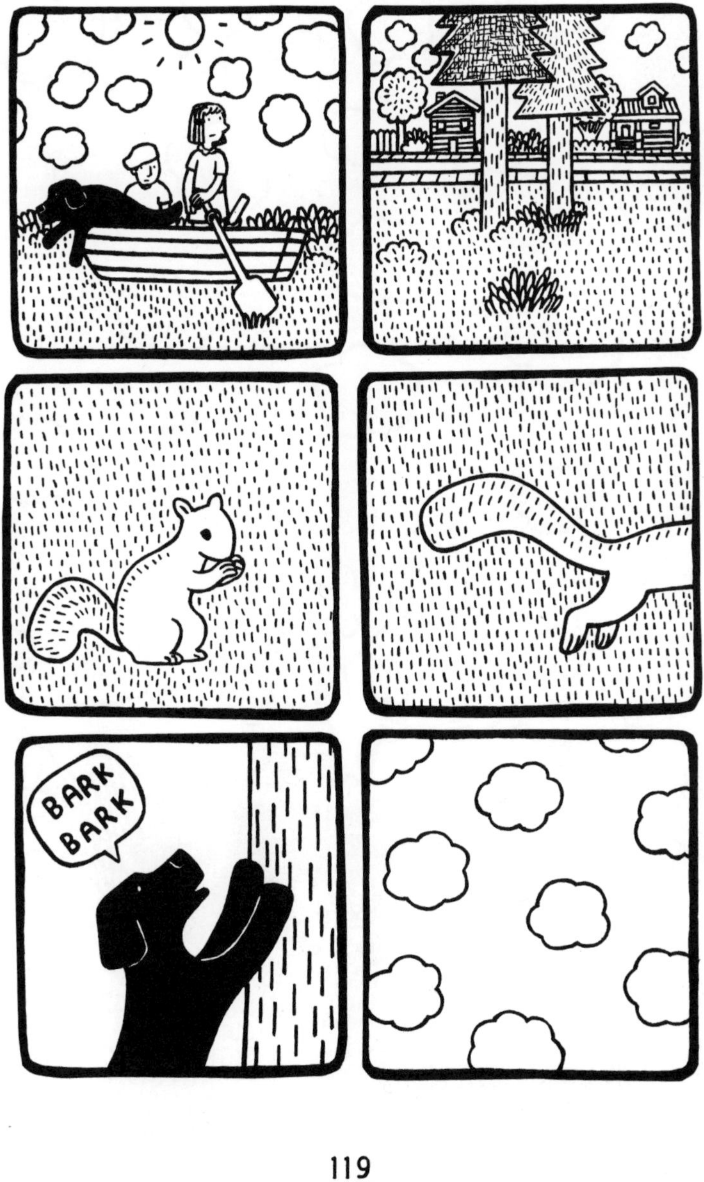
BARK
BARK

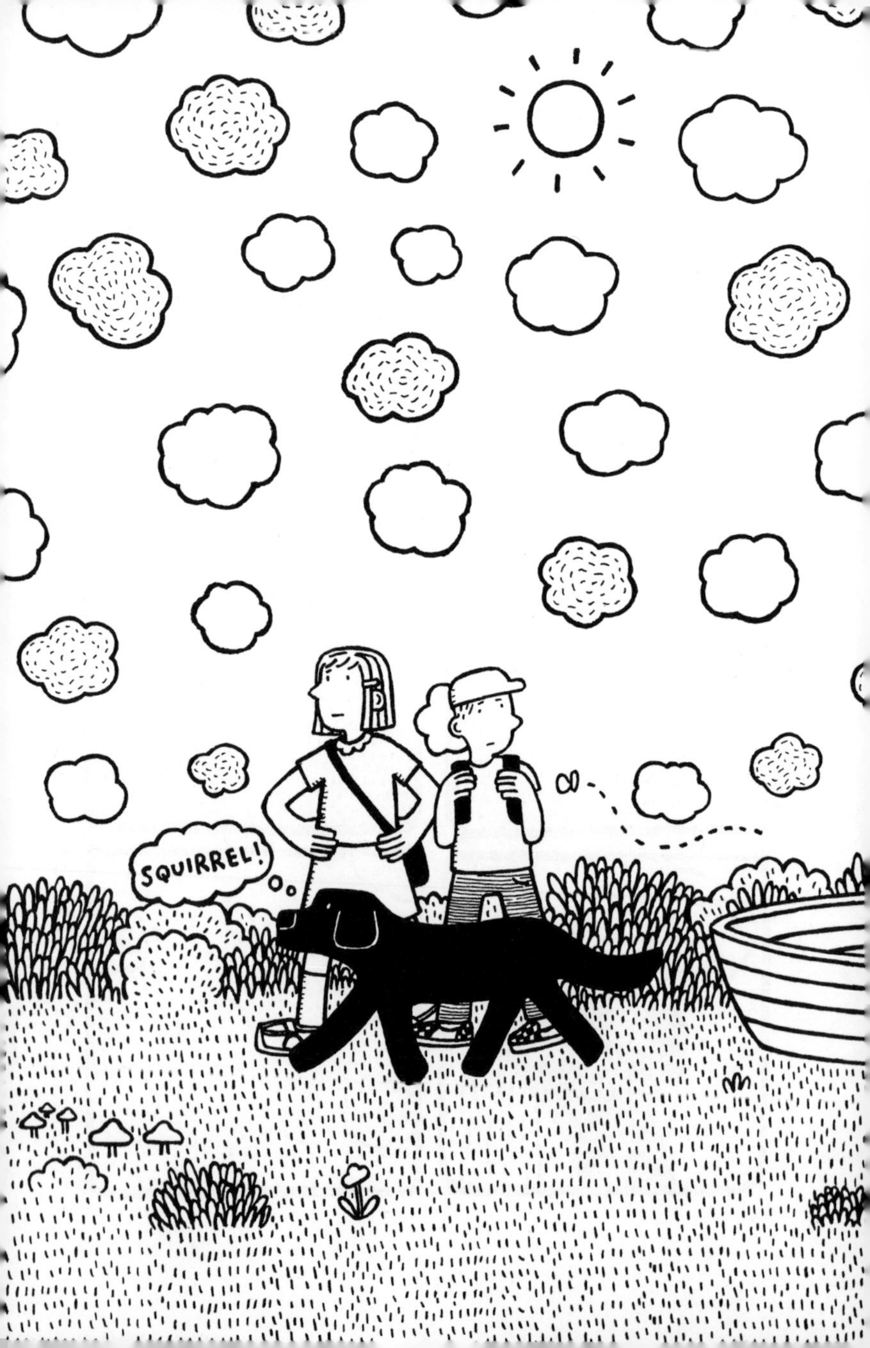
SQUIRREL!

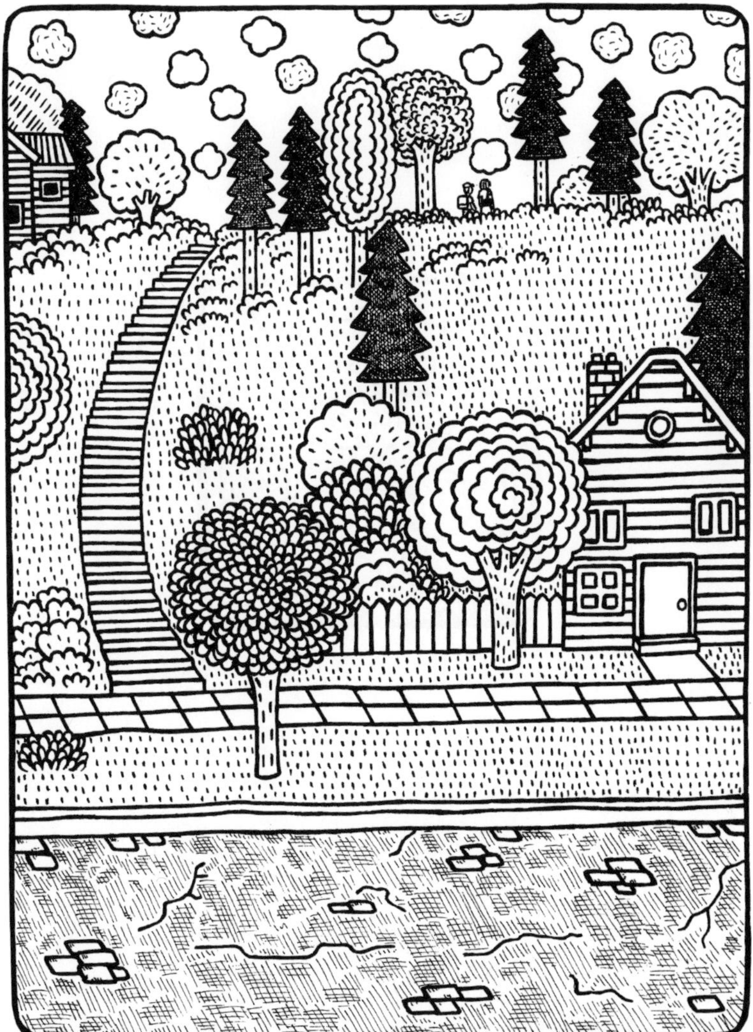

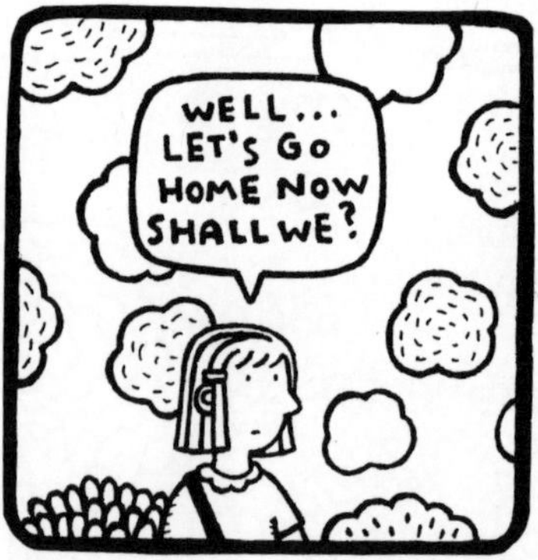
WELL... LET'S GO HOME NOW SHALL WE?

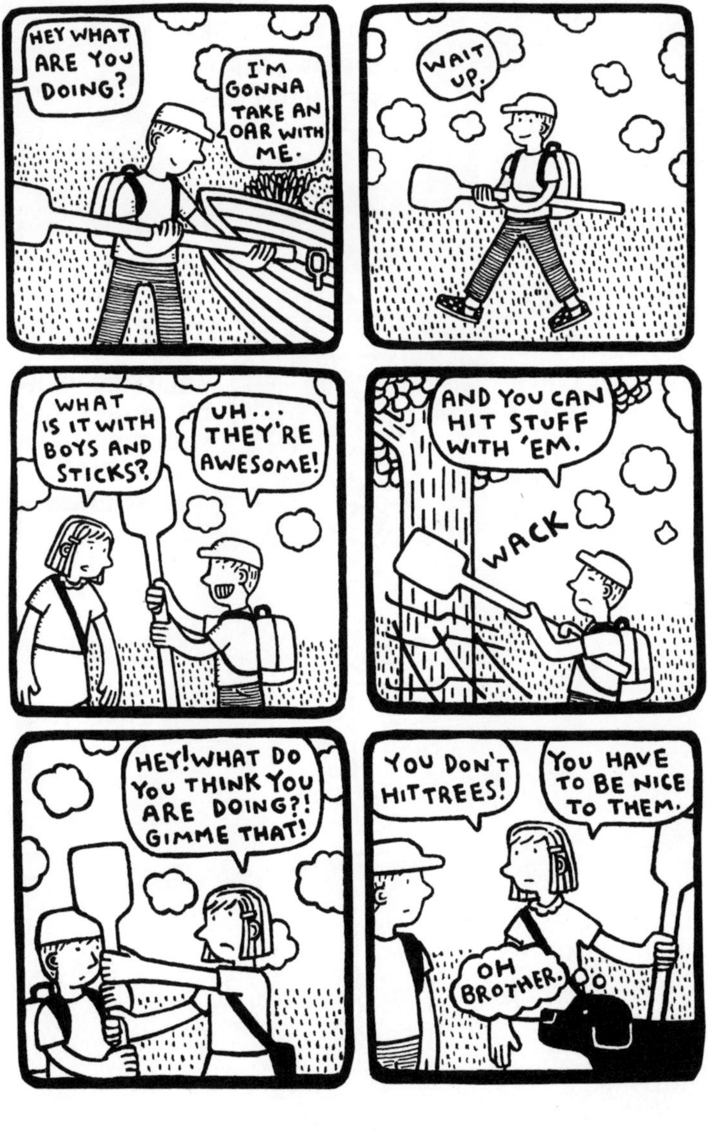
HEY WHAT ARE YOU DOING?
I'M GONNA TAKE AN OAR WITH ME.
WAIT UP.
WHAT IS IT WITH BOYS AND STICKS?
UH... THEY'RE AWESOME!
AND YOU CAN HIT STUFF WITH 'EM.
WACK
HEY! WHAT DO YOU THINK YOU ARE DOING?! GIMME THAT!
YOU DON'T HIT TREES!
YOU HAVE TO BE NICE TO THEM.
OH BROTHER.

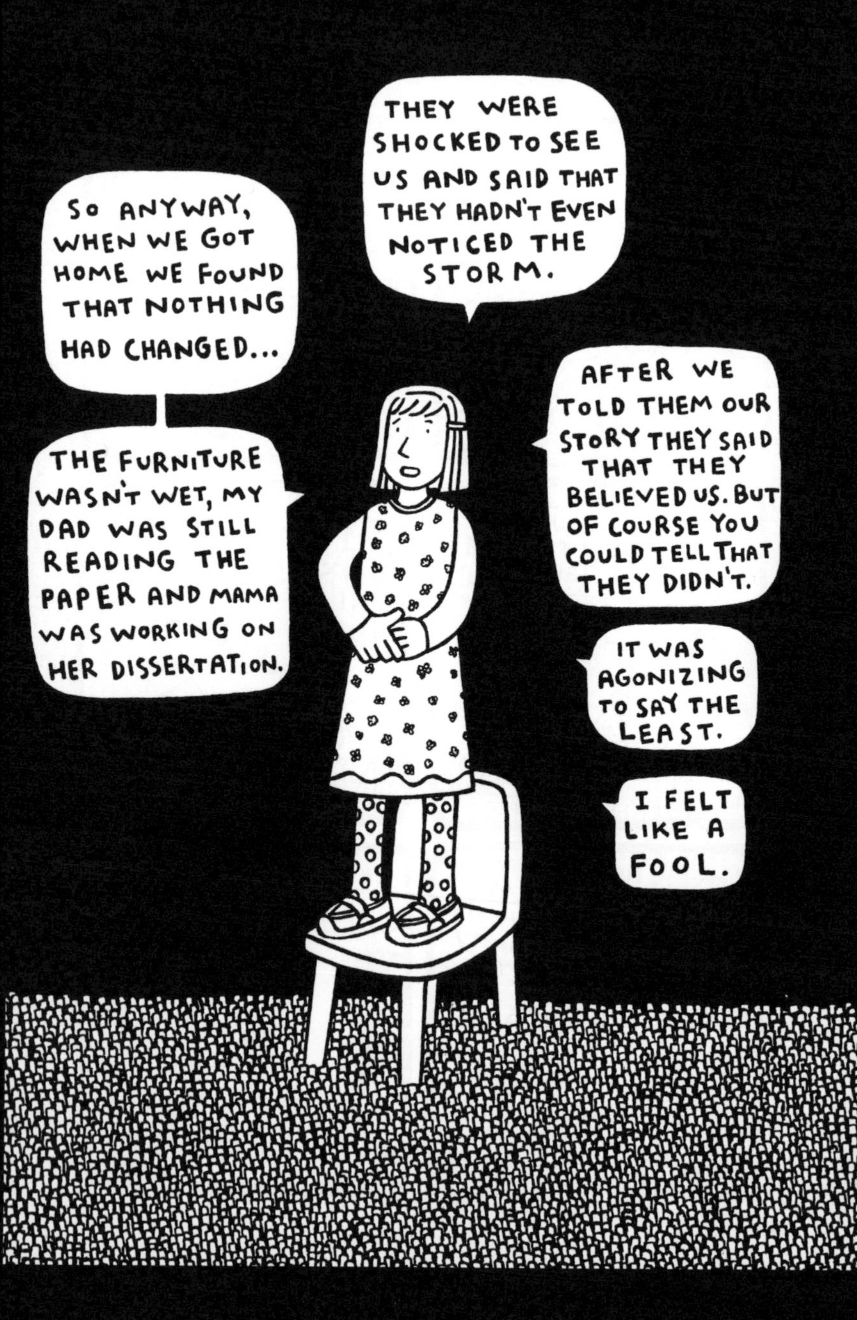
So ANYWAY, WHEN WE GOT HOME WE FOUND THAT NOTHING HAD CHANGED...
THE FURNITURE WASN'T WET, MY DAD WAS STILL READING THE PAPER AND MAMA WAS WORKING ON HER DISSERTATION.
THEY WERE SHOCKED TO SEE US AND SAID THAT THEY HADN'T EVEN NOTICED THE STORM.
AFTER WE TOLD THEM OUR STORY THEY SAID THAT THEY BELIEVED US. BUT OF COURSE YOU COULD TELL THAT THEY DIDN'T.
IT WAS AGONIZING TO SAY THE LEAST.
I FELT LIKE A FOOL.

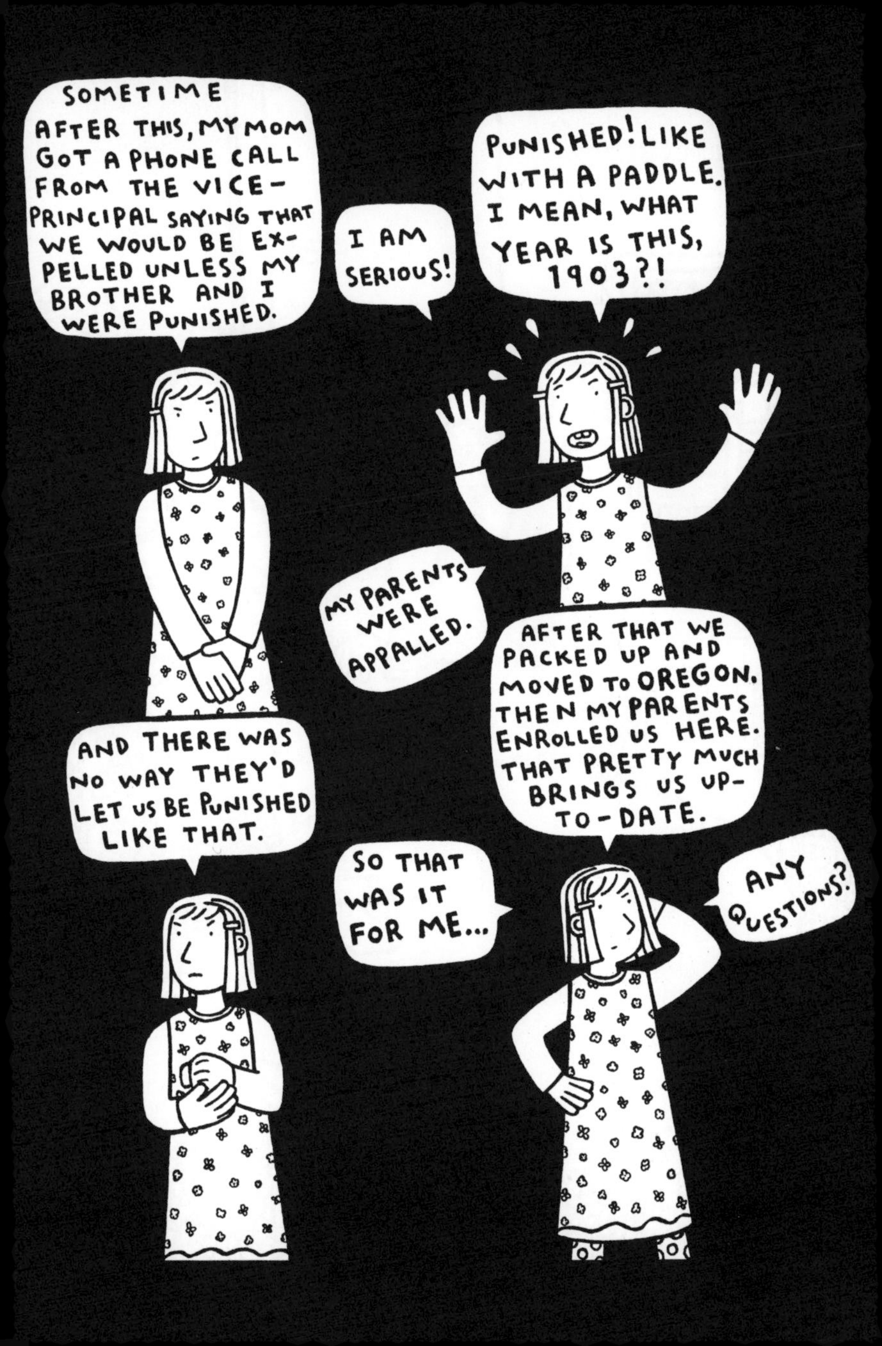
SOMETIME AFTER THIS, MY MOM GOT A PHONE CALL FROM THE VICE-PRINCIPAL SAYING THAT WE WOULD BE EX-PELLED UNLESS MY BROTHER AND I WERE PUNISHED.
I AM SERIOUS!
PUNISHED! LIKE WITH A PADDLE. I MEAN, WHAT YEAR IS THIS, 1903?!
MY PARENTS WERE APPALLED.
AND THERE WAS NO WAY THEY'D LET US BE PUNISHED LIKE THAT.
AFTER THAT WE PACKED UP AND MOVED TO OREGON. THEN MY PARENTS ENROLLED US HERE. THAT PRETTY MUCH BRINGS US UP-TO-DATE.
SO THAT WAS IT FOR ME...
ANY QUESTIONS?

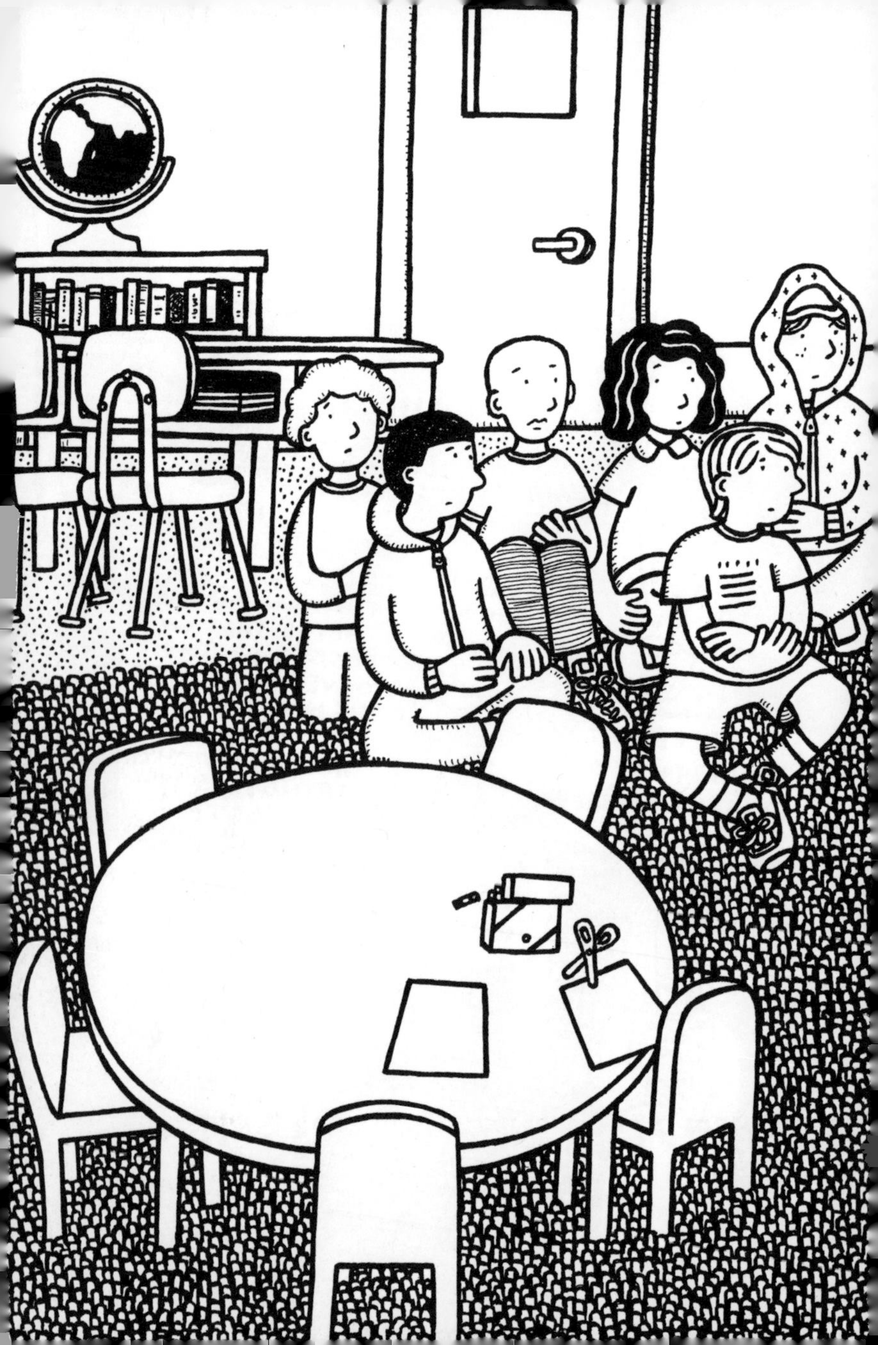

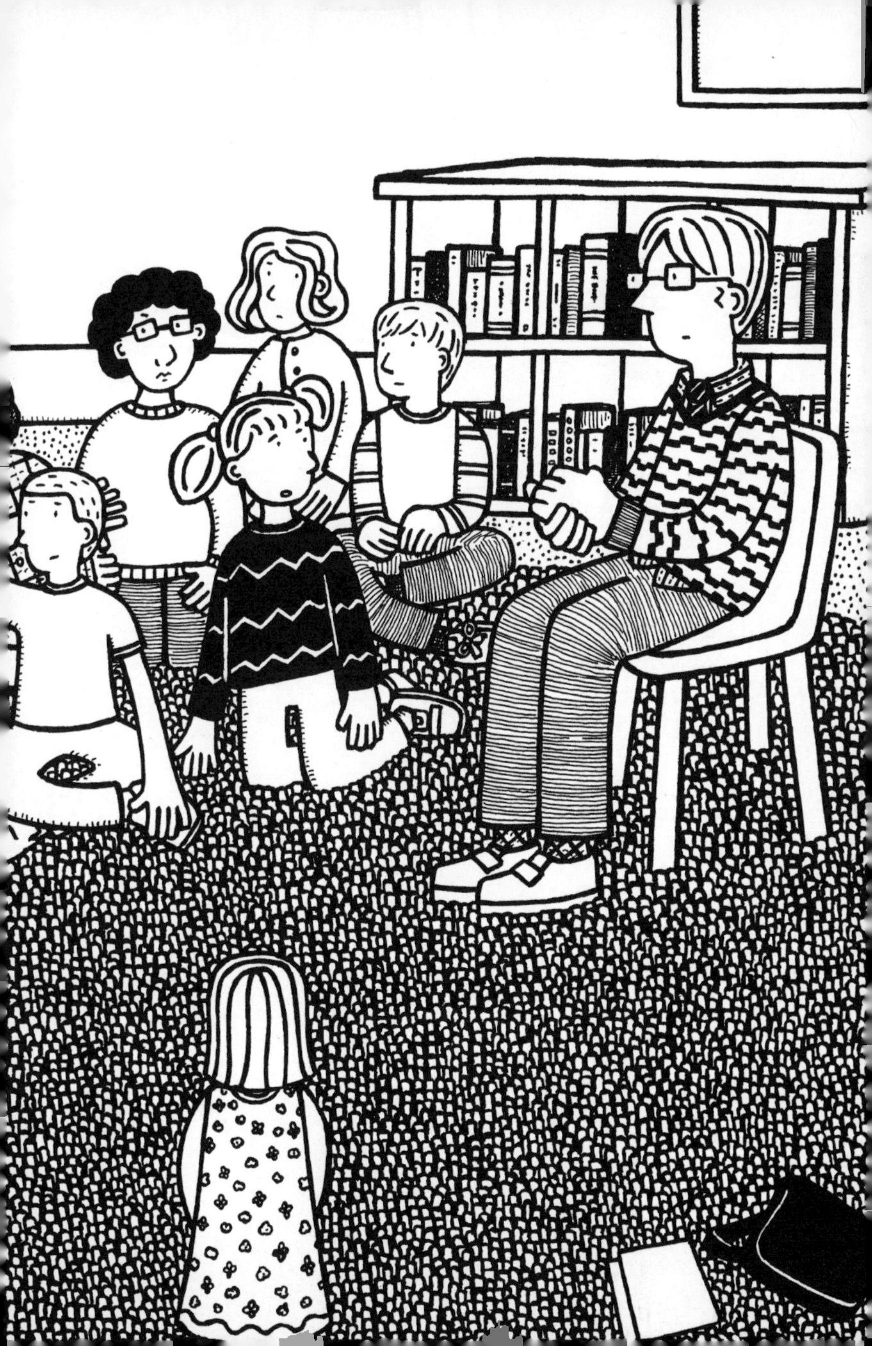

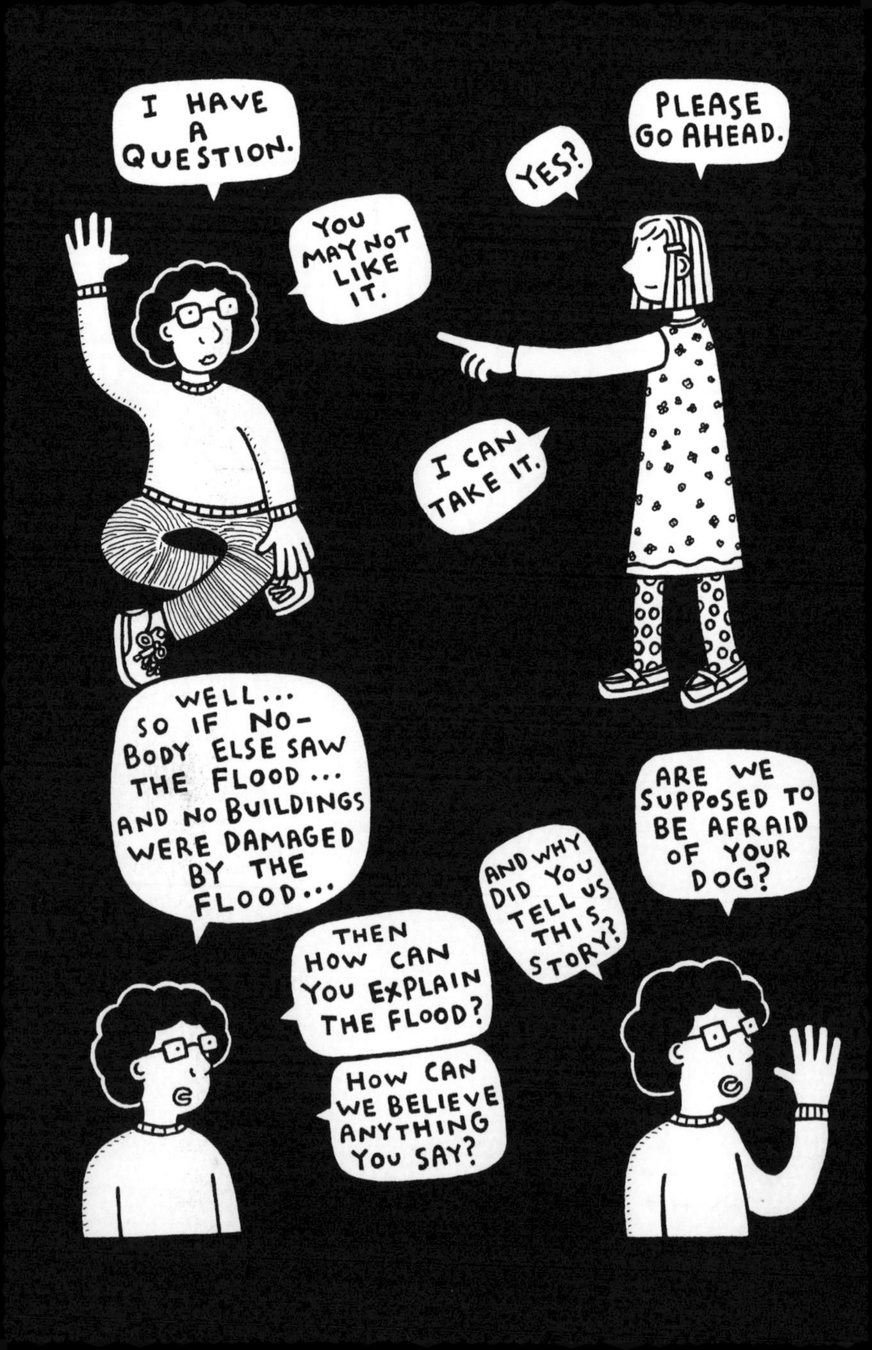
I HAVE A QUESTION.
YES?
PLEASE GO AHEAD.
YOU MAY NOT LIKE IT.
I CAN TAKE IT.
WELL... SO IF NOBODY ELSE SAW THE FLOOD... AND NO BUILDINGS WERE DAMAGED BY THE FLOOD...
THEN HOW CAN YOU EXPLAIN THE FLOOD?
HOW CAN WE BELIEVE ANYTHING YOU SAY?
AND WHY DID YOU TELL US THIS STORY?
ARE WE SUPPOSED TO BE AFRAID OF YOUR DOG?

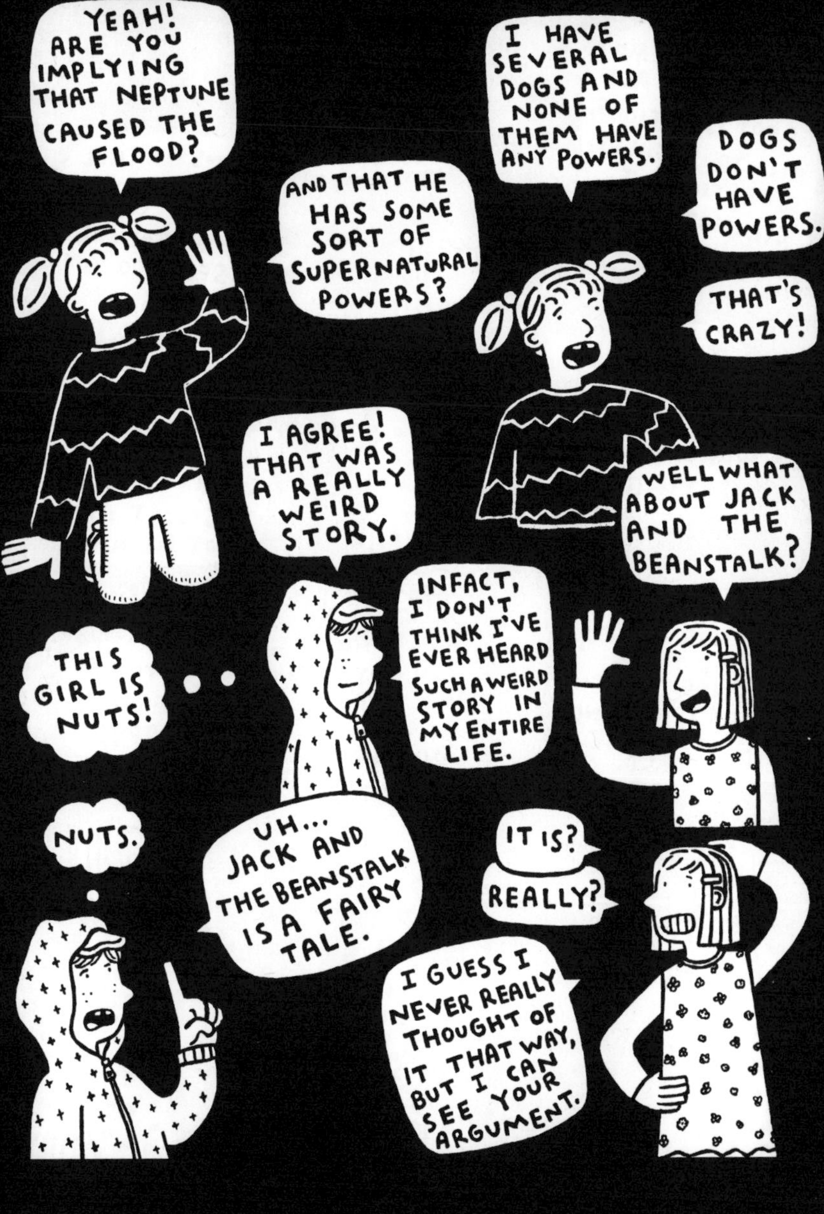
YEAH! ARE YOU IMPLYING THAT NEPTUNE CAUSED THE FLOOD?
AND THAT HE HAS SOME SORT OF SUPERNATURAL POWERS?
I HAVE SEVERAL DOGS AND NONE OF THEM HAVE ANY POWERS.
DOGS DON'T HAVE POWERS.
THAT'S CRAZY!
I AGREE! THAT WAS A REALLY WEIRD STORY.
WELL WHAT ABOUT JACK AND THE BEANSTALK?
THIS GIRL IS NUTS!
INFACT, I DON'T THINK I'VE EVER HEARD SUCH A WEIRD STORY IN MY ENTIRE LIFE.
NUTS.
UH... JACK AND THE BEANSTALK IS A FAIRY TALE.
IT IS?
REALLY?
I GUESS I NEVER REALLY THOUGHT OF IT THAT WAY, BUT I CAN SEE YOUR ARGUMENT.

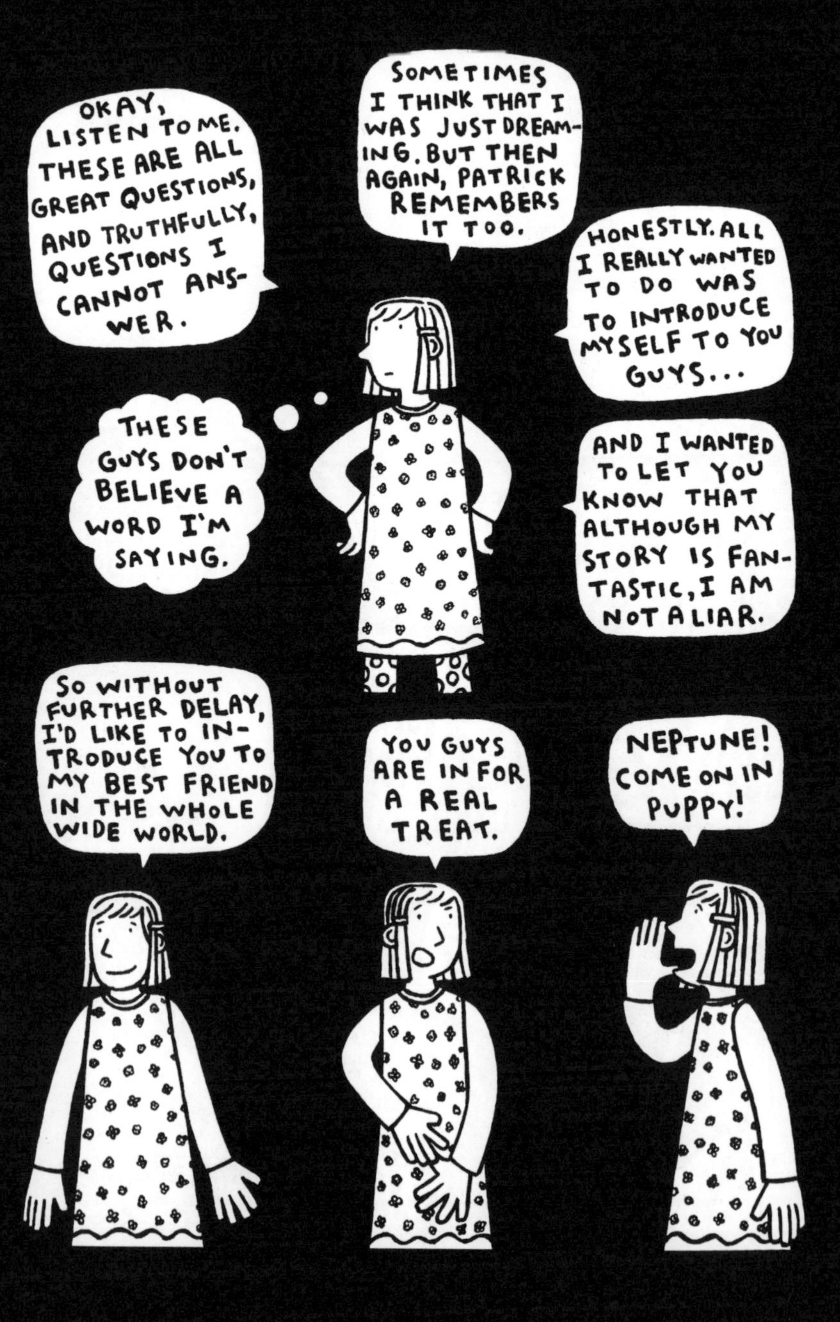
OKAY, LISTEN TO ME. THESE ARE ALL GREAT QUESTIONS, AND TRUTHFULLY, QUESTIONS I CANNOT ANSWER.
SOMETIMES I THINK THAT I WAS JUST DREAMING. BUT THEN AGAIN, PATRICK REMEMBERS IT TOO.
HONESTLY. ALL I REALLY WANTED TO DO WAS TO INTRODUCE MYSELF TO YOU GUYS...
THESE GUYS DON'T BELIEVE A WORD I'M SAYING.
AND I WANTED TO LET YOU KNOW THAT ALTHOUGH MY STORY IS FANTASTIC, I AM NOT A LIAR.
SO WITHOUT FURTHER DELAY, I'D LIKE TO INTRODUCE YOU TO MY BEST FRIEND IN THE WHOLE WIDE WORLD.
YOU GUYS ARE IN FOR A REAL TREAT.
NEPTUNE! COME ON IN PUPPY!

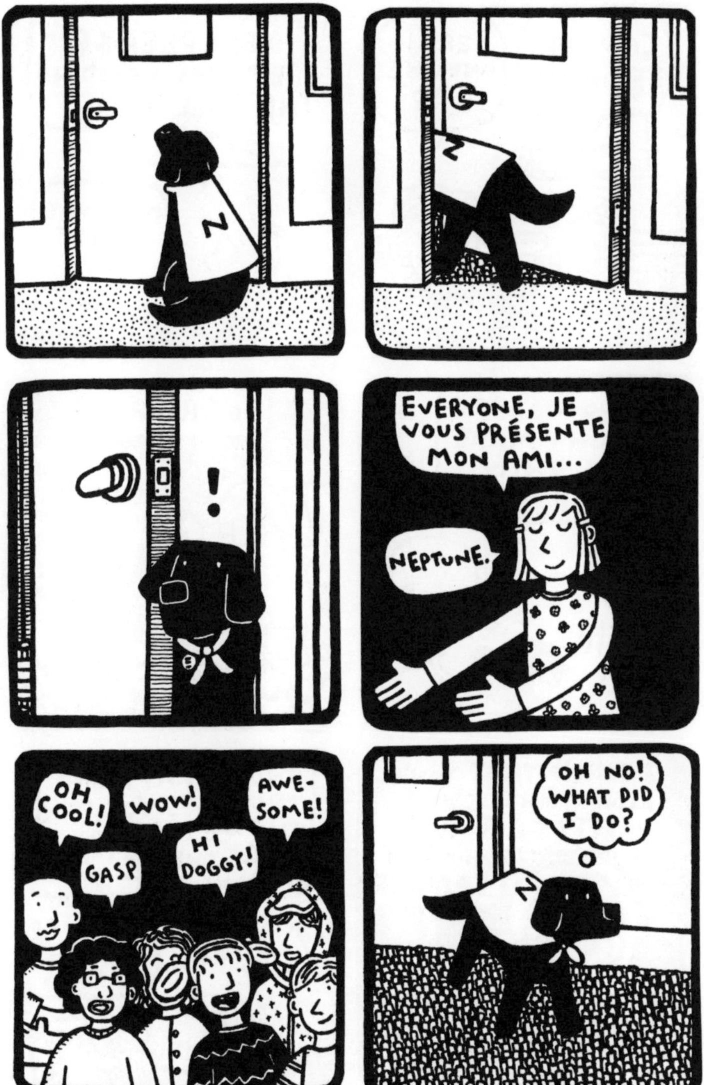
!
EVERYONE, JE VOUS PRÉSENTE MON AMI...
NEPTUNE.
OH COOL!
WOW!
AWE-SOME!
GASP
HI DOGGY!
OH NO! WHAT DID I DO?

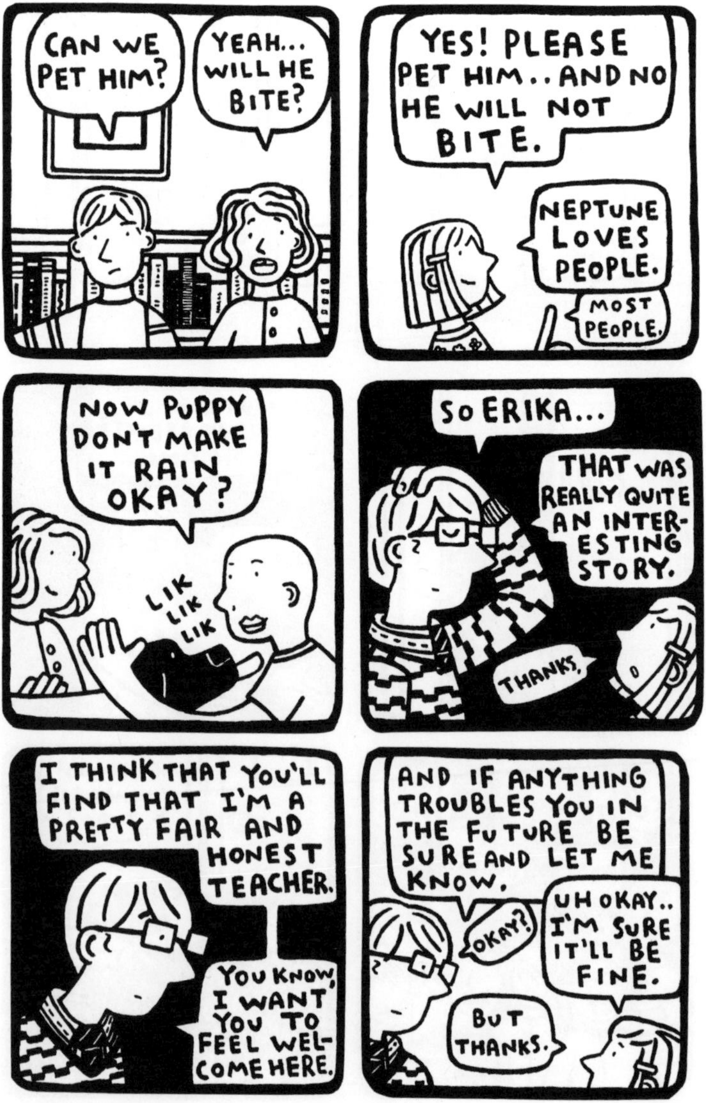

CAN WE PET HIM?
YEAH... WILL HE BITE?
YES! PLEASE PET HIM.. AND NO HE WILL NOT BITE.
NEPTUNE LOVES PEOPLE.
MOST PEOPLE.
NOW PUPPY DON'T MAKE IT RAIN OKAY?
LIK LIK LIK
SO ERIKA...
THAT WAS REALLY QUITE AN INTER-ESTING STORY.
THANKS.
I THINK THAT YOU'LL FIND THAT I'M A PRETTY FAIR AND HONEST TEACHER.
YOU KNOW, I WANT YOU TO FEEL WEL-COME HERE.
AND IF ANYTHING TROUBLES YOU IN THE FUTURE BE SURE AND LET ME KNOW.
OKAY?
UH OKAY.. I'M SURE IT'LL BE FINE.
BUT THANKS.

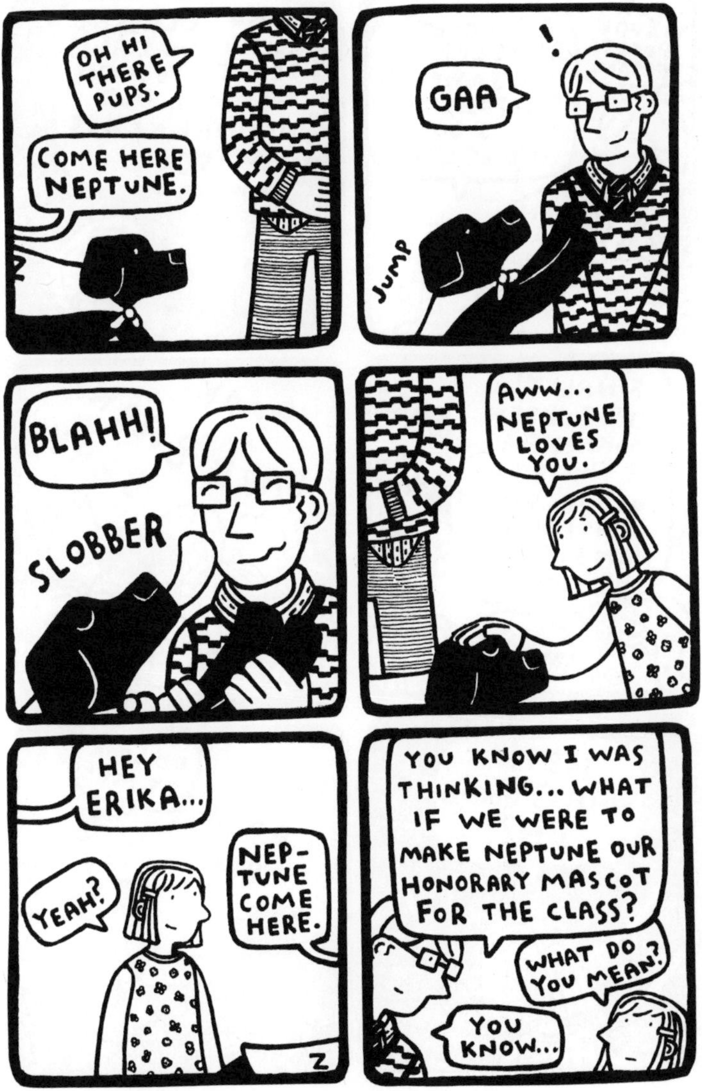
OH HI THERE PUPS.
COME HERE NEPTUNE.
!
GAA
JUMP
BLAHH!
SLOBBER
AWW... NEPTUNE LOVES YOU.
HEY ERIKA...
YEAH?
NEP-TUNE COME HERE.
Z
YOU KNOW I WAS THINKING... WHAT IF WE WERE TO MAKE NEPTUNE OUR HONORARY MASCOT FOR THE CLASS?
WHAT DO YOU MEAN?
YOU KNOW...

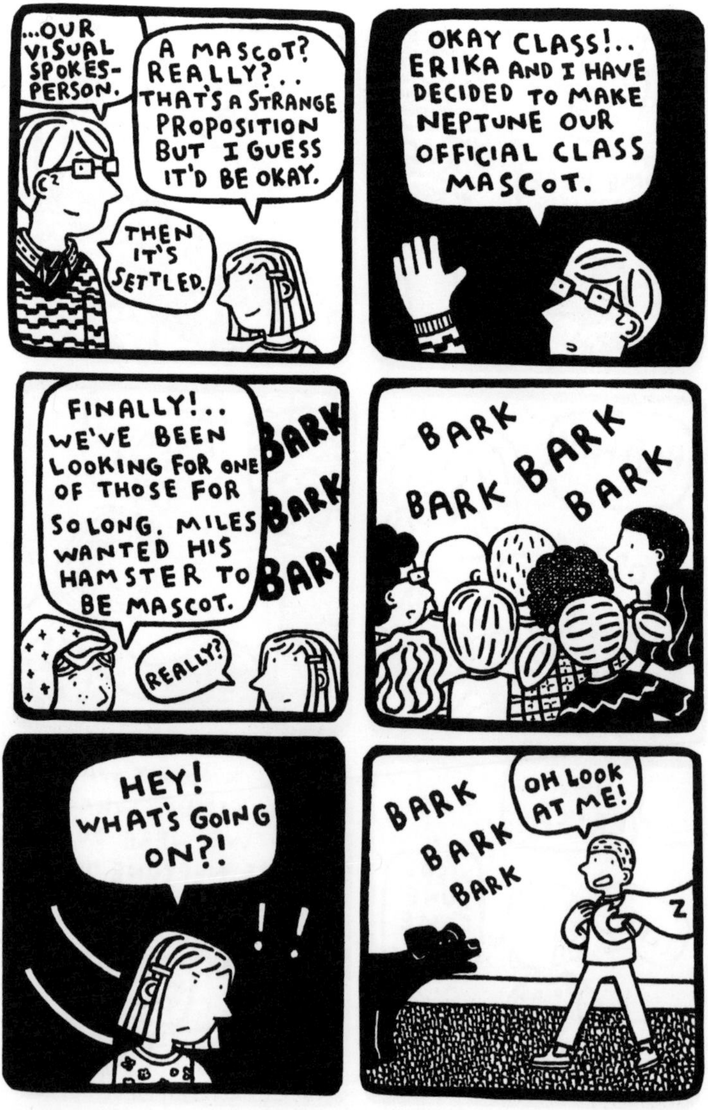
...OUR VISUAL SPOKES-PERSON.
A MASCOT? REALLY?.. THAT'S A STRANGE PROPOSITION BUT I GUESS IT'D BE OKAY.
THEN IT'S SETTLED.
OKAY CLASS!.. ERIKA AND I HAVE DECIDED TO MAKE NEPTUNE OUR OFFICIAL CLASS MASCOT.
FINALLY!.. WE'VE BEEN LOOKING FOR ONE OF THOSE FOR SO LONG. MILES WANTED HIS HAMSTER TO BE MASCOT.
REALLY?
BARK BARK BARK BARK BARK
HEY! WHAT'S GOING ON?!
!!
BARK BARK BARK
OH LOOK AT ME!

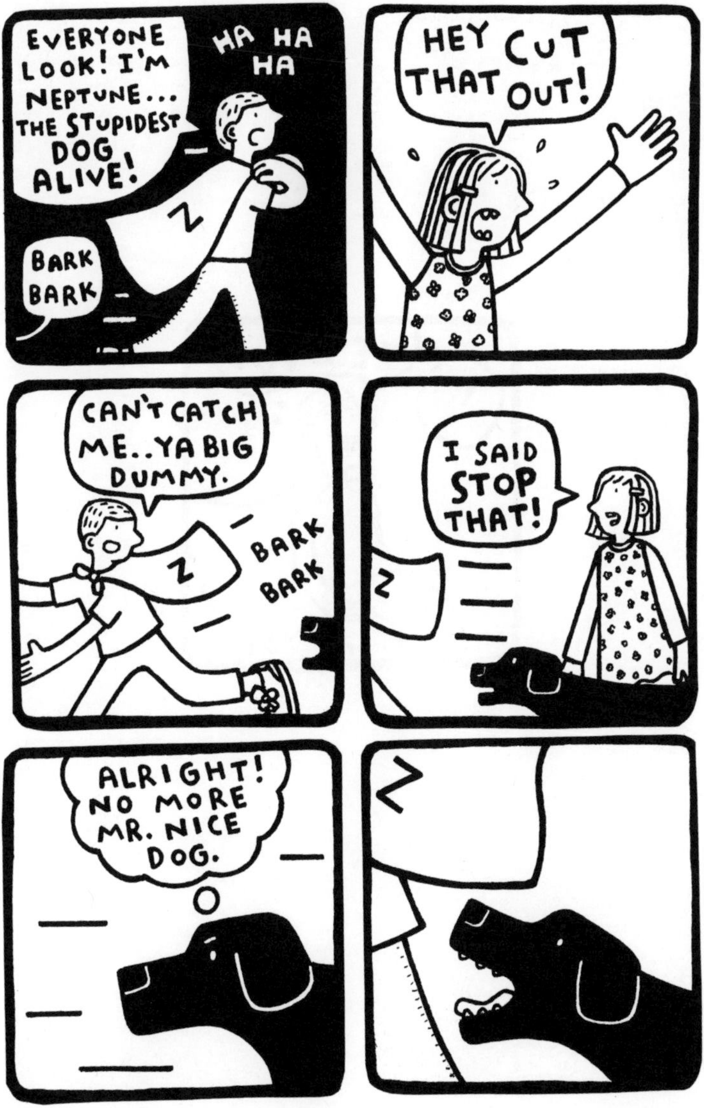
EVERYONE LOOK! I'M NEPTUNE... THE STUPIDEST DOG ALIVE!
HA HA HA
BARK BARK
HEY CUT THAT OUT!
CAN'T CATCH ME..YA BIG DUMMY.
BARK BARK
I SAID STOP THAT!
ALRIGHT! NO MORE MR. NICE DOG.

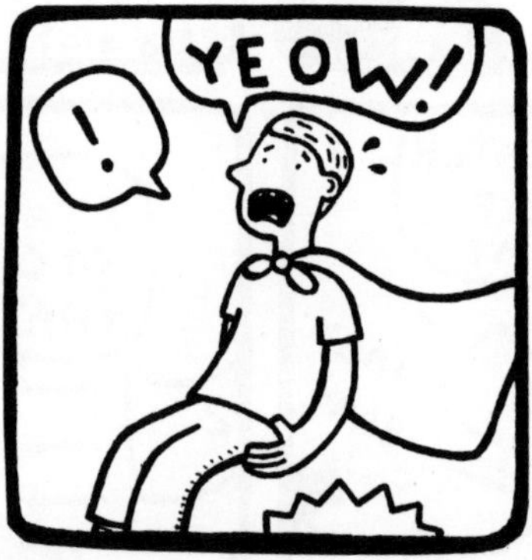
!
YEOW!

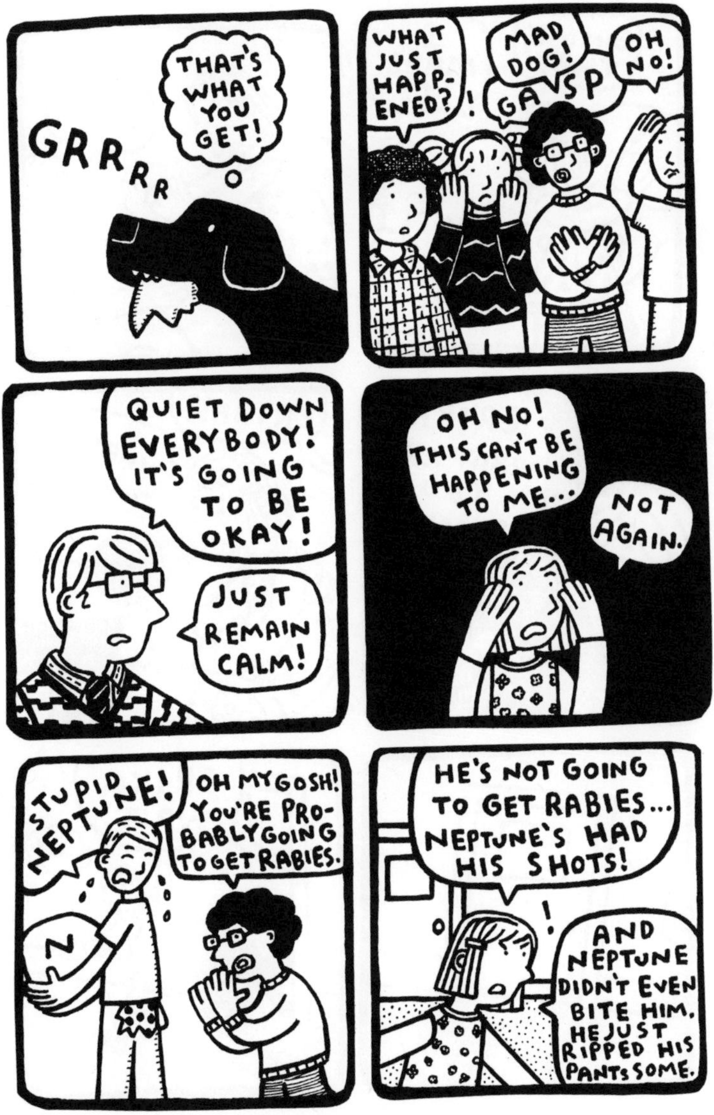
THAT'S WHAT YOU GET!
GRRRRR
WHAT JUST HAPP-ENED?
!
MAD DOG!
GASP
OH NO!
QUIET DOWN EVERYBODY! IT'S GOING TO BE OKAY!
JUST REMAIN CALM!
OH NO! THIS CAN'T BE HAPPENING TO ME...
NOT AGAIN.
STUPID NEPTUNE!
OH MY GOSH! YOU'RE PRO-BABLY GOING TO GET RABIES.
HE'S NOT GOING TO GET RABIES... NEPTUNE'S HAD HIS SHOTS!
!
AND NEPTUNE DIDN'T EVEN BITE HIM. HE JUST RIPPED HIS PANTS SOME.

GIMME THAT!
I MADE IT!
N
SWIPE
WAA!
SHOVE
?
ERIKA! WHAT ARE YOU DOING?!
ERIKA!?
WHAT!?
TIE
ERIKA WAIT!
SORRY.
N

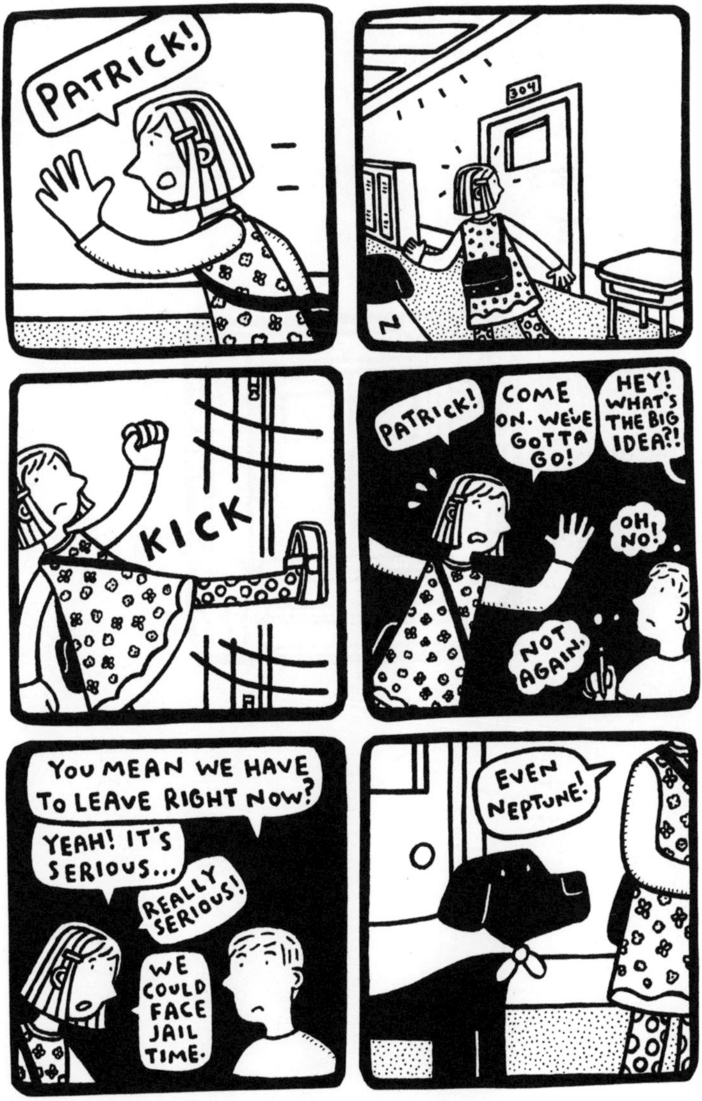
PATRICK!
304
2
KICK
PATRICK!
COME ON. WE'VE GOTTA GO!
HEY! WHAT'S THE BIG IDEA?!
OH NO!
NOT AGAIN.
YOU MEAN WE HAVE TO LEAVE RIGHT NOW?
YEAH! IT'S SERIOUS...
REALLY SERIOUS!
WE COULD FACE JAIL TIME.
EVEN NEPTUNE!

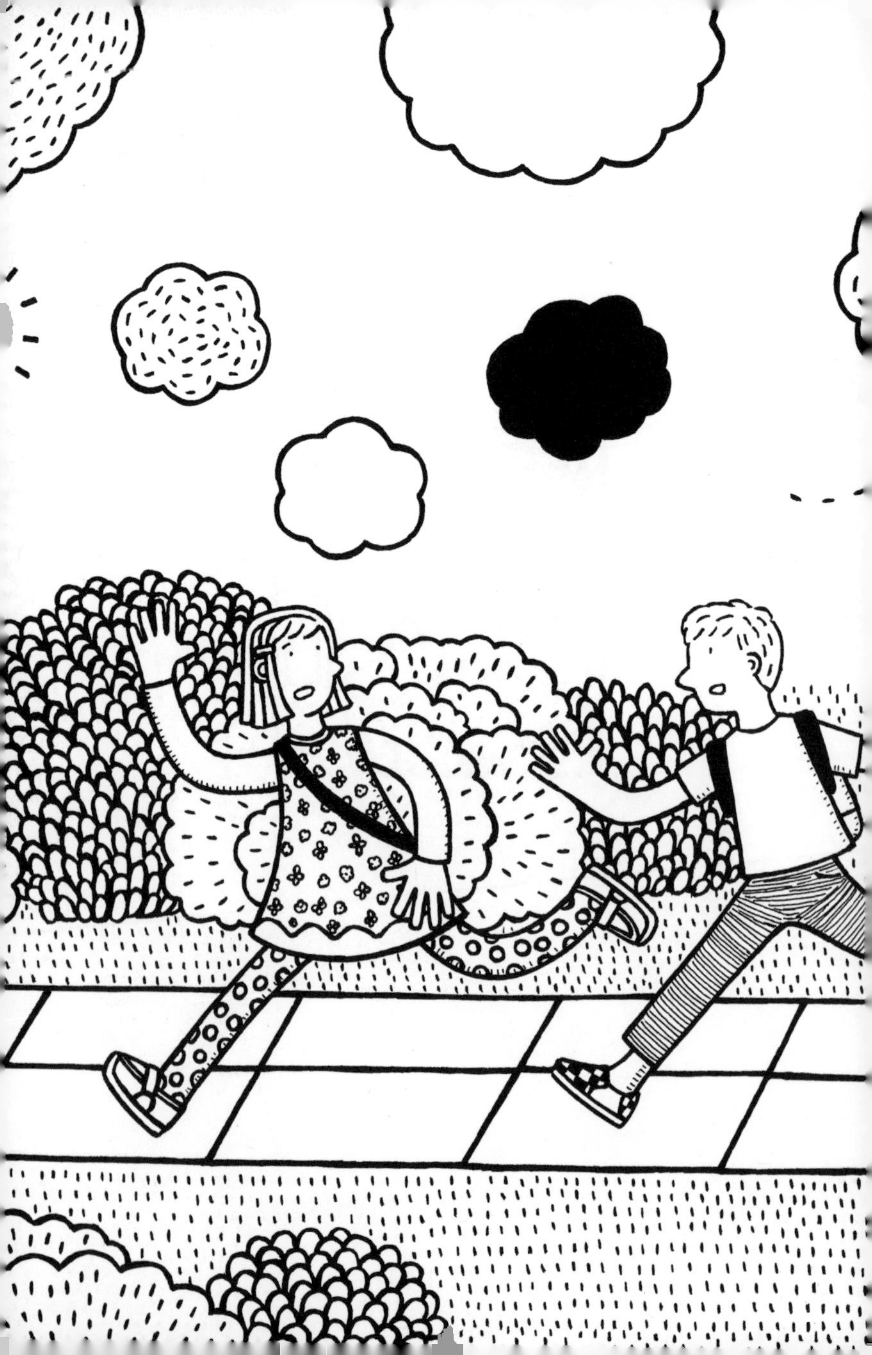

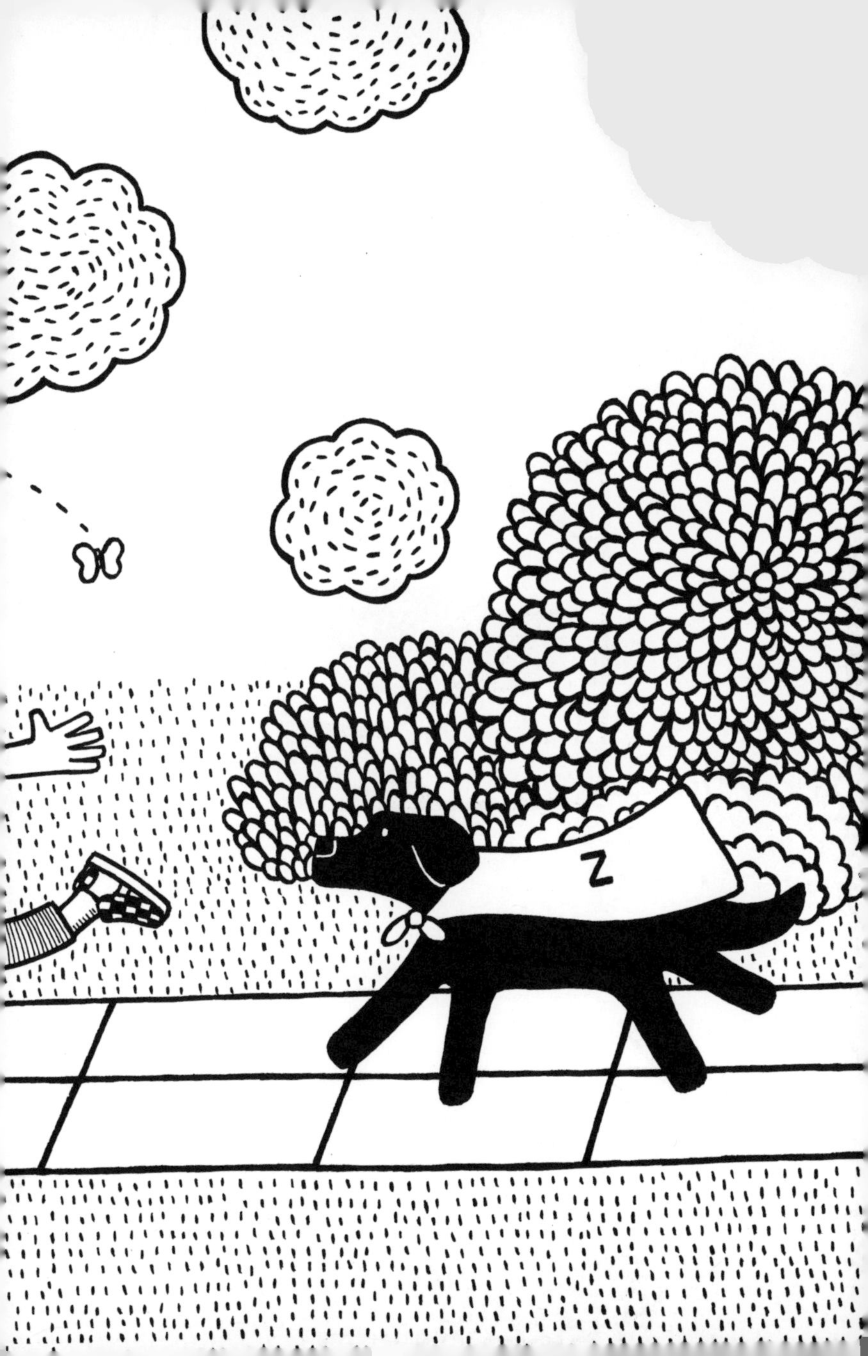
Z

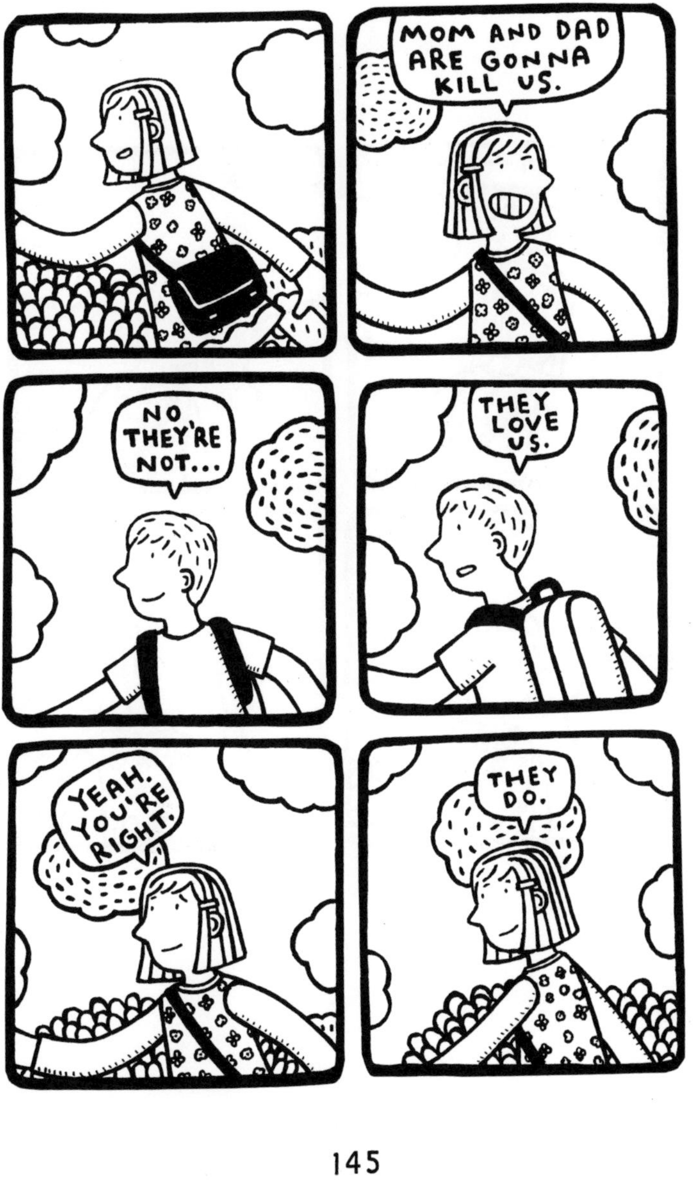
MOM AND DAD ARE GONNA KILL US.
NO THEY'RE NOT...
THEY LOVE US.
YEAH. YOU'RE RIGHT.
THEY DO.

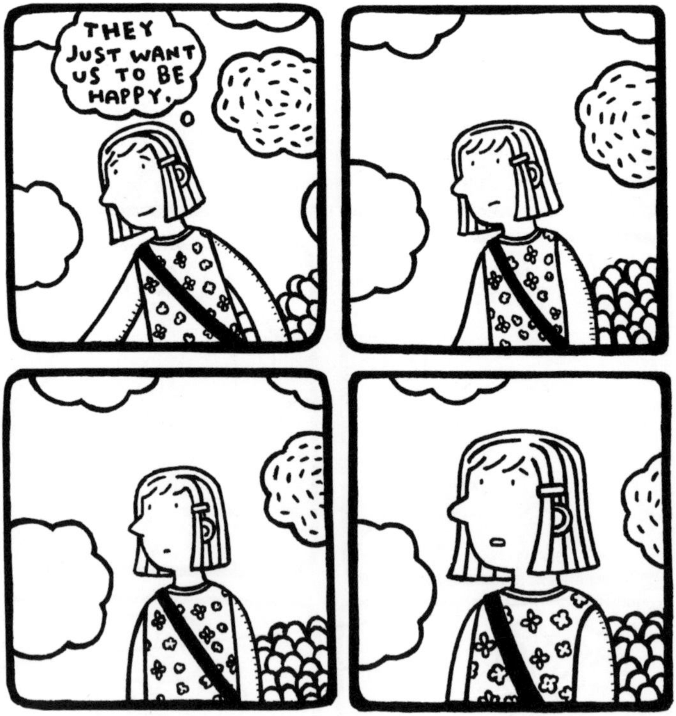
THEY JUST WANT US TO BE HAPPY.

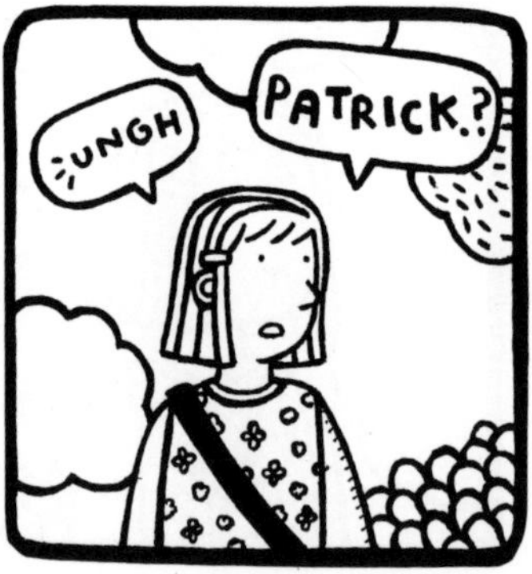
UNGH
PATRICK.?

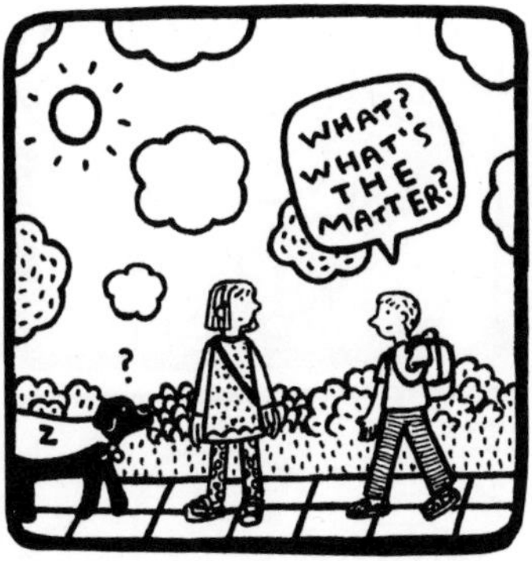
WHAT? WHAT'S THE MATTER?
?
Z

...
NEVER-MIND.
IT DOESN'T MATTER.
... NOT ANY-MORE.

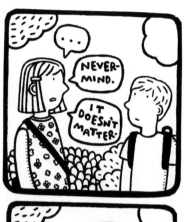

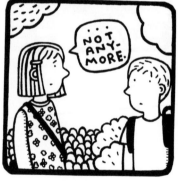

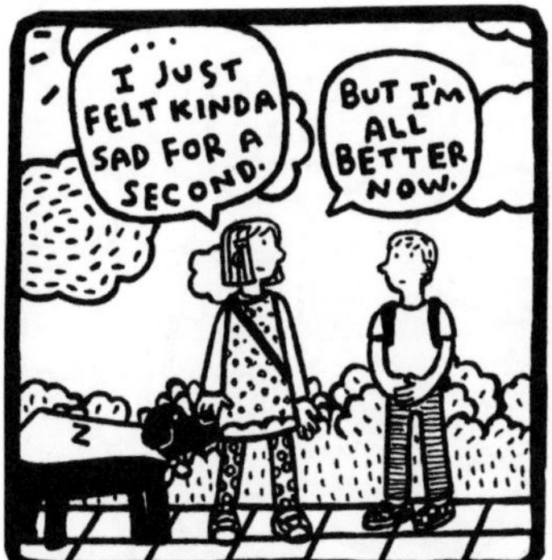
...I JUST FELT KINDA SAD FOR A SECOND.
BUT I'M ALL BETTER NOW.

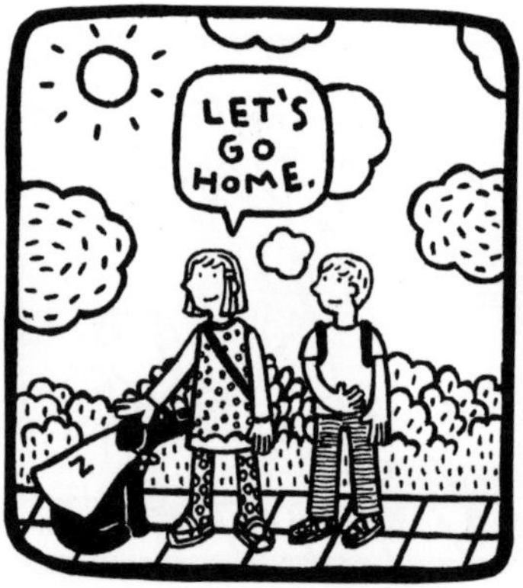
LET'S GO HOME.

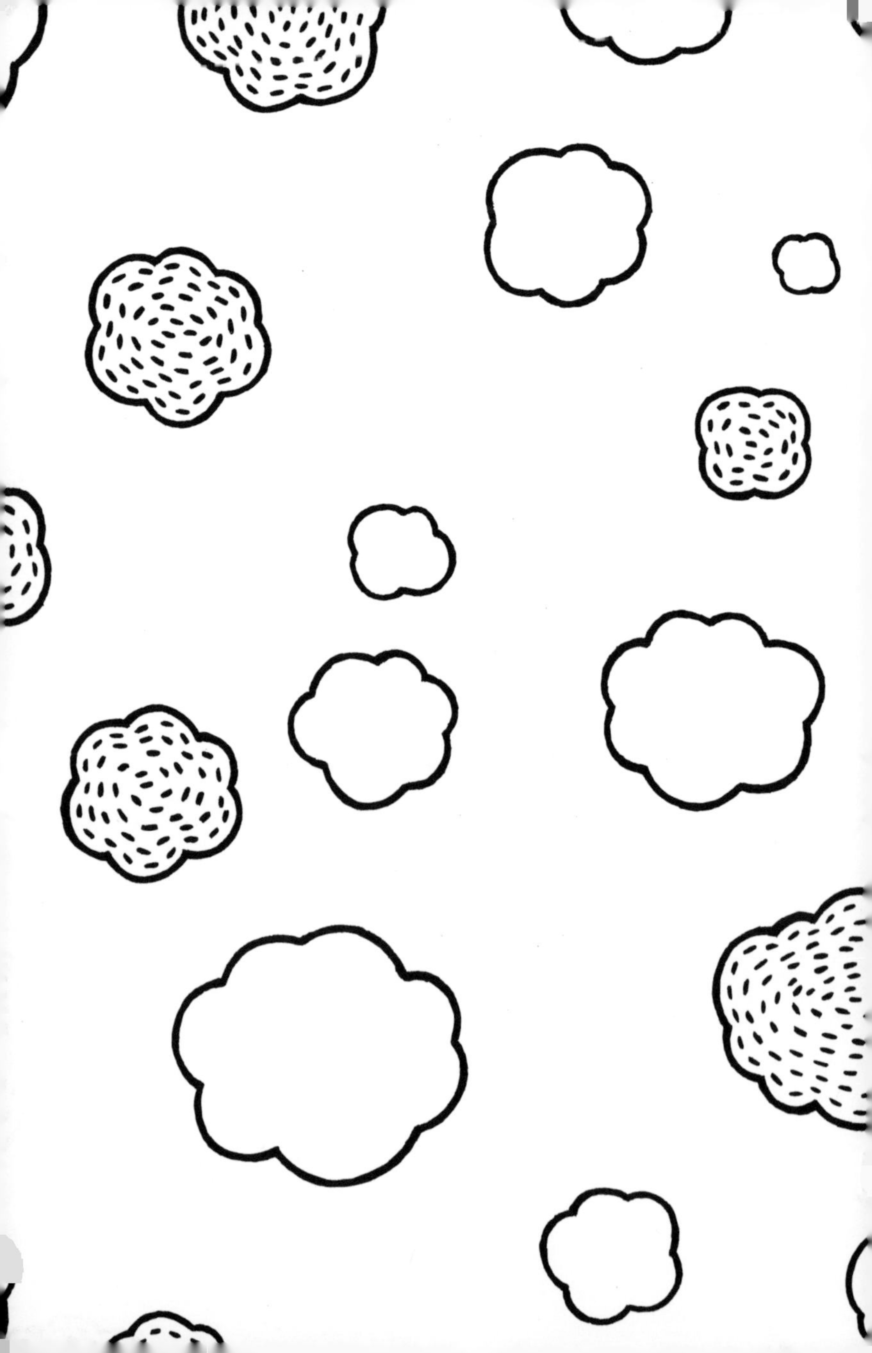

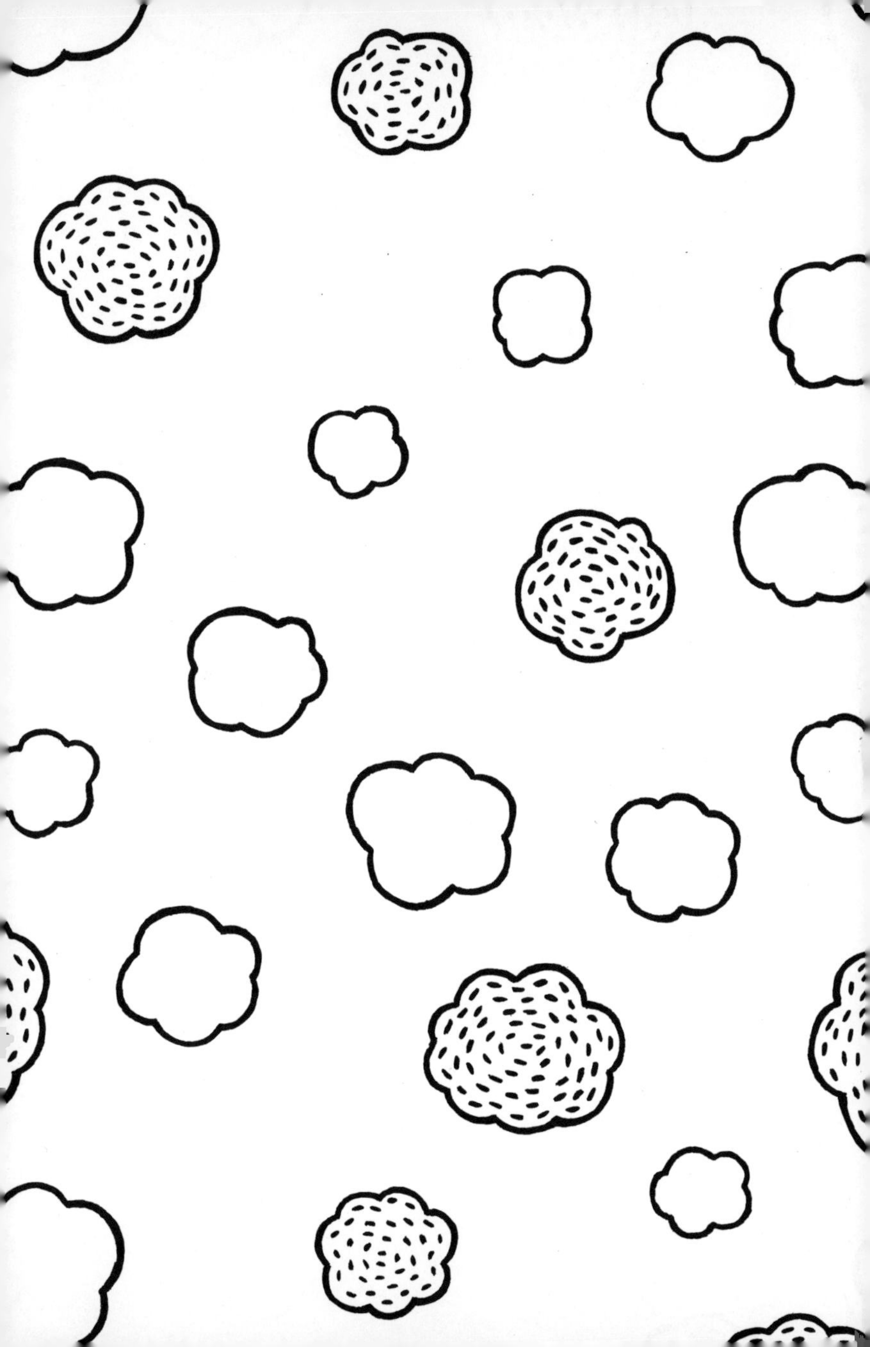

THANK YOU

WITHOUT THE LOVE AND SUPPORT FROM
THE FOLLOWING PEOPLE THIS BOOK WOULD
NEVER HAVE BEEN POSSIBLE...TO ARIEL,
MOM AND DAD, JEREMY AND ANNA, AND
ALL OF MY AUNTS, UNCLES AND COUSINS...
TO DYLAN AND GREG FOR PUBLISHING THIS
BOOK...EDITORIAL ASSISTANCE FROM ARIEL,
EMILY NILSSON, GREG MEANS AND GALEN
LONGSTRETH. THANKS TO JESSE AND ANDRICE,
TIM GOODYEAR, SARAH O, MARTHA, ANGEL,
AUSTIN AND LAURA, NICOLE G., AMY
STEEL, KEVIN SAMPSELL, DIN AND NANCY,
AND ESPECIALLY TO JEREMY AND ALLIE
TIEDEMAN FOR BEING MY FIRST COMICS PALS
IN PORTLAND...TO THE KIDS AT THE
CHILDREN'S MUSEUM SUMMER ART CAMP,
AND MAGGIE'S 5TH GRADE CLASS...ALSO
THANKS TO MUNAF AND EXPLOSIONS IN THE
SKY... THIS BOOK WAS MADE IN MEMORY
OF MY BEST FRIEND SHADOW.